FAMILY LAW PRACTITIONEI

DIVORCE
The Changing Landscape of Divorce in Ireland

AUSTRALIA
Law Book Co.
Sydney

CANADA and USA
Carswell
Toronto

HONG KONG
Sweet & Maxwell Asia

NEW ZEALAND
Brookers
Wellington

SINGAPORE AND MALAYSIA
Sweet & Maxwell Asia
Singapore and Kuala Lumpur

FAMILY LAW PRACTITIONER SERIES

DIVORCE

The Changing Landscape of Divorce in Ireland

Extracted from divisions of the looseleaf work
Family Law Practitioner

Geoffrey Shannon

B.Comm., LL.B., LL.M., Solicitor

ADDITIONAL CONTRIBUTORS

Louise Crowley, *Solicitor and Lecturer in Law* and
Stephanie Coggans, *Solicitor*

Additional material

Siobháin Gallagher and Fergus Ryan

DUBLIN
ROUND HALL SWEET & MAXWELL
2001

Published in 2001 by
Round Hall Ltd
43 Fitzwilliam Place
Dublin 2

Printed in Great Britain by
Pear Tree Press

No natural forests were destroyed to make this product;
Only farmed timber was used and replanted.

A CIP catalogue record for this book is available
from the British Library.

ISBN 1-85800-268-0

DETAILED TABLE OF CONTENTS

DIVISION E: DIVORCE

REFORM

THE RECOGNITION OF FOREIGN DIVORCES

DIVISIONS D & E

FLP R.2: October 2001

INTRODUCTION

This book is extracted from Division E and J of the looseleaf Work *Family Law Practitioner*, edited by Geoffrey Shannon. Page numbers reflect the structure of the looseleaf work and so may not be sequential in this book.

If you are interested in obtaining a copy of the complete looseleaf work, please contact Round Hall Ltd., 43 Fitzwilliam Place, Dublin 2, Ireland (Tel (01) 662 5301; e-mail enquiries@roundhall.ie).

DIVISION E: DIVORCE

INTRODUCTION

The enactment of the Family Law (Divorce) Act 1996 brought to a close **E–001**
several years of protracted campaigning to permit the dissolution of
marriage. Some three years after the event, it is interesting to review the
statistics on divorce which reveal a modest increase in the number of
applications made and granted throughout the country. The legal year
ended July 1997 shows 417 applications were made with 95 decrees granted,
in circumstances where the Act had only come into operation on February
27 of that year. In the year ended July 1998, the numbers had risen to 2,765
divorce applications and 1,452 decrees granted, and in 1999 there were
3,240 divorce applications made with 2,475 divorces granted. In summary, a
total of some 8,000 divorce applications have been sought since the coming
into operation of the Act. It is interesting to note from the available
statistical data that female divorce applications outnumber male applications by two to one. Of the 2,475 divorces granted for the legal year
ended 1999, 1,611 of the applications were made by the wife, while only 864
were made by the husband.

Much has been made of these conservative numbers, but they cannot be **E–002**
altogether surprising in view of certain factors. They are not indicative
themselves of the rate of marital breakdown in Ireland. The figures, to
some extent, reflect the apprehension of people towards relatively new
legislation and their reluctance to reopen existing satisfactory
arrangements.

It is easy to forget, in light of the recent increase of family legislation, **E–003**
that the mechanism for resolving the terms of marriage breakdown has
been availed of by many people since the coming into operation of the
Judicial Separation and Family Law Reform Act 1989, amended and
enhanced by the Family Law Act 1995. Those who may have obtained court
orders under these Acts, or indeed those who entered into comprehensive
deeds of separation, may have found arrangements working well and to the
satisfaction of all concerned. The application for divorce enables all existing
arrangements to be reviewed and revised, and ultimately to be decided by
the court, in exercise of its requirement to ensure that proper provision
exists or will be made for the first family and its dependent members.

FLP R.0: July 2000

E–004   In addition, the strict application of the *in camera* rule in family law proceedings makes it difficult to assess not only people's motives for applying for a divorce, but also the application of the provisions of the legislation by the various Circuit Court judges throughout the country. Ad hoc reporting of family law cases, even with the use of parties' initials, has led to only anecdotal evidence being available as to the approaches of the courts. Consequently, it is difficult to discern whether existing arrangements are being replaced, to the dissatisfaction of one or both parties. It is also not possible to garner a clear picture of what kinds of ancillary relief orders are being made, given that much of the information circulating, outside of reported cases, concerns those where high awards have been made or extraordinary circumstances outlined. It is difficult not to argue the case for some form of relaxation of the *in camera* rule which could serve to promote a more unified approach by both courts and practitioners.

E–005   The plain facts of the situation are that, despite the short period of time which has elapsed since the Family Law (Divorce) Act 1996 came into operation, the courts are carefully examining the facts of each case coming before them and making decisions on the facts as they are presented. It is not possible to state that as a general rule previously existing agreements or court orders will be left in place, unless there are exceptional circumstances. People entering a court to have their divorce application adjudicated upon do not, in the main, know what to expect, even in circumstances where negotiations have produced agreed and settled terms. Given the clear duty imposed on the court by section 5 of the 1996 Act and the fact that there are as many reasons why people would seek to have existing arrangements changed as there are orders which can be made to effect those changes, it is not surprising that uncertainty and hesitancy will bedevil the parties.

THE PATH TO DIVORCE

E–006   The Judicial Separation and Family Law Reform Act 1989 (hereafter referred to as the 1989 Act) represented the first attempt to provide for judicial separation and ancillary reliefs on a statutory footing. The Act operated efficiently and effectively from its introduction, and essentially paved the way for the ultimate introduction of divorce, especially when it was amended by the Family Law Act 1995. Mervyn Taylor T.D., the Minister for Justice, Equality and Law Reform at the time, opined:

> "If we were to single out measures which laid foundations for divorce legislation it was the 1989 Judicial Separation legislation, the 1992 White Paper on Marital Breakdown and the Family Law Act, 1995." [467 *Dáil Debates* Col. 1757].

E–007   Prior to the introduction of the 1989 Act, there was a limited form of separation available in the form of divorce *a mensa et thoro*, granted pursuant to the Matrimonial Causes (Ireland) Act 1870. This was a fault-based relief obtained on the grounds of adultery, cruelty or unnatural practices. The only ancillary reliefs available were limited to orders in respect of alimony and custody, and the issue of succession was dealt with by the granting of the decree, which automatically deprived the "guilty" spouse of his/her right to a share in the estate of the other spouse as provided for in the Succession Act 1965. The court in these cases had no jurisdiction to make orders in relation to property or other issues. Accordingly, it was necessary to make separate applications under each piece of relevant legislation, for example the Married Women's Status Act 1957. The decree of divorce *a mensa et thoro* did not alter the marital status of the parties in any way, but simply relieved them of their duty to cohabit, as became the situation with a decree of judicial separation.

It was, of course, always open to parties wishing to separate to do so by **E–008** entering into a deed of separation, which is probably how most separations were effected prior to the coming into operation of the 1989 Act. During the 1970s and early 1980s, a number of statutes were enacted providing for reliefs in the areas of maintenance, property and domestic violence. The Family Law (Maintenance of Spouses and Children) Act 1976, the Family Home Protection Act 1976 and the Family Law (Protection of Spouses and Children) Act 1981 all marked significant developments in the burgeoning area of matrimonial disputes. Disputes in relation to custody of and access to children were dealt with then, as now, under the Guardianship of Infants Act 1964. Some of the provisions of these earlier pieces of legislation continue in operation today and may, pursuant to section 26 of the Family Law (Divorce) Act 1996 Act, form part of the ancillary reliefs available on divorce.

Given the foregoing piecemeal approach, the introduction of the 1989 **E–009** Act came as a welcome relief to both applicants and practitioners who could now seek a comprehensive range of ancillary reliefs under one piece of legislation, including property adjustment orders, lump sum and periodical payment orders, and orders adjusting succession rights. These reliefs were amended and enhanced by the Family Law Act 1995, which introduced new reliefs such as pension adjustment orders and financial compensation orders.

However effective the provisions of the 1989 Act as amended, it did not provide for re-marriage. It was not until November 1995 that a referendum on the proposed amendment to Article 41 of the constitution was, by a narrow margin, passed. A previous attempt, in 1986, to remove the constitutional ban on divorce failed amid heated – and sometimes divisive – debate. The proposed amendment in 1986 did not differ significantly from the amendment ultimately passed in 1995.

THE CONSTITUTIONAL AMENDMENT

The new Article 41.3.2° was incorporated into the Constitution on June **E–010** 17, 1996 upon the Fifteenth Amendment to the Constitution Bill being signed by the President. This Article now provides that a court designated by law may grant a dissolution of marriage where, but only where, it is satisfied that:

(i) at the date of the institution of the proceedings, the spouses have lived apart from one another for a period of, or periods amounting to, at least four years during the previous five years;

(ii) there is no reasonable prospect of reconciliation between the spouses;

(iii) such provision as the court considers proper having regard to the circumstances exists or will be made for the spouses, any children of either or both of them and any other person prescribed by law;

(iv) any further conditions prescribed by law are complied with.

The provisions of the new Article 41.3.2° have been put into effect by the Family Law (Divorce) Act 1996 (hereafter referred to as the Divorce Act) which became law on February 27, 1997. The Divorce Act is closely modelled on the 1989 Act as amended by the Family Law Act 1995. In fact, the basis and criteria for awards of maintenance on divorce contained in the Divorce Act merely replicate those contained in the 1989 Act as amended.

THE FAMILY LAW (DIVORCE) ACT 1996

E–011   The Family Law (Divorce) Act 1996 [hereinafter the "Divorce Act"] comprises five parts. Part I sets out provisions concerning commencement, interpretation, repeals and expenses. While the date of the coming into operation of the 1996 Act was February 27, 1997, the first divorce granted in Ireland was on January 17, 1997, pursuant to the provisions of Article 41.3.2° of the Constitution [See *R.C. v. C.C.* [1997] 1 I.L.R.M. 401]. This was the first case in which a decree of divorce was granted since ecclesiastical times. The circumstances of the parties in this case were unremarkable. They had sought to order their affairs as amicably as possible with a view to ensuring that there would be no difficulty in complying with the requirement that "proper provision" would be made for the spouses and for any children of either or both of them.

Barron J. considered the various grounds for the granting of a divorce decree. He stated that the court derived its jurisdiction to grant a divorce decree from the Constitution and not from the statute, which had not come into operation at the date of the hearing of the case. It was also clear that there was no statutory provision limiting the power of the High Court to exercise this jurisdiction.

E–012   The court, in *R.C. v. C.C.*, considered the constitutional requirements to be satisfied prior to the granting of a divorce decree. In the case under consideration, all three children of the marriage were adult and no longer dependent. Further, provision had already been made by the applicant husband for his wife and children which essentially resulted in a distribution of almost all the assets of the marriage in their favour. The applicant husband was in a second relationship and had a daughter from that relationship. The court found that there was no reasonable prospect of a reconciliation between the parties, and that it was satisfied that the provisions made for the appropriate parties were proper in the overall circumstances of the family.

An important part of this judgment, and one likely to arise in future applications, was the reference to non-dependent children. The court noted the provisions of Clause 3 of Article 41.3.2° of the Constitution:

". . . such provision as the court considers proper having regard to the circumstances exists or will be made for the spouses, any children of either or both of them and any other person prescribed by law".

This differs from the corresponding statutory provision in section 5(1)(c) of the Family Law (Divorce) Act 1996:

". . . such provision as the court considers proper having regard to the circumstances exists or will be made for the spouses and any dependent members of the family".

E–013 The distinction relates to the issue of dependency, and clearly the wording of the constitutional provision does not preclude the possibility of non-dependent children having provision made for them. This clearly opens the door to applications for divorce being brought under the Constitution in circumstances where a child who does not come within the definition of "dependent member of the family" set out in section 2(1) of the Divorce Act requires provision to be made for him/her. To date no such applications appear to have been made.

The term "dependent member of the family" is defined in identical terms to that in the Family Law Act 1995 and means a child up to the age of 18 years or, if in full-time education, up to the age of 23 years. The requirement to provide for a child suffering a mental or physical disability is not limited by age. The Divorce Act extends the definition of children beyond a child of the marriage, either natural or adopted, to a child in relation to whom either parent is *in loco parentis*. The latter would arise, however, only in circumstances where the spouse *in loco parentis* was aware that he or she was not the parent of the child but nonetheless treated that child as a member of the family. To date there has been no judicial discussion of this point.

E–014 Part II of the Divorce Act deals with obtaining a decree of divorce, and sets out the requirements necessary to comply with the constitutional provisions.

Part III of the Divorce Act contains the comprehensive preliminary and ancillary reliefs available in the context of divorce, and is reviewed in this section in the context of the types of orders which can be made and the factors to be applied by the court in so doing. It is interesting to note that some of the ancillary reliefs available on judicial separation are not necessary, post-divorce, because of the fundamental adjustment in the marital status of the parties, specifically:

(i) the extinguishment of spousal succession rights is no longer necessary;

(ii) there is no need for a similar provision to section 13 of the Family Law Act 1995 in the context of pensions;

(iii) there is no need for provisions similar to those contained in section 4 of the Family Home Protection Act 1976 or section 54(3) of the Family Law Act 1995, as spousal consent to the sale of a family home is no longer necessary.

Part IV of the Divorce Act introduces the necessary taxation reforms to deal with divorce, addressing income and capital taxes, probate and stamp duty.

Part V of the Divorce Act sets out a number of miscellaneous provisions, and amendments to existing legislation.

E–015 With the Family Law (Divorce) Act 1996, Ireland adopted a no-fault system. The scheme of divorce entered into continues the old common law tradition of a life-long spousal support obligation. This acknowledgement that marriage may create permanent support obligations can be viewed as incompatible with the "clean break" doctrine.

FULL AND FINAL SETTLEMENT

E–016 The issue of whether or not a clean break, or a full and final settlement, is facilitated by the divorce legislation also rumbles on with little guidance from the courts, save for the remarks of McGuinness J. in the case of *J.D. v. D.D.* [[1997] 3 I.R. 64]. The case involved the ending of a 30-year long marriage, where there were considerable financial resources available for distribution. The principal issue for determination was the form and level of maintenance to be paid to the wife. The court applied the provisions of section 16 of the Divorce Act to the circumstances of the case in deciding whether it was possible to bring financial issues to a conclusion between the parties by making a "sizeable" lump sum order in favour of the wife. The question posed by the court was whether it should, as a matter of policy, provide a situation of certainty and finality on the irretrievable breakdown of a marriage. In addressing that question, the case of *F. v. F.* [[1995] 2 I.R. 354] (judicial separation) was considered, specifically the judgment of Denham J.:

"Certainty and finality of litigation are important. Some issues in family law are not capable of a final order by law *e.g.* maintenance. However, the fact that some issues in Family Law Courts are not capable of finality does not deprive this area of the law of the important concepts of certainty and finality. Whereas care for dependants requires that there be no finality in some areas the general law regarding certainty should apply unless excluded by law or justice."[*ibid.* at 369].

It should be noted that this judgment was delivered prior to the enactment **E–017** of the Family Law Act 1995 and the Divorce Act. McGuinness J. found herself in agreement with this particular principle in *J.D. v. D.D.* [[1997] 3 I.R. 64]. In that case, however, she noted that no "clean break" provision could be made when financially reordering a broken marriage. She noted that the Oireachtas had legislated to permit repeated applications to court concerning ancillary relief so that finality could not be achieved, and continued:

". . . [I]t appears to me that by the subsequent enactment of the Family Law Act, 1995 and the Family Law (Divorce) Act, 1996, the Oireachtas has made it clear that a 'clean break' situation is not to be sought and that, if anything, financial finality is virtually to be prevented. . . . The court, in making virtually any order in regard to finance and property on the breakdown of a marriage, is faced with the situation where finality is not and never can be achieved. This also appears to mean that no agreement on property between the parties can be completely final, since such finality would be contrary to the policy and provisions of the legislation. The statutory policy is, therefore, totally opposed to the concept of the 'clean break'." [*ibid.* at 89].

The difficulties for both a court and for practitioners in attempting to **E–018** guide a settlement negotiation were acknowledged in this decision. The position in England was referred to, where there is a clear policy of attempting to leave the past behind the separating couple, but McGuinness J. pointed out that "over reliance on the 'clean break' policy has been criticised as causing future hardship on dependent wives".

The court, in *J.D. v. D.D.* [*supra*], went on to order a lump sum payment **E–019** of £200,000 by way of maintenance, in addition to a direction that the husband finance the wife's future residence and that he provide an annual periodic payment of £20,000.

Specific reference to this case was made by White J. in the case of *B.S. v. J.S.* [unreported, Circuit Court (western circuit), February 5, 1999]. A decree of judicial separation had been granted in January 1993, with ancillary orders made on consent between the parties. In October 1997, the wife applied for a divorce with new ancillary orders concerning the family home and a pension adjustment order. The issue arose as to the court's jurisdiction to vacate orders previously made, and the application of the doctrine of *res judicata* to such orders. The court granted the divorce decree and ancillary reliefs sought by the wife, and held that the doctrine of *res judicata* did not apply to such orders. The decision of *J.D. v. D.D.* [see para.

E11

E.–017] was followed, the court stating the comments of McGuinness J. that the Irish statutory policy was totally opposed to the concept of a "clean break" between spouses upon separation or divorce. Indeed, White J. cited with approval McGuinness J.'s statement that financial finality is virtually to be prevented under the legislation.

E–020   The case of *J.C.N. v. R.T.N.* [unreported, High Court, January 15, 1999] demonstrates the difficulties in achieving finality in circumstances of increasing age and decreasing financial resources. The wife was aged 78 and the husband 74. They had separated by deed of separation in 1975, the husband being advised that this was the end of his financial obligations, this being, as McGuinness J. pointed out [at p. 3], "possible under the law as it stood in 1975, prior to the enactment of the Family Law (Maintenance of Spouses and Children) Act, 1976".

E–021   The financial position of both parties had disimproved with the passage of time, with the wife having exhausted the lump sum made available to her on separation, and the husband having retired from his business and now being in receipt of a relatively small pension. He had also been in a second relationship for a long time, having two children from that relationship. The husband had considerable capital, out of which, together with his pension, he discharged a maintenance order to the wife, which she had obtained from the High Court in 1980. Although the court did not refer specifically to the issue of finality or a clean break, the case clearly demonstrated the practical difficulties involved in severing all financial ties where one of the parties remains, despite the passage of time, financially dependent. In granting the decree of divorce, the court went on to adjust the husband's pension by making a form of contingent pension adjustment order, directing that if the husband were to predecease the wife, the trustees were to pay half of the annual pension to the wife, and the other half to the second partner. The existing maintenance position was left as it was, subject to a right to reapply to the court when the taxation position of the parties had been clarified. The most interesting aspect of this case concerns the pension. As the husband's financial circumstances were uncertain, McGuinness J. sought to minimise the disruption of the existing arrangements. Consequently, she granted what can only be described as a contingent pension adjustment order rather than an actual one. While the decision in the case was a sensible one, there appears to be no legislative justification for the order. There is nothing in the Divorce Act to permit a contingent pension adjustment order. There is, however, equally nothing in the Divorce Act that precludes either, and the order could be justified as a pension adjustment order whose operation turns on a condition precedent.

    The issue of whether a "clean break" can be provided by divorce regularly exercises the minds of many participants in the Circuit and High Court. Usually one, if not both, of the parties will be hoping to terminate all aspects of the marital relationship, and it hardly needs pointing out that each case will fall to be determined on its own facts. The onus on the lawyers, therefore, is to clearly advise clients about the uncertainty that surrounds each application and about the potential orders which can be made. It is difficult to see how the concept of a "clean break" will be promoted in future by Irish courts unless there is a radical departure from present judicial interpretation of the existing statutory provisions, a departure which seems unlikely against a background of a society reluctant to promote easy escape from marital obligations.

CONSEQUENCES OF A DECREE OF DIVORCE

The most obvious effect or result of the granting of a decree of divorce is **E–022** set out in section 10 of the Divorce Act, which is that the parties are free to remarry. If the aim of the parties is simply to separate and regulate the terms of the marital breakdown, a deed of separation or application under the 1989 Act and the Family Law Act 1995 would be appropriate.

Another reason widely cited by those looking for a divorce is the desire for a complete cessation of all ties between the parties; in other words, a clean break. It is often said that on divorce, the status of the marriage is irrevocably altered in that the parties are no longer the spouses of one another: the latter part of this sentence is not, however, entirely accurate, as a number of ambiguities arise around the word "spouse", which is referred to in section 2(2)(c) of the Divorce Act in the following terms:

". . . a reference to a spouse includes a reference to a person who is a party to a marriage that has been dissolved under this Act."

The foregoing definition is limited to use in the context of the Divorce Act, **E–023** and is the first indication in the legislation that the word spouse can continue to be used as a description of a person whose marriage has been dissolved pursuant to a decree under section 5 of the Divorce Act. Parties continue to be "spouses" for the purposes of the rights and remedies available to them under the Divorce Act, but not under other Acts. For example, a party who is the beneficiary of a pension adjustment order granted under section 17 of the Divorce Act remains a spouse for that purpose. Indeed, most of the ancillary reliefs available under Part III of the Divorce Act are available to former spouses.

WHEN IS A DIVORCED PERSON STILL A SPOUSE?

After a decree of divorce has been granted, the parties' succession rights **E–024** are severed completely. Accordingly, there is no need for an order extinguishing those rights similar to section 14 of the Family Law Act 1995. It appears that the status of spouse terminates in the general sense of the word, although this is something that could have been clarified by the Divorce Act with a distinction being made in relation to spouses who

FLP R.0: July 2000

remain so for the purposes of the Act. However, it is a striking feature of Irish divorce legislation that the financial obligations of one spouse to another continue beyond the ending of the marriage, except in certain specified circumstances. For example, section 22 of the Divorce Act provides for orders, including maintenance orders, to be varied or discharged if there is a change in circumstances or new evidence. Under the terms of section 22, the court may vary or discharge the following orders:

   (i) maintenance pending suit orders (section 12);

   (ii) periodical payments, secured periodical payments and lump sums orders (section 13);

   (iii) property adjustment orders under section 14(1)(b), (c) and (d);

   (iv) an order under section 15(1)(a);

   (v) a financial compensation order (section 16); and

   (vi) a pension adjustment order (section 17(2)) "retirement benefits".

An explanation of this fact often alarms clients who may have presumed that all ties are being severed and that all connections between them are at an end.

SPOUSAL OBLIGATIONS

E–025   There are circumstances when financial obligations between the spouses will terminate with no possibility of resurrection, that is on the death of either spouse or on the remarriage of the recipient, or beneficiary, spouse. There are also certain reliefs which are denied to a spouse who has remarried, which of course raises the issue of whether all relevant reliefs should be sought at the time of the granting of the divorce decree, in anticipation of remarriage. The court has power to take into account the possible future circumstances of the spouses under section 20(2)(b) of the Divorce Act which contemplates the possibility of remarriage:

"[I]n deciding whether to make an order . . . and in determining the provisions of such an order, the court shall, [in particular, have regard to the following matters including]:
(b) the financial needs, obligations and responsibilities which each of the spouses has or is likely to have in the foreseeable future (whether in the case of the remarriage of the spouse or otherwise)".

The future plans of the spouses may not, however, always be before the court, and therefore may not be taken into account. Accordingly, orders can be made which are incapable of review, such as the provision of a lump sum that is quickly dissipated.

E–026   The orders which automatically stop operating on the death of either spouse or remarriage of the receiving spouse are as follows:

(i) orders for periodic and secured periodic payments under section 13 of the Divorce Act;

(ii) orders for financial compensation pursuant to section 16 of the Divorce Act;

(iii) orders for the payment of a contingency or death-in-service benefit under section 17 of the Divorce Act; and

(iv) orders where periodical payments are being made to the receiving spouse from the proceeds of sale of any property pursuant to section 19(4) of the Divorce Act.

A former spouse is not precluded under the Divorce Act from seeking a **E–027** lump sum order on his or her remarriage. That said, such an order would only be granted in exceptional circumstances, with the court taking all the circumstances into account. This situation whereby a former remarried spouse can nearly always seek the payment of a lump sum presents significant difficulties for lottery winners or persons who have made significant gains in the stock or property markets, and is a striking example of how a "clean break" situation is difficult to achieve.

The following orders may not be sought by spouses who have remarried:

(i) an order for periodical or secured periodical payments pursuant to section 13(1) of the Divorce Act [See section 16(2)(c) of the Divorce Act];

(ii) a property adjustment order pursuant to section 16(2)(c) of the Divorce Act [see section 14(3) of the Divorce Act.];

(iii) a financial compensation order pursuant to section 16 of the Divorce Act [see section 16(2)(c) of the Divorce Act]; and

(iv) a pension adjustment order pursuant to section 17 of the Divorce Act [see section 17(23)(a) of the Divorce Act.].

In summary, support obligations after divorce continue for the lifetime of the spouses, save in very limited circumstances.

GROUNDS FOR DIVORCE

INTRODUCTION

Part II of the Divorce Act comprises sections 5 to 10, which deal with **E–028** obtaining a decree of divorce, pursuant to the provisions of Article 41.3.2° of the Constitution. This Part of the Divorce Act also sets out what are referred to as "safeguards" to ensure that the parties are informed of the alternatives to divorce proceedings and also assists in facilitating reconciliation. Section 5 sets out the legal requirements necessary to obtain a decree of divorce, while section 10 details the effect of the decree. Sections 6, 7 and 8 of the Divorce Act deal with issues of reconciliation, mediation and separation by deed or by decree. These sections also detail actions that can be taken by the court to assist efforts at either reconciliation or at negotiating some of the terms of ancillary relief of the proposed divorce. Sections 6 and 7 are identical in their terms to sections 5 and 6 of the Judicial Separation and Family Law Reform Act 1989, with the obvious addition that judicial separation should be identified as an alternative to divorce. The exact method of imparting this advice by the solicitor is not specified in the Divorce Act, but a certificate pursuant to section 6 must be filed in court with all initiating documentation, and the certificate of the respondent's solicitor must be filed at the same time as the entry of the appearance.

E–029   While advice on reconciliation is clearly meritorious and indeed necessary, what most parties to divorce are seeking is a dissolution of the marriage with the consequent freedom to remarry, if necessary. The four-year waiting period is designed to ensure that the marriage has terminated and that people have had time to consider their positions and their futures. It is unlikely in the context of divorce that reconciliation will be entertained, given that in the course of the four years' separation, the parties will have entered into arrangements dealing with the breakdown of the marriage and may have formed new lifestyles. In the Dáil Debates leading up to the enactment of the Divorce Act, consideration was given to the issue of mandatory counselling and mediation, but these proposals were rejected as being impractical and unenforceable. It can be argued that the provisions of sections 6 and 7 are somewhat unrealistic in so far as most applicants who seek recourse to the Divorce Act are doing so for the express purpose of dissolving the marriage.

E–030   Whatever about the practicalities or otherwise of counselling, mediation may be useful in allowing the parties to negotiate some or all of the terms of the ancillary relief to be granted by the court. It would probably be somewhat unusual for a couple contemplating divorce not to have arrived at some form of mutually acceptable arrangements prior to the expiration of the four-year period, but mediation is likely to be helpful in redefining those terms. Section 9 of the Divorce Act is significant in that it confers evidential privilege on communications made during reconciliation, counselling or mediation, and a similar provision [section 7A of the 1989 Act] in relation to judicial separation was inserted by section 45 of the Divorce Act.

JURISDICTION OF COURTS AND VENUE

E–031   Concurrently with the High Court, the Circuit Family Court can grant decrees under Article 41.3.2° of the Constitution and section 38(1) of the Divorce Act. Both the Circuit Court and the High Court therefore, have an original concurrent jurisdiction to hear divorce applications [section 38(1)

E16

of the Divorce Act]. The court may grant a decree of divorce if either spouse is domiciled (*i.e.* living in a place with the intention of residing in that place permanently) in the State on the date of the institution of the proceedings concerned or, alternatively, either of the spouses was ordinarily resident in the State throughout the period of one year ending on that date [section 39(1) of the Divorce Act]. Most applications will, from the point of view of geographical convenience and a concern for costs, be maintained in the Circuit Court. However, section 38(2) of the Divorce Act facilitates the transfer of the proceedings to the High Court on the application of an interested party where the rateable value of land the subject of the proceedings exceeds £200. An order made prior to the transfer application will be valid unless discharged or varied by the High Court.

It is also possible to transfer proceedings from the High Court to the **E–032** Circuit Court. The circumstances where this will be possible were discussed by Denham J. in the recent case of *M.W. v. D.W.* [unreported, Supreme Court, November 25, 1999]. Denham J. stated [at p. 5] that "[t]he test to be applied is that an order to remit should be in the interests of justice". Delay does not preclude a party seeking to remit an action as an application to remit can be made at any time after an appearance has been entered. However, Denham J. held in the instant case that "delay . . . was an important factor in considering the interests of justice". In refusing to remit the case from the High Court to the Circuit Court, Denham J. stated:

"This is a dysfunctional family, of parents and children, living under one roof, pending the court decision on the action. In light of the circumstances time is an important aspect of this case. Also important is access to court on interim and interlocutory applications to process the case. The probability is that proceedings in [the Circuit Court] would take longer and while the financial affairs on the surface appear not too complex the intricacy arises in the applicant's suspicion as to other assets and intention to try to prove their existence. The court has a discretion. The discretion should be exercised to remit if that be in the interests of justice. In the circumstances of the case the refusal [of the High Court] to exercise the discretion to remit was just. Further delay should be avoided. The case should be decided as soon as it is reasonably possible. Such procedure would be for the benefit of all the family." [*ibid.* at p. 6].

Both parties may consent to the Circuit Court having jurisdiction to deal with applications for ancillary relief orders even in circumstances where the rateable valuation of the property exceeds £200. The proceedings may be issued and the case dealt with on the circuit in which any of the parties (including dependent family members) ordinarily resides or carries on business or occupation [section 38(3) of the Divorce Act]. Whilst not intending to encourage "location shopping", it could be useful in certain circumstances to have a choice of locations in which to bring the proceedings.

DIVORCE DECREE

E–033   Section 5 of the Divorce Act provides that a court designated by law may grant a divorce decree where, on application to it by either spouse, it is satisfied that:

> "(a) at the date of the institution of the proceedings, the spouses have lived apart from one another for a period of, or periods amounting to, at least four years during the previous five years,
>
> (b) there is no reasonable prospect of a reconciliation between the spouses, and
>
> (c) such provision as the court considers proper having regard to the circumstances exists or will be made for the spouses and any dependent members of the family".

E–034   It can be seen from the foregoing that no element of fault needs to be ascribed to either party in order to qualify for a divorce under the section. The parties need only satisfy the requirements of section 5 for a decree to be granted, none of which make any reference to fault or blame, although the issue of conduct arises in the context of matters to which the court shall have regard in deciding whether to make an order for ancillary relief [section 20(2)(i) of the Divorce Act]. Issues relating to conduct may be set out in detail in the endorsement of claim of the family law civil bill, but no matter how dreadful the circumstances, they will not prevent the granting of the divorce if the terms of section 5 are adhered to.

This can of course lead to divorces being granted where one of the parties is very much opposed to it, and where that party may not consider the marriage to be at an end, despite the duration of the separation. It is open to a spouse in such circumstances to plead under section 5(1)(b) of the Divorce Act that there may be a prospect of reconciliation. The court is, however, under no obligation in such a situation other than to adjourn the proceedings under section 8 of the Divorce Act, to enable attempts to be made by the spouses to effect a reconciliation.

LIVING APART

E–035   The apparent simplicity of the key terms of section 5(1)(a) of the Divorce Act is misleading. Such terms have generally not been defined. The absence of a definition of "living apart" has caused particular difficulty. Living apart was first introduced into Irish law in the Judicial Separation and Family Law Reform Act 1989 as a ground for judicial separation. The Act contained an explanation of living apart in section 2(3) such that:

> ". . . spouses shall be treated as living apart from each other unless they are living with each other in the same household, and references to

spouses living with each other shall be construed as references to their living with each other in the same household."

The difficulty with this definition is the word "household", but at least some guidance was provided in the context of judicial separation. Strangely, no such explanation was included in the Divorce Act. In the absence of a legislative definition of living apart, reliance has been placed by the Irish courts on highly persuasive precedents in the English/Welsh jurisdictions. **E–036**

As a starting premise, it appears clear that parties could be held to be "living apart" while continuing to reside under the same roof, perhaps for economic reasons. During the second stage of the Bill to amend the Constitution, Minister Mervyn Taylor T.D. stated:

> "The term 'living apart' is used in the Judicial Separation and Family Law Reform Act, 1989 and it is also a familiar term in many other jurisdictions where it has been held that this phrase will clearly cover whether the spouses have physically separated and are living in different places. The case law also states that where domestic life is not shared it is possible for there to be two households under the one roof."

The court in the case of *Pulford v. Pulford* [[1923] All E.R. 10] determined that the legal concept of living apart does not require a change of address, and was not a withdrawal from a place, "but from a state of things". **E–037**

In *Hopes v. Hopes* [[1949] 2 All E.R. 920], it was stated that spouses will be considered to be "living apart", when, although each is living in the family home, they have ceased "to be one household and become two households".

In the case of *Bartram v. Bartram* [[1949] 2 All E.R. 270] the issue arose in the context of desertion, when the parties separated by way of desertion by the wife. Subsequently, unable to find alternative accommodation, the wife returned to the house where the husband was residing with his mother, and commenced living there in a separate bedroom from the husband, whom she avoided at all times other than for meals. The court held that despite the return of the wife, the desertion had continued and the issue of whether the parties intended to set up matrimonial home together was relevant. Accordingly, the desertion was held to be ongoing. The court stated: **E–038**

> "The question is: Do the facts proved establish that it [the desertion] was brought to an end? In my view, it can only be brought to an end if the facts show an intention on the part of the wife to set up a matrimonial home with the husband. If the facts do not establish any intention on the part of the wife to set up a matrimonial home, the mere fact that, as a lodger, she went to live under the same roof as her husband, because she had nowhere else to go, does not remove the desertion which she had already started and which continued to run."[*ibid.* at 272].

It was held, in that case, that the requisite three years' desertion had been established by the husband and the decree was granted. Although desertion cannot be equated to "living apart", the fact that the parties did not intend to live as a married couple was relevant.

In the case of *Mouncer v. Mouncer* [[1972] 1 W.L.R. 321], the parties had continued to live together for the sake of the children. The court held that in those circumstances, applying a test of physicality as opposed to intent, the parties were living together and, accordingly, no divorce was granted.

E–039   The case of *Santos v. Santos* [[1972] 2 All E.R. 246] contained an analysis of the authorities in circumstances where the couple were not living in the same house and the question to be determined was whether this in itself was enough to qualify as "living apart". The court held that something more than physical separation was required, and that the attitudes of mind of the parties in each particular case had to be considered.

The case of *Holmes v. Mitchell* [[1991] S.T.C. 25] is the most recent instructive English authority on "living apart". In this case, the English Inspector of Taxes issued the following very helpful guidelines as to the questions to be asked to determine whether a couple are "living apart under the same roof":

(i)   how is the house divided up and what are the arrangements for using kitchen and bathroom facilities?

(ii) what services do the couple provide for each other, for example, cooking, cleaning, etc.?

(iii) what financial arrangements have been made in relation to the alleged separation?

(iv) what do the husband and wife do to avoid meeting each other in the house?

E–040   The first judicial guidance on the no-fault ground of "living apart" in Irish divorce procedings came in the case of *McA. v. McA.* [[2000] 2 I.L.R.M. 48]. The case was also the first reported contested divorce in this country dealing with ancillary reliefs as well as the issue of "living apart". Since the coming into operation of the Divorce Act, there had been little or no defintion of the term "living apart", despite much discussion amongst lawyers in that regard. Indeed, the concept of "living apart" caused some controversy during the divorce referendum, with anti-divorce campaigners claiming that it could be used unilaterally by a spouse to claim a divorce while continuing to live with the respondent. The applicant and the respondent were married in October 1968. They had two children who were no longer dependent. In 1988 the applicant discovered the respondent was having an affair with another woman. In September of that year, the respondent left the family home to continue the affair. The respondent ended the second relationship in 1991 and returned home to live with the applicant and their two children. On his return, he agreed to pay the applicant wife a sum of £750 per month in cash and later increased this sum

E20

to £1,000 per month. He also covered her car and motoring expenses. The applicant stated that she was happy with his return and had never considered the marriage to be finished. The respondent said his primary motive for returning was to develop his relationship with his then 18-year-old son.

The parties slept in separate bedrooms, even when on holidays with the children. They did not recommence sexual relations. While living together they were civil to each other and, when both were present, they ate meals together. When the children were present, the respondent took a full part in household arrangements. The respondent often retired to his bedroom early to watch television and had a telephone installed in that room. The respondent often left at weekends and only saw the applicant for a few hours a week.

In 1995, whilst they were still living together in the same house, the applicant began a relationship, including a sexual relationship, with another man. In 1996, the respondent began a relationship with a woman.

The respondent had established a successful business, of which the holding company was 85 per cent owned by him and 15 per cent owned by the applicant. The value of the business had reached its peak and the respondent had diversified his business in Ireland and abroad. The new businesses were in the respondent's sole name. The respondent had assets of some £2 million in addition to the old business, with an annual income of some £120,000. The respondent had agreed before the court hearing to transfer the family home and an apartment in Tenerife into the sole name of the wife. He had also agreed that the applicant should have the shop that she had been managing for many years and the house adjoining it. The respondent further agreed that the applicant could become the sole owner of another house in Dublin and agreed to purchase the applicant's 15 per cent share in the business, at a price to be agreed with the court.

The applicant sought a decree of judicial separation and the respondent **E–041** counterclaimed for divorce; the date of the institution of divorce proceedings was August 16, 1999. The respondent's entitlement to a divorce was contested by the applicant on the ground that they had not lived apart for four of the five years preceding the date of the institution of proceedings.

The net point therefore was: did the applicant and respondent "live apart" from one another for at least four years during the previous five years at the date of the institution of proceedings.

McCracken J. considered the law on living apart. He noted that the **E–042** Divorce Act did not provide any definition guidance and sought assistance from highly persuasive precedents in the English/Welsh jurisdictions. He considered the judgments given in *Mouncer v. Mouncer* [[1972] 1 W.L.R. 321] and *Santos v. Santos* [[1972] 2 All E.R. 246]. McCracken J. in *McA. v. McA.* [[2000] 2 I.L.R.M. 48] distinguished the *Mouncer* case where the spouses were deemed to have lived as a single household "from the wholly admirable motive of caring properly for their children". The *Santos* case was accepted by McCracken J. as a case which clearly expressed "the view that the intention of the parties is a very relevant matter in determining issues of whether they live apart of whether there has been desertion" [*ibid.* at p. 7]. In support of the proposition that intention was a very relevant matter in determining whether the parties had been living apart, McCracken J. noted that there are a number of instances in which the matrimonial relationship continues even though the parties are not living together under one roof, such as while one party is in hospital or obliged to spend a lot of time away from home for the purposes of employment. He referred to the judgment of Sachs J. in *Santos* wherein the latter stated:

"[L]iving apart . . . is a state of affairs to establish which it is in the vast generality of cases . . . necessary to prove something more than that the husband and wife are physically separated. For the purposes of that vast generality, it is sufficient to say that the relevant state of affairs does not exist whilst both parties recognise the marriage as subsisting. That involves considering attitudes of mind and naturally the difficulty of judicially determining that attitude in a particular case may on occasion be great . . . identification of an attitude of mind is required". [[1972] 2 All E.R. 246 at 255].

E–043 McCracken J. accepted this approach in *McA.* in recognising that just as "there is a mental element to" living apart other than mere physical separation, there is more to living together than being physically in the same house. In this case, the husband's return to the family home in 1991 was not activated by a desire to restart the marriage, but to develop his relationship with his children. Accordingly, he had no intellectual attachment to the marriage, although he did live in the same house as the wife. They ate and holidayed together, though that was in the interests of the children. McCracken J. stated [at p. 8] in relation to the test for "living apart":

"I do not think one can look solely at where the parties physically reside, or at their mental or intellectual attitude to the marriage. Both of these elements must be considered, and in conjunction with each other".

E–044 In essence, this is a mixed test: one that encompasses an objective element, though it is primarily subjective in any case where the parties have physically separated. If one cannot look solely at physical separation then the real determinant becomes mental attitude, which must be subjective. In this case, for example, there was no analysis of who looked after the house, who did the shopping and the other mundane activities that express the realities of everyday life.

A larger element of objectivity would in all likelihood enter the equation if the couple were still living under the same roof, or had only physically separated for a short time. More importantly, the real strength of the subjective approach in this case prevented objective factors such as dining together and going on holidays from blocking "living apart" as a state of mind.

FLP R.0: July 2000

It is probable that the broad approach to "living apart" was permitted **E–045** because the mental attitude was common to both husband and wife. In *McA.*, McCracken J. found that the wife, too, had withdrawn from the marriage, as evidenced by forming a new relationship. In granting the divorce, McCracken J. referred to the mental attitude of the parties, which tends to show the need for both to share this view. Given the subjective approach favoured in *McA.*, this is probably necessary, but would not be the end of the argument on the matter. The Act requires the spouses to live apart from each other, and in theory this could be achieved by the unilateral withdrawal of one of the spouses. In such a scenario, a more objective approach would be desirable.

In summary, following the *McA.* judgment, it appears that "living apart" **E–046** means something more than physical separation; the mental attitude of the parties is of considerable relevance. "Marriage", post *McA.*, is not concerned with where the parties live or whether they live under the same roof, and just as physically separated parties can maintain a full matrimonial relationship, parties who live under the same roof may live apart from one another. In determining whether the parties are living apart, it now appears that the court must look to both where the parties reside and their mental attitude to the marriage.

The *McA.* judgment has the potential to prompt practitioners to adopt a more relaxed approach to the four-year rule. It must be emphasised that the dangers inherent in this practice could lead to a situation where a decree is refused and proceedings have to be re-instituted, with the attendant implication for costs.

NO REASONABLE PROSPECT OF A RECONCILIATION

Section 5(1)(b) of the Divorce Act sets out the second imperative for **E–047** qualification for a decree of divorce. The court must be satisfied that "there is no reasonable prospect of a reconciliation between the spouses", something that seems to be set out more in hope than expectation in light of the requirement for a four-year separation. The direction to the court is, however, enshrined in the Constitution. Therefore, there is a duty on the court to establish in each case that there is no possibility of a reconciliation [see *E.P. v. C.P.*, unreported, High Court, November 22, 1998, where McGuinness J. was satisfied that the breakdown of the marriage was irretrievable when she stated: "Both parties accept that there is no reasonable prospect of a reconciliation"]. In granting a divorce decree in *J.C.N. v. R.T.N.* [unreported, High Court, January 15, 1999], McGuinness J. stated [at p. 2]: "There is clearly no prospect of a reconciliation; the husband lived in a permanent second relationship since 1978".

As with the issue of living apart, it is likely that each case will turn on its **E–048** own facts, and the degree of acrimony or amicability in each case will assist the court in deciding the issue. In the later case of *Moorehead v. Tiilikainen* [unreported, High Court, O'Sullivan J., June 17, 1999], one of the issues to be determined was whether a reconciliation had been effected between the parties, although this was in the context of a previous separation agreement. In this case, it was held that the intention of the parties was relevant in determining whether a reconciliation had taken place, which could be seen as the flipside of *McA*.

The relevant word in the subsection is "reasonable", and the court is not charged with the task of ensuring that every last remnant of civility between the parties has been abandoned. The insertion of the word reasonable ensures that a party who does not want a divorce under any circumstances will not be able to disrupt matters by claiming a possibility of a successful reconciliation when clearly there is no such possibility.

That is not to say, however, that the court does not have jurisdiction to refuse to grant a decree of divorce where it believes there is a reasonable prospect of reconciliation. In such circumstances, should the court decide not to adjourn the proceedings under section 8 of the Divorce Act, it would appear to be open to the court to simply refuse to grant a decree, and the matter would then have to be dealt with on appeal. It is unlikely, however, that such a refusal could be envisaged in the absence of agreement from the parties to the proceedings.

PROPER PROVISION FOR THE SPOUSE AND DEPENDENT MEMBERS OF THE FAMILY

E–049   By virtue of section 5(1)(c) of the Divorce Act, the court must be satisfied that such provision as the court considers proper, having regard to the circumstances, exists, or will be made for the spouses and any dependent members of the family. Section 2(1) of the Divorce Act defines a "dependent member" as any child under the age of 18 years [or 23 years if in full-time education] of both spouses, or adopted by both spouses or in relation to whom both spouses are *in loco parentis,* so long as the other spouse is aware that he or she is not the parent of the child and has treated the child as a member of the family. It is surprising that whereas this subsection alludes to "dependent members of the family", Article 41.3.2° of the Constitution refers to "any children of either or both" of the spouses. In the case of *R.C. v. C.C.* [[1997] 1 I.L.R.M. 401; see also above at paras E–012 and E–013] Barron J. confirms that there is little doubt that the latter interpretation will prevail:

> "Since the jurisdiction invoked is that contained in the Constitution and not that amplified by the Act, it is necessary for the court to consider the position of the children. While I do not purport to determine that non-dependent children should necessarily have provision made for them, I am satisfied that in the particular circumstances of the present case it is proper that certainly the two daughters of the marriage should have provision made for them in the interests of the family as a whole".

E–050   The reference to "any children" in the Constitution is clearly capable of a much wider interpretation than that of "any dependent members of the family" as set out in the Divorce Act, where the term is defined as anyone under the age of 18 years, or if over 18 but below 23, is in full-time education. There are no such limitations on the interpretation of "child" used in the Constitution. It is therefore possible to envisage circumstances whereby a divorcing parent could be ordered to continue maintenance payments in respect of an adult child where he/she no longer wishes to do so, in order that the court might be satisfied that proper provision exists or will be made for the "children" of the marriage.

It must be remembered that the requirement of proper provision must be in place to the satisfaction of the court, prior to the granting of the divorce decree. The court, cannot decide to grant the decree first and then examine the issue of ancillary reliefs, but the court need not ensure that the provision exists at the time of the making of the decree, if it is satisfied that it will be in place in the future. The reference to "all the circumstances" means that a subjective view will be taken of each family's situation and there are no standards or guidelines in place as to what constitutes proper provision in general.

The case of *McA. v. McA.* [[2000] 2 I.L.R.M. 48] is instructive in terms of   **E–051** the ancillary reliefs ordered by the court to form "proper provision". The court in that case referred to the provisions of section 20 of the Divorce Act, and also to the fact that the wife's share of the company being 15 per cent was worth £1.2 million which she would receive as it was hers as of right. The court went on to direct the lump sum payment of £300,000 in recognition of the full value of the husband's business interests, and also made a periodic payments order of £4,500 per month. Issues concerning property had been agreed between the parties prior to the hearing. The manner in which McCracken J. ordered the ancillary reliefs will be of guidance to practitioners in advising wealthy clients.

It would appear that the court is not constrained to consider only the financial circumstances (including property) of the marriage but also the behaviour of the parties might be taken into account and the post-divorce circumstances in which the children are likely to find themselves. Certainly the court is charged with taking conduct into account in deciding whether to make orders for ancillary reliefs under section 20(2)(i) "if . . . in the opinion of the court it would in all the circumstances of the case be unjust to disregard it [the conduct]". However, while the court may take cognisance of all the circumstances of the case in deciding whether proper provision exists, or has been made under section 5(1)(c), it cannot refuse to grant a decree on the basis of conduct, if the three requirements set out in section 5(1) have been adhered to.

The criteria set out in section 20 of the Divorce Act bear close   **E–051A** resemblance to those contained in section 25 of the Matrimonial Causes Act 1973, which governs divorce applications in England and Wales. In *White v. White* [[2000] 3 F.L.R. 555], the House of Lords emphasised the need for equality and fairness in the division of assets. The parties in that case, who were both farmers had been married for over 30 years and had

had three children. The wife claimed that as well as contracting a marriage, she had contracted an equal farming partnership. They both brought money to the undertaking. One farm was in joint names, although the husband's father had played a significant part in providing the initial capital. Another farm was inherited later by the husband, as his share of the father's estate. The assets were worth £4 to 5 million. While the High Court accepted that the farm was run in partnership over the entire period of the marriage, the Court rejected the wife's claim for an equal division of the farm, which would have enabled her to run an independent farm. Instead, the Court focused on the wife's "reasonable requirements". Adopting this approach, the Court awarded the wife approximately one fifth of the total wealth. The wife appealed to the Court of Appeal. The Court of Appeal accepted that the dominant feature of the case was that from first to last, the parties traded as equal partners. However, the Court did not consider it appropriate to divide the assets equally, as the husband's father had made a significant contribution to the acquisition of the farm. Instead, having regard to the parties' contributions and the goal of overall fairness, it increased the wife's share to reflect approximately, two fifths of the estate. Both parties appealed unsuccessfully to the House of Lords.

The House of Lords held that in the division of assets on divorce, the Court should approach the case from the point of view of fairness between the parties. [This "yardstick of equality" was applied again by the House of Lords in the subsequent decision of *Cowen v. Cowen*.] All of the factors set out in the statutory guidelines were relevant to the determination of the claim. Lord Nicholls (with whom the other Law Lords concurred), stated that as a general guide, equality should be departed from only if, and to the extent that, there is good reason for doing so. Lord Nicholls also stated that there should be no bias in favour of the money earner as against the homemaker and child carer. The absence of financial need should not be determinative of the award. In this regard, he noted that there was nothing either in the statutory provisions or in the underlying objective of securing fair financial arrangements, which would lead him to suppose that the available assets of the Respondent became immaterial once the claimant's financial needs were satisfied. Where assets exceeded the financial needs of the parties, there was no reason why the surplus should automatically belong to one party rather than the other. On the facts of a particular case, there may be a good reason why the wife should be confined to her needs and the husband left with the much larger balance, but the mere absence of financial need could not, by itself, be a sufficient reason. Regarding the decision of the Court of Appeal in the case before the House, Lord Nicholls noted that in exercising its discretion, the Court had in mind all the available assets, the contribution made by the husband' father, the wife's dual role as business partner and as wife and mother and the overall goal of fairness. In his view, the amount of the award was well within the ambit of the Court of Appeal's discretion.

E–052   If proper provision does not exist at the time of the application for the divorce decree, it is probable that it will be brought about by the court by way of orders for ancillary relief. If a court is not satisfied as to proper provision, it may re-examine and amend previous agreements or orders, regardless of whether these were operating to the satisfaction of the parties or not. This is one of the most controversial aspects of the Divorce Act. The power of the court to refuse to grant a decree of divorce unless satisfied with the terms of the orders agreed or being proposed has led to practical difficulties, with some judges adopting an interventionist approach despite the agreement of the parties to future financial arrangements. Difficulties also arise in that regard for practitioners who may have participated in settlement negotiations on behalf of their clients and considered the resulting heads of agreement to be worthy of recommendation to their client. Confidence in hard-fought terms of agreement may then be eroded by the refusal of the judge to make the order. It would appear in such circumstances that there is little option but to renegotiate the terms, not always a welcome proposal for at least one of the parties.

The documentation to be supplied to the court to help it assess whether proper provision has or has not been made will be examined in the section on procedure. It is also instructive to look at the provisions of section 20 of the Divorce Act, which set out in detail the matters to which the court shall have regard in deciding whether to make orders for ancillary reliefs, as doubtless the same matters will be considered by the court in deciding on the issue of "proper provision". The status of a subsisting separation agreement and court orders will be of relevance in deciding the status of the existing "proper provision", and these can be revisited and reviewed to obtain the desired result.

The situation in relation to judicial separation is somewhat different. **E–053** Provided the parties come within one of the grounds set out in section 2 of the Judicial Separation and Family Law Reform Act 1989, then the decree of judicial separation will be granted. It seems ironic that parties who might have obtained a decree of judicial separation on the basis of having no normal marital relationship for only one year could then avail of almost identical ancillary reliefs to those available on divorce, without, obviously, the right to remarry. However, in circumstances where there are dependent children in a family, the court is again mandated to ensure proper provision exists or has been made for the welfare of the children. The original terms of section 3(2)(a)(i) of the Judicial Separation and Family Law Reform Act 1989 were amended by section 45 of the Divorce Act.

Finally, although not a constituent ground for obtaining a decree of divorce, the provisions of section 5(2) of the Divorce Act must be examined in so far as they permit the court to make, of its own motion, directions in relation to the welfare, custody of or right of access to any dependent family members in any case before it. This power is in addition to the power of the court to make such orders under sections 11 (preliminary orders) and 15 (ancillary orders) of the Divorce Act provided applications in relation to such matters have been brought before it.

E–054   In summary, the implications of section 5(1)(c) of the Divorce Act are obvious. The court has the power to refuse to grant a decree of divorce in circumstances where it is not satisfied that proper financial arrangements have been put in place to ensure that the spouses and dependent family members have been catered for and, in this regard, the court may refuse to direct that a settlement agreement entered into by the parties be made a rule of court. This can have very practical consequences for parties who have arrived at such an agreement, in so far as the court has the jurisdiction vested in it by section 5(1)(c) to interfere with a hard-fought settlement. A similar jurisdiction is vested in the court in the context of judicial separation, pursuant to section 3(2)(a)(i) of the Judicial Separation and Family Law Reform Act 1989 as amended by section 45 of the Divorce Act.

SECTIONS 6 AND 7 OF THE DIVORCE ACT

E–055   Sections 6 and 7 of the Divorce Act set out the duties of the solicitor acting for either applicant or respondent in relation to advising the client of the alternatives to divorce. Section 6 sets out the obligations towards an applicant while section 7 details the obligations towards a respondent. In all other respects, the sections are identical.

These safeguards first appeared in sections 5 and 6 of the Judicial Separation and Family Law Reform Act 1989. The duties of solicitors relating to divorce are only different in so far as the client must be advised of the possibility of a judicial separation as an alternative to divorce. The solicitor must, before the institution of proceedings, furnish the client with a list of persons qualified to assist in the reconciliation process [sections 6(2)(a) and 7(2)(a) of the Divorce Act]. [See Division J]. The possibility of engaging the services of a mediator to help bring about a separation or a divorce on agreed terms is also to be discussed with the client, who must be provided with a list of suitably qualified mediators for that purpose [sections 6(2)(b) and 7(2)(b) of the Divorce Act]. [See also Division C].

E–056   During the course of Dáil and Seanad debates on this part of the Divorce Act, much was made of the possibility of obliging the parties to attend for counselling before permitting them to obtain a decree of divorce. Deputy Woods, at the Second Stage of the Bill, [467 *Dáil Debates* Col. 1778] was of the opinion that:

> "The Bill should contain a provision placing an obligation on the spouses initiating a separation or divorce process to participate in counselling, proof of which could take the form of a certificate from the counselling service, or other similar document".

These proposals, while laudable, were rejected. Indeed, it is difficult to see how applicants for divorce could have been forced to attend counselling sessions, after a period of four years' separation during which time people would presumably have moved on to develop their own lives. In addition to the practical difficulties, there might also have been constitutional difficulties associated with compelling a person to attend for counselling which they did not want.

Sections 6(2)(c) and 7(2)(c) of the Divorce Act impose a duty on the **E–057** solicitor to discuss with their client the possibility of separating by way of a deed of separation. It is probable that most parties seeking relief specifically under the Divorce Act will have rejected the deed of separation as a means of resolving the issues surrounding the marital breakdown. Indeed, some parties may already have entered into a deed of separation by the time of application for divorce. Nonetheless, the obligation remains on the solicitor to outline this possibility to their client and presumably to promote the desirability of same.

A similar situation pertains in relation to judicial separation, pursuant to sections 6(3) and 7(3) of the Divorce Act. However, this would appear to be a more realistic exhortation to the solicitor, who can advise their client of the advantages of orders available under the Judicial Separation and Family Law Reform Act 1989, and the Family Law Act 1995, in comparison to the Divorce Act. A client may wish, for example, to avail of relief pursuant to section 13 of the Family Law Act 1995 [preservation of pension entitlements], a relief not available under the Divorce Act.

Solicitors for both applicant and respondent must file a certificate with **E–058** the originating proceedings confirming that they have fulfilled their duties under sections 6 and 7 of the Divorce Act. It is useful as a practice to have a list of professional persons and bodies which may be furnished to the client before signing the certificate. It is unwise to adopt a cavalier attitude to compliance with sections 6 and 7 as it is clearly open to the court to make detailed enquiries in this regard. However, the exact manner in which the information is imparted by solicitors in relation to these matters is at their discretion.

A copy of the relevant certificate must accompany the family law civil bill on service of same, and the entry of appearance when being filed on behalf of the respondent.

The Divorce Act is silent as to how lay litigants are to be made aware of the alternatives to divorce, as indeed the 1989 Act was in relation to judicial separation. It is possible that under section 8 of the Divorce Act the court may adjourn the proceedings to allow a person explore the alternatives, but this would clearly not extend to an obligation on the court to dispense advice in relation to these matters.

The provisions of section 6(6) of the Divorce Act should be noted, which state that the Minister "may" establish a register of professional bodies qualified to act as reconciliation counsellors, but so far this has not been effected, and there are many areas of the country which are badly served in this regard.

ADJOURNMENT OF PROCEEDINGS TO ASSIST RECONCILIATION OR AGREEMENT AS TO TERMS

E–059   Section 8 of the Divorce Act permits the court to adjourn proceedings before it for the purposes of assisting parties to reconcile, or to agree some or all of the terms on which the divorce would be granted. The important words in section 8(1) and (2) of the Divorce Act are "if they [the parties] both so wish". Clearly, the consent of both spouses to such a course of action is required and the section therefore, will not facilitate a party opposed to the proceedings to delay or frustrate them. Section 8(3) of the Divorce Act directs that if the proceedings are adjourned under section 8(1) or (2), either of the spouses may, at any time, request their resumption, and if such a request is made, then the court "shall" resume the hearing, subject to any other power of adjournment the court may have.

Section 8(5) of the Divorce Act contains a power for the court to advise or to recommend to the parties that they obtain the assistance of a third party, presumably a marriage guidance counsellor or mediator, to help either effect a reconciliation or agree some or all of the terms of the divorce.

SECTION 9 OF THE DIVORCE ACT

E–060   Section 9 of the Divorce Act was not included in the Divorce Bill as originally drafted, but was added at Committee Stage in the Seanad. A similar provision in respect of judicial separation has been inserted into the 1989 Act by section 45 of the Divorce Act. The section provides that any oral or written communications entered into between the parties and any third party in the course of their efforts either, to effect a reconciliation, or to attempt to agree the terms of the proposed divorce shall not be admissible as evidence in any court. The use of the term "any court" would appear to preclude the evidence being given not only in the divorce proceedings, but in any other proceedings which could arise in connection with the breakdown of the marriage. The section stipulates that the communications need not have been made in the presence or with the knowledge of the other spouse.

The new rule was long overdue and there can be no doubt as to its desirability. Prior to the coming into operation of section 9, it was not uncommon for evidence to be given in relation to agreements entered into during mediation which subsequently failed, or in relation to discussions which took place between parties in attempting to settle their own affairs. It was, and remains the case, that without prejudice, correspondence and discussions between solicitors attempting to resolve the terms of a marriage breakdown are inadmissible, but difficulties had arisen with evidence being admitted in relation to discussions between the parties themselves.

The issue of whether privilege attached to communications with a marriage guidance counsellor arose in the case of *E.R. v. J.R.* [[1981] 1 I.L.R.M. 125], where Carroll J. held that privilege did attach. Section 9 therefore clarifies the position with regard to all forms of communication entered into between the spouses for the purposes set out above. The inadmissibility also extends to records of the communications.

FACTORS TO BE CONSIDERED BY THE COURT

INTRODUCTION

On the introduction of divorce the courts were granted unfettered **E–061** discretion to deal with the economically valuable assets of the parties to the marriage. This discretion is exercisable within a framework of criteria as well as the constitutional and statutory requirement that proper provision be made for the spouses and dependent children of the marriage. Section 20 of the Divorce Act sets out those individual factors which must be taken into account by the court before deciding to make any order of ancillary relief. The specific criteria contained in section 20 apply to the making of orders under sections 12, 13, 14, 15(1)(a), 16, 17, 18 and 22 of the Divorce Act.

ADEQUATE AND REASONABLE PROVISION

The introductory requirement set out in section 20(1) of the Divorce Act **E–062** requires the court to:

". . . ensure that such provision as the court considers proper having regard to the circumstances exists or will be made for the spouses and any dependent member of the family concerned."

This general standard is not defined any more clearly by the legislature, thus increasing the level of discretion afforded to the judiciary in these cases. Without having an adverse effect on the generality of this clause and the obvious need for adequate and reasonable provision to be provided where possible, section 20(2)(a) to (l) contains a list of 12 factors, to which the court is obliged to pay particular regard. Each factor will be considered in turn.

1. INCOME AND GENERAL FINANCIAL RESOURCES

Section 20(2)(a), the first of those criteria to be considered, requires the **E–063** court to have regard to:

". . . the income, earning capacity, property and other financial resources which each of the spouses concerned has or is likely to have in the foreseeable future".

E31

This requirement directs attention to the actual and potential financial resources of each party. Under this subsection, the court is obliged to have regard to all income from whatever source and all property, whether bought, inherited or otherwise acquired. The "marital cake", which must be divided up on separation includes anything, which is capable of being owned, such as farms, livestock, milk quotas, forestry, fishing rights, holiday homes, investment property, businesses, shares in private and publicly quoted companies, investments, furniture, antiques, artworks etc.

E–064   In order to ensure that the Court is adequately equipped to exercise its discretion under section 20, section 38(6) of the 1996 Act obliges each spouse to give to the other spouse or any dependent member of the family concerned or the representatives of any such member:

> "such particulars of his or her property and income as may reasonably be required for the purposes of the proceedings."

Such disclosure is made by the filing of an Affidavit of Means. If the Affidavit of Means is prepared comprehensively and accurately and vouching documentation is supplied, it should provide much of the information, which the Court requires in order to exercise its discretion. The parties and their legal advisers are afforded some discretion however, as the disclosure requirement only pertains to "such particulars . . . as may reasonably be required for the purposes of the proceedings". What is deemed to be reasonably required by the applicant in any particular case may of course be deemed by the respondent to be grossly superfluous. In the majority of cases heard by the courts, the income, property and financial resources of each spouse will be clearly identified in the affidavit of means of each party. But in some cases, particularly where one or both of the spouses is self-employed or has substantial assets, this may prove more difficult as was evidenced in the case of *J.D. v. D.D.* [[1997] 3 I.R. 89] where the behaviour of the respondent husband in not disclosing many of his assets was strongly criticised by McGuinness J. [Budd J. in *P.O.D. v. J.O.D.*, unreported, High Court, Budd J., March 31, 2000 cited with approval the approach adopted in *J.D. v. D.D. ibid.* See also *B.(S.) v. B.(R.)* [1997] 3 Fam. L. J. 66 (Circuit Court) and *P.P. v. A.P.* unreported, High Court, December 14, 1999]. Clearly, in financial terms, justice can only be assured where full disclosure is made by both parties. Thus, the importance of discovery in the context of ancillary relief cannot be overstated.

The court is also required to consider the present and probable future earnings of each spouse. The granting of ancillary financial orders will depend greatly on the potential earning capacity of (in particular) the applicant spouse. Judge McGuinness (as she then was) stated in *S.B. v. R.B.* [[1997] 3 Fam. L.J. 66] that the decision of the court in determining the value of the financial order was influenced by the fact of the wife's heart condition which made it "at least difficult for her to earn anything substantial outside the home." Such a disability was not even necessary in the view of Lynch J., who stated in *B.F. v. V.F.* [unreported, High Court,

Lynch J., May 20, 1993] that he was "satisfied that it is reasonable and proper for the wife at the present not to seek work outside the home. She provides a home for the three children of the marriage . . . that is a full-time occupation in itself." Therein, Lynch J., on appeal from the Circuit Court, increased maintenance payments to the applicant wife by £13,325 per annum (gross) to £25,000 (gross) and, in addition, ordered a lump sum payment of £14,000. The Respondent's state of health may also be a relevant factor for the Court to consider when making ancillary financial orders. In *P.P. v. A.P.* [unreported, High Court, McCracken J., December 14, 1999], McCracken J. in determining the level of maintenance, which was to be paid to the Applicant wife accepted that a very high maintenance award might effectively prevent the Respondent, who had a heart condition, from cutting down on his work or retiring and accordingly, he stated that he would take that matter into account.

The significance of the individual facts of every case was highlighted in the High Court case of *J.C. v. C.C.* [[1994] 1 Fam L.J. 22]. When determining what periodical payments to order, Barr J. stated that the applicant wife would not have much difficulty in utilising her qualifications as a Montessori teacher. He stated this in view of his belief that "such employment would seem suited to her present circumstances and would not interfere with her duties as a mother." [*ibid.* at 25]. All property owned by the spouses, both before and after the marriage, is also highly relevant to the issue of ancillary orders. For example, where an affluent spouse owns property other than the family home, or has a substantial income, the court, in viewing the property, income and earning capacity of the wealthy spouse as a whole, may transfer the home to the wife for her use and the use of the dependent children of the marriage. **E–065**

2. FINANCIAL NEEDS

Section 20(2)(b) of the Divorce Act requires the court to have particular regard to: **E–066**

". . . the financial needs, obligations and responsibilities which each of the spouses has or is likely to have in the foreseeable future (whether in the case of the remarriage of the spouse or otherwise)".

In *S. v. S.* [[1977] 1 All E.R. 56], Ormrod L.J. stated that when attention is concentrated primarily on the actual needs of the parties involved, the calculation of financial provision then becomes easier, more logical and constructive. Thus, the courts are likely to place a greater emphasis on the needs of the spouses when determining the orders to be made. In assessing these needs the court will take account of the parties' obligations and responsibilities to one another. The primary financial need of any spouse is to be supported and maintained. If there are dependent children, they will also be included in this calculation of needs. The needs stated can be met by both regular maintenance payments and infrequent payments such as educational expenses every September or an annual payment for car insurance and/or a summer holiday.

E–067   The calculation of what constitutes the reasonable needs of both parties is a matter to be determined in each case. This important aspect is also relevant to section 20(2)(c), which refers to the past standard of living. Facts particular to each case may give rise to additional needs that must be provided for, *e.g.* the poor health of one spouse. In *R.K. v. M.K.* [unreported, High Court, Finlay P., October 24, 1978] Finlay P. (as he then was) accepted that a wife who was suffering from motor neuron disease, with resulting depression and anxiety, would require hired help in addition to the other essentials of life.

The family home is often the sole major asset and the arrangements concerning the home can be of vital importance. Although a means of facilitating a cleaner financial break could be through the sale of the family home and the division of the proceeds, this approach fails to take account of the need of the custodial parent (if applicable) to maintain a stable home for any dependent children.

3. STANDARD OF LIVING

E–068   Section 20(2)(c) of the Divorce Act refers to:

". . . the standard of living enjoyed by the family concerned before the proceedings were instituted or before the spouses commenced to live apart from one another, as the case may be".

One of the practical realities of divorce, in particular where the parties are of limited or average means, is that both parties will inevitably face a reduction in living standards following the grant of the decree. This was recognised in the Supreme Court by Finlay C.J. in *R.H. v. N.H.* [[1986] I.L.R.M. 352] where he stated that the parties suffering a significant diminution in their overall standard of living was inevitable, particularly, he noted, where there are children involved. In some ways section 20(2)(c) is probably more relevant where there are substantial assets involved. In particular, this subsection will allow the court to ensure that the dependent spouse of a very wealthy person will not necessarily lose their financial status and can, despite the departure of the affluent spouse, be adequately provided for and continue to enjoy a luxurious lifestyle. In *G.H. v. E.H.* [unreported, High Court, Barr J., February 9, 1998], Barr J. confirmed the applicant's "right to the benefit of a reasonable lifestyle commensurate with that available to the respondent", and thus affirmed her entitlement to maintenance from the respondent of £200 per week. [See also *McA. v. McA.*, unreported, High Court, McCracken J, January 21, 2000, where the High Court, in granting a divorce, made a maintenance order for the sum of £4,500 per month and a further lump sum payment of £300,000].

Essentially, section 20(2)(c) aids the court in determining the type of **E–069** lifestyle the separated spouses are entitled to lead and the needs that they are likely to have. In *L.B. v. H.B.* [unreported, High Court, July 31, 1980] despite the wife living in a stately home in the west of Ireland, receiving £50 weekly maintenance, having shop credit accounts which were met by her former husband and an annual flight to London, Barrington J., in fixing weekly maintenance at £300, agreed with the applicant wife that she was not being properly maintained. Similarly, in an earlier English case of *Caulderbank v. Caulderbank* [[1976] Fam. 93], the affluent wife was ordered to pay £10,000 to her former husband who was without property. This was to enable him to buy a house that was comparable to his wife's standard of living. However, O'Toole ["Introduction to the Judicial Separation and Family Law Reform Act 1989" (1990) Fam. L.J. 12] notes that the English courts have generally held that following a decree of divorce, the standard of living of neither party should be above that which would have existed if the marriage had continued. Where a decree of divorce/separation is granted two houses will be necessary and both spouses will inevitably suffer financially. This is repeatedly recognised by the courts. In *H.D. v. E.D.* [unreported, High Court, January 1, 1994], Costello J. noted that "[a] broken marriage inevitably means a lowering of the living standards of both parties which can be very considerable in some instances." Similarly, in *B.F. v. V.F.* [unreported, High Court, Lynch J., May 20, 1993], Lynch J. stated:

"It is inevitable that all the parties will suffer a significant diminution in the overall standard of living. The necessity for two separate residences to be maintained and two households to be provided for makes this an inescapable consequence of the separation."

4. AGE OF SPOUSES AND LENGTH OF COHABITATION

Section 20(2)(d) of the Divorce Act requires the court to consider: **E–070**

". . . the age of each of the spouses, the duration of their marriage and the length of time during which the spouses lived with one another".

In *C. O'R. v. M. O'R.* [unreported, High Court, September 19, 2000], the fact that both husband and wife were still relatively young and that the marriage had only lasted three and a half years were among the factors, which O'Donovan J. cited in refusing to direct the transfer of the family home to the wife. The importance of these factors will vary with the particular facts of each case. In *Gengler v. Gengler* [[1976] 2 All E.R. 81], it was held that to attempt to state when a marriage should be classed as short, not very short, long or not very long, is rather like trying to define the length of a piece of string. The age of the spouses will also be relevant as they will shed light on the financial position of each spouse and particularly on their future earning capacity. Age may have a substantive bearing on their employability or, if already employed, will determine the likely length of future employment. The longer the future employment period, the more likely the applicant spouse will be capable of self-support. An older applicant has a greater need for financial security for his or her future. In addition, the type of financial relief afforded to the parties may be influenced by the age of the parties, *i.e.* periodical payments or a lump sum order. In *Page v. Page* [reported in *The Times*, January 30, 1981], when considering the amount of capital provision which could reasonably be made for an elderly wife, the court noted that her requirements might be provided for by a smaller capital sum than would be needed by a younger wife with a greater life expectancy.

E–071   In respect of the period of marriage, it is likely that an applicant spouse will be made a more substantial payment if the marriage and prior cohabitation (if any) existed for a lengthy period. The courts in Britain have proved reluctant to award large payments where the marriage is of short duration, especially when the parties are childless. The time during which the spouses cohabited, both prior to and during the marriage, is also relevant to a court when deciding what, if any, ancillary orders should be made. Although on a simplistic level, a court is likely to be more willing to make substantial awards in respect of a lengthy marriage than one that was short-lived, a scenario with extenuating circumstances could contradict this entirely. Clearly, this factor can, where relevant, have a considerable bearing on the decision of a judge. In the English case of *Krystman v. Krystman* [[1973] 3 All E.R. 247], the court made no order in favour of the wife. Although they had been married for 26 years, they had only lived together for two weeks.

5. PHYSICAL OR MENTAL DISABILITY

E–072   Section 20(2)(e) of the Divorce Act refers to "any physical or mental disability of either of the spouses". Where one or other of the parties to the proceedings suffers from a physical or mental disability, the court is likely to regard this as a burden of that spouse, which necessitates greater financial provision. Certainly, a disability which prevents or inhibits a spouse from working will result in the making of a greater periodical payments order in favour of that dependent spouse.

6. PAST AND FUTURE CONTRIBUTIONS

E–073   Section 20(2)(f) of the Divorce Act requires the court to have regard to:

". . . the contributions which each of the spouses has made or is likely in the foreseeable future to make to the welfare of the family, including any contribution made by each of them to the income, earning capacity, property and financial resources of the other spouse and any contribution made by either of them by looking after the home or caring for the family".

FLP R.2: October 2001

This factor represents the growing tendency of the legislature and the **E–074** courts to look beyond the financial contributions of each spouse. It places an onus on the courts, when making ancillary orders, to distribute the assets on the equitable basis of both financial and non-financial contributions. In *F. v. F.* [unreported, High Court, December 2, 1999], O'Neill J. held that the Applicant wife who had assisted the husband in the administration of his business in the early days was entitled by virtue of her joint shareholding pre-1989 to a disposal of the assets on a 50/50 basis of her equity in the marital property and in other property. Accordingly, he made an order transferring the family home (which represented roughly 50 per cent of the value of the assets) to the wife free of encumbrances. He declined to transfer any additional property to the wife as this would have led to "a gross imbalance" between the husband and wife. A similar approach was taken in *P. O'D. v. J. O'D.* [unreported, High Court, March 31, 2000]. In that case, Budd J. accepted the evidence of the Applicant that she had made a significant contribution to the building up of her husband's property portfolio and held that the justice of the case required that the property should be divided equally. The real value of non-financial "home-maker" contributions was clearly stated by Lord Denning M.R. in *Wachtel v. Wachtel* [[1973] 1 All E.R. 829]:

> "The wife who looks after the home and family contributes as much to the family assets as the wife who goes out to work. The one contributes in kind, the other in money or money's worth. If the court considers that the home has been acquired and maintained by the joint efforts of both, then when the marriage breaks down, it should be regarded as the joint property of them, no matter in whose name it stands."

This reference by Lord Denning M.R. to the non-earning spouse contributing as much as an earning spouse, may be regarded by some financially-minded persons as unrealistic. However, in practice, the division of the matrimonial assets has very much reflected this notion. Although such "domestic" contributions are difficult, if not impossible, to value financially, they clearly have an impact on any court assessment of the periodical payments or lump sum orders to be made. Practically speaking, the court often equates domestic contributions to mortgage payments. In this way such contributions are viewed by the court in terms of comparable financial value.

Section 20(2)(f), which gives credit to a non-earning spouse, is a **E–075** relatively new concept, with its origin in the Judicial Separation and Family Law Reform Act 1989. Section 20(2) of the 1989 Act is worded very similarly to section 20(2)(f) of the Divorce Act and when introduced in 1989 was viewed as a major development in the area of family law. The High Court case of *J.D. v. D.D.* [[1997] 3 I.R. 64] is an excellent example of a scenario where the applicant wife remained in the family home to rear the children and provide for the respondent husband while he worked outside the home. McGuinness J. ordered ". . . a reasonably equal division

E37

of the accumulated assets . . ." as the application for an order of judicial separation followed a 30-year marriage and was so ordered because of the husband's long-term acceptance of their respective traditional roles as financial provider and homemaker.

Furthermore, section 20(2)(f) refers to "the foreseeable future" and the contributions that are likely to be made during that period. An example of this, involves the court including in its calculations future contributions in respect of the caring required for any children remaining in the custody of one or other of the spouses. Both this subsection and section 20(2)(g) seek to protect the traditional position of women in the home and to reward them for their share and effort in the development and acquisition of the family's wealth. Budd J. in *M.Y. v. A.Y.* [unreported, High Court, December 11, 1995] acknowledged this issue in making several lump sum orders in favour of the applicant wife. The learned judge made the following financial orders: monthly maintenance of £1,300 being £500 in respect of the dependent son and £800 in respect of the wife; £26,000 being a lump sum order in respect of arrears of maintenance; a payment of £4,273.19 in respect of monies due; and, finally, a lump sum of £85,000 for the purchase by the wife of a home and contents "to be in satisfaction of the plaintiff's interest in the business assets of the plaintiff and the defendant and in respect of her contribution to the acquisition of those assets".

7. MARITAL RESPONSIBILITIES

E–076   Section 20(2)(g) of the Divorce Act requires the court to take account of:

> ". . . the effect on the earning capacity of each of the spouses of the marital responsibilities assumed by each during the period when they lived with one another and, in particular, the degree to which the future earning capacity of a spouse is impaired by reason of that spouse having relinquished or foregone the opportunity of remunerative activity in order to look after the home or care for the family".

This provision clearly authorises the court, in making ancillary orders, to take account of, and to compensate accordingly, a spouse's past and future earnings lost due to his/her assumption of marital and domestic responsibilities.

8. STATUTORY INCOME AND BENEFITS

E–077   Section 20(2)(h) of the Divorce Act refers to "any income or benefits to which either of the spouses is entitled by or under statute" and requires the court to take such payments into account. In order to ensure the making of a fair and appropriate periodical payments or lump sum order, the court is obliged to take all income which is received by both parties into account. This subsection includes all social welfare payments as well as children's allowance, old age pension and other benefit payments. This section, particularly as it deals with social welfare payments, is likely to become relevant in cases where the parties to the proceedings are of limited means. Where there are little or no assets available for distribution, the parties may ultimately rely for the most part on State payments after the granting of the decree of divorce.

9. CONDUCT

Section 20(2)(i) of the Divorce Act requires the court to take account of: **E–078**

". . . the conduct of each of the spouses, if that conduct is such that in the opinion of the court it would in all the circumstances of the case be unjust to disregard it".

This provision, which mirrors the equivalent provision in the Family Law Act 1995, is a broader version than that contained in the Judicial Separation and Family Law Reform Act 1989, which required the court to disregard the conduct of each spouse, unless it would in all the circumstances of the case be repugnant to justice to do so. Clearly, the court when making ancillary orders, is now afforded greater scope to take account of misconduct by either spouse. In the earlier case of *E.M. v. W.M.* [[1994] 3 Fam. L.J. 93], McGuinness J. considered that the respondent husband's behaviour was relevant to her decision. Similarly, Budd J. in *M.Y. v. A.Y.* [unreported, High Court, December 11, 1995] approved of the approach taken by Costello J. in *E.D. v. F.D.* [unreported, High Court, October 23, 1980] in relation to the issue of misconduct when determining the issue of maintenance:

"Where a husband deserts his wife and children, the court should be concerned to ensure that their financial position is protected, even if this means causing a drop in the husband's living standards." [*ibid.* at 4.]

10. ACCOMMODATION NEEDS

Section 20(2)(j) if the Divorce Act requires the court to have particular **E–079** regard to "the accommodation needs of either of the spouses". In every case in which a decree of divorce is granted, two homes are required to replace one. This fact will invariably have a great bearing on the financial orders to be made by the court which is statutorily obliged under section 15(2)(b) to ensure that:

". . . proper and secure accommodation should, where practicable, be provided for a spouse who is wholly or mainly dependent on the other spouse and for any dependent member of the family."

This requirement to consider the accommodation needs of each spouse will not necessarily result in a right of residence or complete transfer being awarded automatically to one spouse. The needs of both spouses must be considered, which can result in the sale of the family home and the division of the net proceeds. This was deemed by McGuinness J. to be both the appropriate and necessary measure in the case of *O'L. v. O'L.* [[1996] 2 Fam. L.J. 63]:

> "In all the circumstances I am satisfied that common sense and justice require that the family home be sold and that the proceeds of sale be divided so as to provide as far as possible for the purchase by the wife of a smaller house . . . and to provide for the husband something towards a deposit on the purchase by him of suitable accommodation for himself."

In this case, it should be noted that the learned judge believed the child would be relatively unharmed by the move. Alternatively, where the facts of a case necessitate minimal change, the sale of the family home can be postponed to a more appropriate future time.

11. LOSS OF FUTURE BENEFITS

E–080   Section 20(2)(k) of the Divorce Act requires the court to take account of:

> ". . . the value to each of the spouses of any benefit (for example, a benefit under a pension scheme) which by reason of the decree of divorce concerned, that spouse will forfeit the opportunity or possibility of acquiring".

This subsection, which requires the court when making an order for divorce to take account of the loss of a benefit such as a pension scheme, is a significant legislative development. As a factor to be considered by the court prior to the making of any ancillary orders, it includes benefits not only already received by either spouse, but also those that the spouse may possibly acquire in the future. The term benefit is not defined in the Divorce Act and this is likely to result in a broad approach being adopted by the courts. In effect, the courts are likely to compensate a spouse for the loss of most potential benefits. Financial experts will be required to give evidence to the court as to the value of these future losses.

12. RIGHTS OF OTHER PARTIES

E–081   The final factor contained in section 20 is subsection (2)(l) which requires the court to take account of "the rights of any person other than the spouses but including a person to whom either spouse is remarried." The remedy of divorce by its very nature permits both parties to remarry once the decree is granted. Consequently, any financial resources or assets that become available by way of a new relationship to one of the parties to the application must be taken into account by the court when making any ancillary orders.

PRIOR EXISTING SEPARATION AGREEMENTS

The importance of a separation agreement existing between the parties **E–082** prior to their application for a decree of divorce is again highlighted in section 20(3) of the Divorce Act which requires the court, in deciding whether to make an order for ancillary relief, to have regard to the terms of such an agreement (which is still in force). Further, the court is also obliged under section 20(4)(f) to consider such an agreement when making an order in respect of a dependent member of the family. In *M.G. v. M.G.* [unreported, Circuit Court, Buckley J., July 25, 2000], Buckley J. considered the factors, which a Court should take into account when faced with an application for ancillary relief, which will have the effect of varying the terms of a prior separation agreement. He noted that the 1996 Act obliges the Court to consider every aspect of the parties' financial and family situation before granting the decree while having regard to any existing agreements entered into between them. Buckley J. examined a similar statutory provision in the Canadian Divorce Act, 1985 and looked to the jurisprudence of the Canadian Supreme Court for guidance. He noted that Canadian case law requires that before varying a prior agreement, the Court should be satisfied that there was a "sufficient change" in circumstances. Such a change was to be defined in terms of the overall financial circumstances of the parties and the fact that a change was objectively foreseeable did not necessarily mean that it was contemplated by the parties. Buckley J. went on to state that in cases where the parties are intelligent persons who have had the benefit of legal advice before entering an agreement, which is of recent date, a Court should be very slow to make radical alterations unless there have been sufficient changes in the circumstances of the parties. Moreover, the Court should be slow to make any radical changes, which would affect the stability of the children's home life.

The parties in that case had entered into a separation agreement in April, 1995. Pursuant to the terms of the agreement, the Applicant transferred his interest in the family home (which at the time had a gross value of £200,000) to the Respondent for a sum of £20,000, which was to be payable in the future. Moreover, the Applicant was to pay maintenance. In 1996, the Applicant wished to obtain a foreign divorce in order to remarry and in consideration of the Respondent's consent, the Applicant waived his entitlement to the £20,000 and agreed to hold the money in trust for the three children of the marriage. The Applicant subsequently remarried. In 1998, the Applicant lost his job and at the time of the hearing was finding it difficult to obtain employment other than short-term contracts. The family home had at this stage increased in value to £800,000. The Applicant sought to vary the terms of the separation agreement on the basis of his remarriage, his unemployment and the increase in the value of the family home. Judge Buckley refused to alter the financial provisions of the agreement. He held that the seeking of a divorce was foreseeable at the time the agreement was entered into. Moreover, the loss of the Applicant's job may have been reasonably foreseeable as he had suffered a similar loss before. However, he considered that it could not have been in the contemplation of the parties at the time they entered into the supplemental agreement that there would be such a remarkable increase in the value of the family home. Accordingly, he declared that in any future sale of the family home, the Applicant was to receive 10 per cent of the net sale price, after all encumbrances and costs of sale had been deducted.

DEPENDENT MEMBERS

E–083   Without prejudice to the generality of section 20(1) of the Divorce Act and to the extensive factors to be considered by the court as outlined in sections 20(2)(a)–(l), section 20(4)(a)–(g) requires the court to take account of seven further elements when considering whether to make any ancillary orders in favour of a dependent member of the family. "Dependent member of the family" is defined in section 2 of the Divorce Act and includes any child or adopted child of the spouses or any child in relation to whom either parent is acting *in loco parentis*, the child being under 18 years old or under 23 years old if in full-time education, or any member of the family who has a mental or physical disability to such an extent that it is not reasonably possible for him/her to look after himself or herself. As well as the financial needs, status, income and earning capacity of the dependent member, this subsection also refers to specific matters, such as education, disabilities and accommodation. Furthermore, section 20(4)(f) requires the court to consider section 20(2)(a)–(c) and section 20(3) specifically in the light of the needs of the dependent person. The recent decision of McGuinness J. in the case of *E.P. v. C.P.* [unreported, High Court, November 27, 1998], highlights the importance attached by the court to the needs of the children of the marriage. There the court ordered that the family home was to be transferred to the applicant wife, as the security and welfare of the children and their need for a secure home was the most important aspect of the case. Thus, the various needs of any dependent member of the family must be considered by the court prior to the making of any order for ancillary relief on application for a decree of divorce.

ULTIMATE NECESSITY FOR JUSTICE

E–084   Finally, section 20(5) of the Divorce Act forbids the making of any order that is not in the interests of justice. Although the legislature outlined almost 20 independent factors to be considered, this is not an exhaustive list and, ultimately, the decisions of the court can only be made, if they comply with this overriding requirement. Clearly, although the inclusion by the legislature of specific matters to be considered ensures that all specific aspects of the case are dealt with, the ultimate necessity for justice to be done is a requirement which must be met in all cases.

THE FAMILY HOME

INTRODUCTION

A dispute in relation to the family home is central to almost every **E–085**
application for a decree of divorce. In Ireland this problem is often
magnified because of the unique importance of the family farm to Irish
society. An order in respect of the family home is usually necessitated, it
often being the largest family owned asset. The relevant legislative provisions relating to divorce and the family home, contained for the most part
in the Divorce Act, are set out in this chapter. The practical application of
these provisions will be highlighted, particularly in the light of the
interpretations adopted by the judiciary.

DEFINITIONS

The term "family home" as interpreted by the Supreme Court in **E–086**
National Irish Bank v. Graham [[1995] 2 I.R. 244] is restricted to the precise
terms of the Family Home Protection Act 1976 (hereinafter the Family
Home Act). Section 2(1) of this Act specifies the family home as:

> ". . . primarily a dwelling in which a married couple ordinarily reside.
> The expression comprises, in addition, a dwelling in which a spouse
> whose protection is in issue ordinarily resides, or if that spouse has left
> the other spouse, ordinarily resided before so leaving."

The Supreme Court stated that the definition of "family home" cannot be
extended by the judiciary beyond the words of the Family Home Act. In
National Irish Bank v. Graham Finlay C.J. held that the definition should
not be given a liberal or alternative interpretation beyond the words used in
section 2. This basic meaning was adopted in full by the Divorce Act with
the modification that the references to a spouse in section 2 of the 1976 Act
shall be construed as references to a spouse within the meaning of the
Divorce Act. In an effort to identify the practical meaning of a family
home, section 54(1)(a) of the Family Law Act 1995 defines a dwelling as:

[THE NEXT PAGE IS E41]

". . . any building or part of a building occupied as a separate dwelling and includes any garden or other land usually occupied with the dwelling, being land that is subsidiary and ancillary to it, is required for amenity or convenience and is not being used or developed primarily for commercial purposes, and includes a structure that is not permanently attached to the ground and a vehicle or vessel, whether mobile or not, occupied as a separate dwelling."

STATUTORY PROVISIONS

Preliminary orders

Section 11 of the Divorce Act allows the court to make certain **E–087** preliminary orders in proceedings for a decree of divorce. Such preliminary orders can be applied for by either party to the divorce proceedings and if granted by the court shall remain effective until the hearing of the action. Among these, section 11(c) empowers the court to make an order under section 5 or section 9 of the Family Home Act. Section 5 of the Family Home Act allows the court to make any order it considers proper where it believes that one spouse is guilty of conduct which could lead to the loss of the family home. Section 9 of the Family Home Act allows the court to place a restriction on the disposal of any household chattels.

Property adjustment orders

Section 14 of the Divorce Act allows the court on granting a decree of **E–088** divorce or at any time during the lifetime of the respondent spouse to make a property adjustment order. Section 14(1) restricts the time in which an application can be made under this section to during the lifetime of the respondent spouse. This section grants the court the power to make one or more of the following property adjustment orders:

(i) the court can order the transfer of property from one spouse to the other spouse, or to any dependent member of the family, or to a specified person for the benefit of such a member;

(ii) the court can order the settlement of any property for the benefit of one or both of the spouses or for any dependent member;

(iii) the court can make an order varying any previously agreed settlement of property;

(iv) the court can make an order extinguishing or reducing any interest held by either spouse under any such settlement.

Section 14 of the Divorce Act permits the court, upon application to it, **E–089** to make an order, not only at the time of the granting of the decree of divorce but also at any time thereafter. Both spouses retain a right to apply at any time into the future, during the lifetime of the other spouse. Section 14(3) of the Divorce Act, however, provides that if either spouse remarries, the court can no longer make an order under section 14 in favour of the re-married spouse. Section 14(4) deals with the practicalities following the making of a property adjustment order by the court. This section requires the lodging of a true copy of the court order by the registrar of the court pursuant to section 69(1)(h) of the Registration of Title Act 1964. Section 14(5) of the Divorce Act provides for the situation where a spouse who is directed by the court to transfer land under section 14 refuses to execute the necessary deeds. An order under this section allows a person nominated by the court to execute the necessary documents. Section 14(6) states that the court shall retain discretion in respect of the costs of such an application. Significantly, section 14(7) prevents the court from applying the provisions of this section to a family home in which, following the decree of divorce either of the spouses concerned, having remarried, ordinarily resides with his or her spouse.

Miscellaneous ancillary orders

E–090   Section 15 of the Divorce Act deals with miscellaneous ancillary orders including orders relating to the family home. Section 15(1)(a)(i) permits the court to make an order conferring on one spouse for life or other period of time (definite or contingent) the right to occupy the family home to the exclusion of the other spouse. Section 15(1)(a)(ii) allows the court to make an order for the sale of the family home subject to any conditions it considers proper. Section 15(1)(b) introduces a power to the court in relation to the family home, allowing the court to make an order under section 36 of the Family Law Act 1995 which relates to the determination of any issue of ownership of any property between spouses. Section 15 allows such an order or any order under section 15, to be made by the court on the granting of a decree of divorce or at any time during the lifetime of the other spouse. Section 15(1)(c) reiterates in part the aforementioned section 11 of the Divorce Act, save in so far as section 15 applies to the making of orders by the court on the granting of the decree of divorce or thereafter whereas section 11 is concerned with preliminary or interim orders. In addition to section 11(c), section 15 permits the court to make an order under section 7 of the Family Home Act, which in turn empowers the court to postpone proceedings issued by the mortgagor or lessor of the family home where repayments and/or arrears are overdue. In relation to the accommodation needs of both spouses and any dependent members of the family, the legislature recognised that when making any ancillary order relating to the family home that the court must have regard to the welfare of both spouses and any dependent children and must take into considera-tion that where a decree of divorce is granted the spouses will no longer reside together. Consequently, section 15(2)(b) of the Divorce Act requires the court to ensure that, where practicable, proper and secure accommo-dation is provided for a wholly, or mainly, dependent spouse and for any

E42

dependent members of the family. This section represents a change in the attitude of the legislature. Section 19 of the Judicial Separation and Family Law Reform Act 1989, which is now repealed, had required the court to have regard to the welfare of the family as a whole. The requirement, which the court must now consider, is the needs of the dependent spouse and children.

Orders for the sale of property

Section 19 of the Divorce Act is concerned with the ancillary powers of **E–091** the court where an order for the sale of property has been made. It sets out the number and type of consequential and/or supplementary provisions which such an order can contain. Essentially, an order for the sale of property can contain whatever provisions the court considers appropriate. However, without prejudice to the generality of this power as set out in subsection 3(a), section 19(3)(b) contains the following provisions which may be included in an order made under section 19:

(i) a provision specifying the manner of sale and some, or all, of the conditions applying to the sale of the property;

(ii) a provision specifying the person or class of persons to whom the sale of the property is to be offered;

(iii) a provision directing that the sale not have effect until the occurrence of a specified event, or the expiration of a specified period;

(iv) a provision requiring the making of a lump sum payment, or periodical payments, to a specified person or persons from the proceeds of sale; and

(v) a provision specifying the division of the proceeds of sale between the spouses and any other person(s) having an interest therein, as the court considers appropriate.

Section 19(4) provides that a payment to a spouse under this section shall **E–092** not be made where the recipient spouse has died or remarried except where payments are due on the date of the said death or remarriage. Section 19(5) states that where a spouse has a beneficial interest in the property at issue and where a third party also claims a beneficial interest in the said property, the court in considering what order to make, must allow that other person to make representations to the court and those representations shall be among the matters to be considered by the court.

Finally, it should be noted that by exercising its power under this section the court cannot, under subsection 2 thereof, affect a right of a spouse to occupy the family home. Similarly, section 19(6), in an attempt to protect a spouse's second family, provides that section 19 shall have no application to a family home where, after the granting of a decree of divorce, either of the spouses having remarried ordinarily resides with his or her spouse.

FLP R.0: July 2000

Variation of orders

E–093   The final aspect of the Divorce Act which relates to the family home is contained in section 22 which deals with the variation of orders made under Part III of the Divorce Act. In relation to the family home the orders which are open to variation under section 22 are a property adjustment order under section 14, an order under section 15(1)(a)(ii) relating to the sale of the family home and an order under section 15(1)(a)(i) conferring an exclusive right of residence on one spouse. Section 22 allows the court, on application by either spouse, or in the case of the death of either spouse, on application by a person deemed by the court to have sufficient interest (normally a dependent child), or in the case of the remarriage of either spouse, by his or her spouse, having regard to any change of circumstances and any new evidence, to make an order to vary, discharge, temporarily suspend or revive an order to which this section applies. Thus, in changed circumstances, an order granting a spouse sole occupation rights in the family home could be replaced by an order for the sale of the home or could be granted to the spouse originally excluded sole occupation rights in the home. In circumstances where the sale of the family home results in an unexpected substantial increase in net proceeds the court may, upon application being made to it, see fit to vary under section 22 the sum to be received by each spouse. As a result, no order relating to the family home, except perhaps an order for sale which has already been complied with, can be viewed as being unquestionably final. Even in the case where the family home has already been sold to a third party, the court can use its powers under section 22 to make an order in relation to the proceeds of the sale.

GENERAL COMMENTARY AND JUDICIAL INTERPRETATION

Right of residence

E–094   Section 15 of the Divorce Act authorises the making of miscellaneous ancillary orders and includes specific references to the family home which enable a court to make one or more orders relating to the family home. The first is an order under section 15(1)(a)(i), providing for the conferral on one spouse either for life or for such other period (whether definite or contingent) as the court may specify, of the right to occupy the family home to the exclusion of the other spouse. Under this section an order can be made giving one spouse the exclusive right to occupy the family home for his/her lifetime, or for a lesser period of time, or until further order of the court. This granting of an exclusive right to reside in the family home is well established, being initially provided for in section 16(a) of the Judicial Separation and Family Law Reform Act 1989 and more recently by section 10 of the Family Law Act 1995. The decision of the court to grant such an order to one spouse over the other is often based on a desire to provide stability and continuity for the children of the marriage. Similarly, where

E44

one spouse is substantially better off, it is open to the court to grant sole occupancy in the family home to the financially weaker spouse. In fact, the need to provide separate accommodation for both spouses is recognised in section 15(2)(a) of the Divorce Act which highlights the impossibility of spouses who are now divorced residing together. However, as the facts of each case will vary, so too will the orders of the court, highlighting the importance of the court's discretionary powers in this area. In *A.K. v. P.K.* [unreported, High Court, March 13, 2000], where the children of the marriage were of full age and part of the Respondent's medical practice was conducted at a surgery attached to the family home, Murphy J. granted the Respondent husband the right to occupy the family home and surgery to the exclusion of the Applicant for so long as he remained in practice or until he attained the age of 65, whichever was earlier.

In *F. v. F.* [[1994] 2 I.L.R.M. 401], the High Court, and on appeal the **E–095** Supreme Court, rejected the contention that the power given to the court, when making a decree of judicial separation, to exclude a spouse from occupying the family home was unconstitutional. Murphy J. in the High Court stated [at 417–418]:

"In the area of family law, the family home has . . . two important functions. First it provides the ordinary residence for the family, and secondly, it represents or may represent an asset of significant value. In addition to the immediate and practical value of the right to reside in a family home—particularly for a non-income earning spouse—and the possible asset value of the family home, the courts have long identified the psychological value of the family home in providing a point of unity around which the children of a broken marriage may preserve or rebuild some of the physical and personal relationships on which the development of the family would depend".

However, Murphy J. also stated [at 418] that a right of residence, incorporating an exclusionary order, "may be an immediate practical necessity but in general it is unlikely to be a permanent solution to the problem for either spouse." To highlight the complications involved, Murphy J. referred to his earlier High Court judgment of *L.C. v. A.C.* [[1994] 1 Fam L.J. 19]. In that case, the Circuit Family Court granted to the wife the right to occupy the family home to the exclusion of the husband for life or until further order of the court. On appeal to the High Court, Murphy J. noted that in so far as the Circuit Court order gave a right of residence to the wife for life, it was unfair to the husband and unsatisfactory for the wife. If the wife was to have full enjoyment of the property, her husband's equity had no value and if the wife was to have a mere right of residence and not a property right, then her right would lapse if a sale was necessary. The learned judge's determination of a price, which took account of the interests of both parties and allowed the wife to buy out the husband's interest, resolved the issue in a satisfactory manner. Clearly, by allowing the applicant to buy out her husband's share in the family home the court ensured that a more permanent solution was obtained.

E45

E–096   Similarly, the court when granting an exclusive right of residence, can incorporate with such an order a transfer of all or part of a spouse's title in the property to the residing spouse. Such a scenario occurred in the case of *C.C. v. J.C.* [[1994] 1 Fam. L.J. 22] where Barr J., on foot of an application for judicial separation, granted a right of residence in the family home to the dependent wife for her lifetime and transferred the house which was in the husband's sole name into their joint names. In the circumstances, however, Barr J. declined to make an order giving the applicant wife an absolute title in the family home.

It should be noted that any order made by the court under section 15(1)(a)(i) only remains binding until the court determines it appropriate to vary the order. When the original order of the court is made not for the lifetime of a spouse, but rather for a specified period, the order will be open to review and/or change after that specified period, or more likely upon the occurrence of a particular event. In practice, this particular event is usually when the youngest child attains majority or when the youngest child's participation in full-time education ends. In addition to the immediate and practical value of the dependent spouse obtaining a right to reside in the family home, the court in *B. v. B.* [[1975] I.R. 54] identified the psychological value of the family home in providing a point of unity around which the children of a broken marriage may preserve or rebuild some of the physical and personal relationships on which the development of the family would depend. O'Dalaigh C.J. [at 60] recognised that for the son of the union "remaining at the family home will serve . . . as a stabilising influence and should help minimise the upset which must necessarily have been suffered". In a similar vein, O'Donovan J., in *C.'O'R. v. M.O'R.* [unreported, High Court, September 19, 2000], referred to the trauma and disruption, which can be suffered by a child who has to leave surroundings with which he or she has been familiar for most of his or her life. In making an Order giving the Applicant spouse the exclusive right to occupy the family home until such time as the children had completed their full time education, O'Donovan J. expressed the view that where there was a breakdown of a marriage and there are children of that marriage, the better interests of those children demands that they should not have to leave the home, which they have known all their lives unless the financial position of their parents requires that the family home be sold. [See also the views expressed by Murphy J. in *F. v. F., Ireland and the Attorney General* [1995] 2 I.R. 354].

Order of sale of the family home

E–097   Another order which the court is empowered to make in relation to the family home is governed by section 15(1)(a)(ii) which directs "the sale of the family home subject to such conditions (if any) as the court considers proper and providing for the disposal of the proceeds of the sale between the spouses and any other persons having an interest therein". Under this section, the court can order the sale of the family home, subject to the imposition of conditions which the court deems to be appropriate. A typical example, could involve the court making provision for the dependent or financially weaker spouse by ordering the payment to him/her of a specific sum of money from the net proceeds of sale, for the purchase of a new home. This power under section 15(1)(a)(ii) is not new to the court, such a right already existed under section 18 of the Family Home Act. The right to order the sale of the family home and make an award of all or part of the proceeds has been applied regularly by our courts in family law disputes. An examination of some such cases will provide an illustration of the application of section 15(1)(a)(ii).

In *J.D. v. P.D.* [unreported, High Court, Lynch J., August 9, 1994], the **E–098** court ordered the sale of the family home and required that the net proceeds be divided 83 per cent to the wife and 17 per cent to the husband. Lynch J. explained that this division was to provide:

". . . for the purchase by the wife of a smaller house in a more convenient location for schools and generally, and to provide for the husband, something towards a deposit on the purchase by him of suitable accommodation for himself."

Similarly, in *S.B. v. R.B.* [[1996] I.F.L.R 220], McGuinness J. ordered the **E–099** sale of the family home and in so doing, required that the sum of £85,000 be paid to the wife out of the estimated net proceeds of £94,000, to enable her to acquire a new home. Thus, although at first glance the division of proceeds may seem grossly unjust, in each case the court has taken account of all relevant facts and has utilised its discretion to divide the proceeds of sale as is necessary in the circumstances. In so doing, and in refusing to sell the family home in *T.T. v. T.T.* [unreported, Circuit Family Court, March 1995], McGuinness J. somewhat unusually held that the court could take into account the position of the older children of the family still residing in the home, who were no longer "dependent" within the meaning of the Judicial Separation and Family Law Reform Act 1989, but who were "either in full-time education or merely starting on their careers." This case is an interesting illustration of the extent of the discretion exercised by the judiciary when deciding such matters, and highlights the importance of their role in the context of ancillary orders. It should be further noted that this decision was based upon the provisions of the 1989 Act which contained a narrower definition of what constituted "dependent", and the definition has since been extended by both the Family Law Act 1995 and the Divorce Act. A dependent child now reaches the age of majority at 18 years, or 23 if he/she remains in full-time education. The case of *C.N. v. R.N.* [[1995] 1 Fam. L.J. 14] is a further example of the discretionary powers of the court as they apply to an order for the sale of the family home. In this case, as the farmhouse represented the largest matrimonial asset, McGuinness J. ordered that the family home was to be sold and that the house purchased from the proceeds of sale for the applicant wife was to be placed in the joint names of the parties. Thus, despite the decree of judicial separation it was ordered that the wife's home be held by both parties as joint tenants.

Factors to be considered by the court

E–100   Section 15(2) of the Divorce Act sets out factors that the court must take into account in the event that it makes an order relating to the family home under section 15. Section 15(2) requires the court to have regard to the welfare of the spouses and any dependent member of the family and to take into consideration two particular factors. First, where a decree of divorce is granted it is recognised that it is impossible for spouses to continue to reside together. Secondly, the court is obliged to ensure that proper and secure accommodation is provided, where practicable, for a wholly or mainly dependent spouse and any dependent members of the family. It is interesting to note that the equivalent section 19 of the 1989 Act required a court to not only take these particular factors into account but also to consider the needs of the family as a whole. Perhaps from this distinction we can make an assumption that the legislature in drafting the Divorce Act (and similarly the Family Law Act 1995) has placed a greater emphasis on protecting the position of the dependent spouse and children, rather than the family as a whole, when granting a decree of divorce.

E–101   Section 20 of the Divorce Act sets out in detail 12 factors which must be considered by the court when making, *inter alia*, an ancillary order which relates to the family home. This section requires the court when making an order, *inter alia*, under section 15(1)(a) to have regard to matters including the income and earning capacity of each of the spouses concerned as well as their future earning capacity. More importantly, in this context, the court is required to take account of any contributions made by either spouse in looking after the home, or caring for the family and the consequential extent to which their future earning capacity has been impaired. This provision, in conjunction with the court's obligation to take account of the standard of living previously enjoyed by the family is likely to introduce a slight bias in favour of the financially weaker spouse.

The provisions of the Divorce Act, specifically sections 14 and 15 represent an admirable effort by the legislature to provide several options for the courts, from which the most viable and fair order(s) can be made in relation to the family home. They provide various options, which allow for the making of the most appropriate order in every case. The inclusion of a residual power to vary, discharge, revoke or suspend an order under section 22 is also vital to ensure that fairness can be guaranteed in all circumstances. The Divorce Act, as it relates to the family home, contains a well-rounded, all inclusive selection of provisions.

MAINTENANCE

INTRODUCTION

At common law the wife acquired the right to be supported by her **E–102** husband throughout the marriage. Lord Penzance justified the survival of this right following the granting of a decree of divorce in the Victorian case *Sidney v. Sidney* [(1865) 4 Sw. & Tr. 178]:

> ". . . the duty of a husband as consists in the maintenance of his wife may be justly kept alive and enforced upon you in favour of her whom you have driven to relinquish your name and home."

Furthermore he stated that "no man should, in my judgment, be permitted to rid himself of his wife by ill-treatment, and at the same time escape the obligation of supporting her." The relevant provisions of the Divorce Act ensure that this legal duty to maintain a spouse survives equally on the granting of a decree of divorce.

LEGISLATIVE PROVISIONS

Preliminary orders

Section 12 of the Divorce Act permits the making of a preliminary **E–103** maintenance order prior to the hearing of the action. It empowers the court, upon application to it for the grant of a decree of divorce, to require either of the spouses concerned to make, either a lump sum payment, or periodical payments, for the benefit of the other spouse and/or dependent children as the court considers proper. Such interim orders of maintenance cannot commence earlier than the date of application and must end by the date the court determines whether to grant the decree of divorce. The court, under section 12(2), is empowered to make the order subject to such terms and conditions as it considers appropriate.

Periodical payments and lump sum orders

On the granting of a decree of divorce, or at any time thereafter during **E–104** the lifetime of the spouse, the court may, on application by either spouse, make one or more orders under section 13 of the Divorce Act. Section 13(1)(a) governs the making of a periodical payments order to either spouse under subsection (i) thereof and to a dependent member of the family under subsection (ii). Section 13(1)(b) provides similarly for the making of a periodical payments order to a spouse under subsection (i) thereof and to a dependent member of the family under subsection (ii), but in this case the order made is secured. Section 13(1)(c)(i) empowers the court to make an order that either of the spouses shall make a specified lump sum payment(s) to the other spouse while section 13(1)(c)(ii) provides for the making of such an order in favour of a dependent member of the family. Section 13(2)(a) empowers the court to make a lump sum order in respect of any liabilities or expenses reasonably incurred by the applicant spouse before the making of an application under section 13(1). Section 13(2)(b) allows the court to order a spouse to pay a lump sum to a specified person to meet any liabilities or expenses reasonably incurred prior to the making of the application under section 13(1) by or for the benefit of a dependent member of the family. Furthermore, section 13(3) provides that an order for the payment of such a lump sum can be made by instalments as specified by the court and such instalment payments can be secured if so ordered by the court.

E–105   Section 13(4) provides that a payment made on foot of any order under section 13(1) shall not commence before the date of the application for the said order and shall end no later than the death of either spouse or dependent member of the family in whose favour the order is made, if relevant. Under section 13(5)(a) the remarriage of the applicant nullifies any order previously made under subsection (1) except in respect of payments due at the date of the marriage. Furthermore, the remarriage of a spouse acts as a bar under section 13(5)(b) to the court making any further order under section 13(1) in favour of that spouse. Finally, section 13(6) deals with the procedures involved in securing an order made under section 13. The court must ensure that the person against whom an attachment of earnings orders is made is a person to whom earnings fall to be paid. Before deciding whether to make such an order, the court must give the spouse concerned an opportunity to make representations, first as to whether he/she is a person to whom earnings fall to be paid and, secondly, whether he/she would make the payments to which the relevant order relates.

GENERAL COMMENTARY AND JUDICIAL INTERPRETATION

Introduction

E–106   Section 13(1)(a) allows the court to make a periodical payments order against one spouse for the benefit of the other or any dependent children, to last as long as the court specifies. Alternatively, or in addition, the court may order, pursuant to section 13(1)(b) that such periodical payments in favour of a spouse or dependent child should be secured.

Periodical payments order

E–107   An order for periodical payments is in practice a relatively common order in proceedings for a decree of divorce. In cases where the Order is made on consent, care should be taken by practitioners to ensure that there is no ambiguity regarding the terms of the Order. In *M.P. v. A.P.* [2001] 1 I.L.R.M. 51, a dispute arose between the parties as to the meaning of the words "net of income tax", which had been used in connection with a provision for maintenance in the terms of a settlement, which were attached to an Order of the High Court in proceedings under the Guardianship of Infants Act 1964 and the Judicial Separation and Family Law Reform Act 1989. The consent provided for "maintenance of £1,800 net of income tax per month" and further provided that the wife would be liable for income tax on any income she may have from any source in addition to maintenance of £1,800 net of tax per month as adjusted thereafter. It was submitted on behalf of the wife that the agreement meant that the Defendant was obliged to pay her a gross sum which, after deduction of the income tax payable by her, would leave her with the net sum of £1,800 per month. It was claimed on behalf of the Defendant however, that it meant that the tax payable by the wife in respect of the sum of £1,800 was to be deducted by him and transmitted to the Revenue and the balance to be paid to the wife. In the High Court, Costello J. favoured the Plaintiff's interpretation and held that the words meant that the wife was entitled to be paid the sum of £1,800 and to be under no liability to income tax in respect of that sum. On appeal to the Supreme Court however, this finding was overturned. The Supreme Court stated that had the parties used the well known formula under which the spouse making the periodic payments undertakes to pay the other spouse such a sum as, after the deduction of income tax at the standard rate, would leave a sum of X pounds, the contention on behalf of the Plaintiff wife would have been unanswerable. The same result would have followed if the payment of £1,800 per month was to be "free of income tax". However, the Court held that no such clear significance could be attributed to the expression "net of income tax". In the Court's view, these words were not a sufficiently clear indication that the Defendant husband was obliged by the terms of the agreement to pay the gross sum claimed by the Plaintiff. At best, from the wife's point of view, the expression was ambiguous. In those circumstances, the Court remitted the matter back to the High Court for a determination as to whether, in the light of such oral evidence as might be relevant and admissible, the consent annexed to the Order should be rectified so as to give effect to what was claimed on behalf of the Defendant to have been the intention of the parties to the consent.

Where default occurs in respect of the payment of a periodical payments order the practical procedure for the enforcement of unsecured periodical payments is not very effective. The onus is placed on the paying spouse to make these payments directly to the recipient spouse or, alternatively, through the local District Court office. The recipient spouse in turn collects the money from the District Court clerk. There is no onus on the District Court clerk to take action should the paying spouse default. Rather the onus is placed on the recipient spouse to request a summons to be issued for the arrest of the defaulting spouse. Too often the dependent spouse is reticent to be seen to cause trouble for their estranged spouse and the matter goes unpunished. Thus, it is clear that the making of an order against a spouse to financially support his/her spouse and dependent children may not be adequate and, in reality, may fail to secure an income for those in financial need following the grant of a decree of divorce.

Lump sum orders

E–108 Section 13(1)(c) of the Divorce Act empowers the court to order either spouse to make a lump sum payment to the other spouse under the terms as specified in the order for the benefit of the recipient spouse, or a dependent member of the family, allowing the court flexibility to deal with a variety of situations. It takes into account the practical difficulties of raising a large sum immediately and allows the court to order the lump sum payment to be made at various times and even in varying amounts. In addition, the court can also require such instalment payments to be secured. Where a lump sum is paid by way of instalments, tax benefits arise for the paying spouse, because stage payments are tax deductible. The type of lump sum order made by the court is dependent on the particular circumstances of the case. A lump sum may be ordered to finance future purchases such as a home, to discharge outstanding debts and liabilities or to reimburse a spouse for specific expenditure. In addition, section 13(2)(a) empowers the court to make a lump sum order in respect of expenses already reasonably incurred prior to the making of an application under section 13. For example, in proceedings for judicial separation, *J.C. v. C.C.* [[1994] 1. Fam. L.J. 22], Barr J. ordered the husband to pay a lump sum of £15,500 to the wife in respect of money unfairly withheld during the marriage. The lump sum related, *inter alia*, to money already spent by the wife on the maintenance and improvement of the family home and on health care for a dependent son since the breakdown of the marriage. In the more recent case of *E.P. v. C.P.* [unreported, High Court, November 27, 1998], McGuinness J. chose to exercise the court's power to make a lump sum order in proceedings for a decree of judicial separation. In so doing the learned judge acknowledged that although a lump sum of maintenance was desirable for the children sufficient funds were not available to allow for this. In the circumstances, McGuinness J. ordered the payment of arrears in the sum of £10,000 together with the sum of £30,000 to cover maintenance for the children for a period of four years and thereafter the applicant could apply for further maintenance. This order was made by the court in light of the history of non-payment of maintenance by the respondent husband. Clearly, in such circumstances, McGuinness J. sensibly foresaw the likelihood of the respondent falling into arrears once more if a periodical payments order was made. More recently, in *P.P. v. A.P.* [unreported, High Court, December 14, 1999], McCracken J. in determining the amount of the lump sum to be paid to the wife took into account the fact that the maintenance payments would be cut back within a few years because of the husband's intention to cut back on his work due to his health problems.

Secured periodical payments

The object of a secured periodical payments order is to require the **E–109** paying spouse to set aside a fund of capital, to be vested in trustees, and to execute a deed of security. This fund could then be resorted to, if the maintenance payments were not made as they fall due. Clearly, the advantage of a secured payments order is the increased likelihood of enforcement. Although the fund and the income therefrom remains the beneficial property of the husband, it is available for use should the husband default in his payments. If necessary, in the event of such a default the fund can be sold in order to pay the arrears due.

Attachment of earnings order

As stated in relation to secured/unsecured periodical payments orders, **E–110** the making of a secured order greatly increases the chance of enforcement. Another means of facilitating easier enforcement is to make an attachment of earnings order. As distinct from section 10 of the Family Law (Maintenance of Spouses and Children) Act 1976, whereby an attachment of earnings order may only be made where a spouse has defaulted on a maintenance order made against him, section 13(6) of the Divorce Act entitles the court to make such an attachment order at the time of the making of the periodical payments order. Thus, the court need not wait for default to occur and be proven. Section 13(6)(b) directs the court to give the spouse against whom the order is proposed an opportunity to make such representations as he/she feels are necessary. Unfortunately, this order cannot be used to ensure payment where the paying spouse is self-employed or where he/she works on an irregular contractual basis.

How is maintenance assessed and calculated by the Irish courts?

The calculation of what constitutes appropriate maintenance in each case **E–111** is ultimately left to the court to decide. In attempting to strike the proper balance, a court will take into account all the circumstances it considers proper. Section 20(2)(a) to (l) of the Divorce Act provides a non-exhaustive list of criteria to be taken into account by the court when deciding whether to make an order under, *inter alia*, sections 12 and 13. These factors apply to the needs and circumstances of the claimant and respondent spouse. In addition, section 20(4)(a) to (g) provides a non-exhaustive list of factors to be considered by the court when deciding to make an order under, *inter alia*, sections 12 and 13 in favour of any dependent members of the family. Ultimately, whatever order is made by the court under section 12 and 13, section 20(1) requires the court to endeavour to ensure that such provision is made for each spouse concerned and for any dependent member of the family as is proper, having regard to all of the circumstances in the case. However, despite the extensive factors contained in the Divorce Act, no practical formula has been proposed. Although a definite formula may not apply in every case, some method of calculation is necessary in order to provide a level of predictability.

The formulae used to calculate maintenance levels in the United Kingdom

E–112 The English one-third rule stems from Lord Denning's dictum in *Watchel v. Watchel* [[1973] 1 All E.R. 829]:

"In view of [a wife's] call on [her husband's] future earnings, we do not think she can have both half the capital assets, and half the earnings . . . giving it the best consideration we can, we think that the fairest way is to start with one-third of each. If she has one-third of the family assets as her own and one-third of the joint earnings, her past contributions are adequately recognised, and her future living assured so far as may be".

In practice, the English courts have only applied this formula in limited circumstances. It can only be applied in the clearest of cases and it fails to take account of the possibility of dependent children.

Another formula, which has been applied is the reasonable needs formula. In *Preston v. Preston* [1982] 2 F.L.R. 331, Lord Justice Ormrod expressed the view that it was wrong in principle to adopt a mathematical approach since all the circumstances of a case and all of the factors set out in the statutory provisions should be considered before making an appropriate financial order. He also stated that the word "needs" in section 25(1)(b) of the Matrimonial Causes Act 1973 was equivalent to "reasonable requirements". In *F. v. F. (Ancillary Relief: Substantial assets)* [1995] 2 F.L.R. 45, which concerned an application for maintenance pending suit, Thorpe J. stated that in determining the wife's reasonable needs on an interim basis, it was important as a matter of principle that the Court should endeavour to determine reasonableness according to the standards of the ultra-rich and accordingly, he thought it necessary to establish a yardstick that more nearly reflected the standard of living, which had been the norm for the wife ever since the marriage. In *Dart v. Dart* [1996] 2 F.L.R 286, the reasonable needs model was affirmed. In the course of his judgment, Thorpe L.J. stated that there must be an objective appraisal of what the Applicant subjectively requires to ensure that it is not unreasonable. He went on to state that this objective appraisal must have regard to the other criteria of section 25 including what is available, the standard of living to which the parties are accustomed, their age and state of health and perhaps, less obviously, the duration of the marriage, contributions and pension rights, both as affected by the marriage and as accrued or likely to accrue. [But see *White v. White* [2000] 3 F.L.R. 555, E—051A, wherein the House of Lords criticised the reasonable requirements model and stressed the importance of achieving equality and fairness between the parties.]

In respect of low-income couples, the subsistence level approach has **E–113** been adopted. O'Farrell ["Dividing Matrimonial Assets on Marital Breakdown: Guidelines from English Case-law" [1994] 3 Fam. L.J. 74 at 77] notes that this principle was established in England to ensure that the effect of a maintenance order in favour of a wife should not be to depress the maintaining spouse below subsistence levels. Under this approach, the court calculates the net available income of the maintaining spouse and considers the effect of the proposed order for periodical payments on his ability to meet his own living expenses. In so doing, it compares the sum he would receive if in receipt of supplementary benefit to ensure that he is not left below that figure.

In response to calls by the English Court of Appeal for expert guidance in cases involving wealthy couples, the "Duxbury computations" were introduced in *Duxbury v. Duxbury* [[1987] 1 F.L.A. 7]. O' Farrell notes that it involves the use of computer-based, actuarial evidence to calculate lump sums sufficient to generate future annual income for one spouse. Thus, in *B. v. B.* [[1990] 1 F.L.R. 20], the Court of Appeal made a lump sum order in favour of the wife for £300,000, sufficient to produce an annual income of £15,000. The court in *Gojkovic v. Gojkovic* [[1990] 2 All E.R. 84, *per* Butler-Sloss L.J.], approved of this formulation as "a helpful guide" but, in so doing, emphasised that it should not be elevated to a rigid mathematical calculation.

The development of methods by the English judiciary is an admirable **E–114** attempt to establish consistency in the area of maintenance for divorced families. However, the development of different formulae serves to highlight the varying circumstances of every situation. As Scarman L.J. stated in *Calderbank v. Calderbank* [[1975] 3 All E.R. 333 at 340], "every case will be different and no case may be decided except upon its particular facts . . . the proportion of the division is dependent on circumstances." The non-precise nature of the statutory guidelines and the obligation on the court to have regard to the circumstances that exist invariably result in the existence of a questionable level of judicial discretion. While such broad criteria, as the ability of a spouse to pay, and the needs of the other spouse and any dependent children have been relied upon to date, it is not altogether clear what weight the courts attach to the various factors present in individual cases. Although retaining an element of judicial discretion always allows for extenuating or unusual circumstances to be accommodated, the failure of the Irish legislature to provide any system for the calculation of maintenance allows absolute judicial discretion to be applied in every situation, and not just those with extenuating circumstances. In the Report of the Joint Oireachtas Committee on Marriage Breakdown, the Committee expressed concern at evidence of "judicial inconsistency in administering the law in the area of maintenance". Furthermore, the Committee emphasised the importance of "uniform judicial interpretation" as to the level of such awards. However, once again despite this criticism no means of attaining judicial consistency by way of agreed formula was proposed.

E–115   An order for periodical payments made pursuant to the Divorce Act means that although the union of the parties is no longer recognised the ongoing obligation to maintain a spouse results in an undeniable link remaining between the parties. This obligation to maintain a spouse after the granting of a decree of divorce is governed by legislation that effectively mirrors the pre-existing provisions governing maintenance granted with a decree of judicial separation. Thus, although the marriage is deemed to be no longer in existence, no corresponding alteration has been made to the law governing the ancillary relief of maintenance. The legislature's failure to take account of the need for change and, more importantly in the case of divorce, the need for a "clean break" to exist between the parties to a marriage that is long since over is clear. The recent introduction of divorce should have involved a reassessment of the basis on which maintenance is paid to former spouses. The legislature's failure to provide for a "clean break" division in appropriate cases is a shortfall in our law. In fact, the radical change introduced in Irish law by the Divorce Act should have engendered a debate on the nature of the obligations owed to a former spouse. However, the legislature not only failed to provide a rationale to underpin grants of maintenance where spouses can be declared legally free of each other and capable of remarriage, but it has failed to do so since the inception of the first legislation governing maintenance *i.e.* the Family Law (Maintenance of Spouses and Children) Act 1976, which transferred the duty to pay maintenance from a common law duty to a statutory foothold.

E–116   McGuinness J., in *N.(C.) v. N.(R.)* [unreported, High Court, January 15, 1999], notes that variability rather than finality is the general characteristic of family law matters. Indeed, in *J.D. v. D.D.* [[1997] 3 I.R. 64], McGuinness J. held that no "clean break" provision could be made when financially re-ordering a broken marriage. She noted that the Oireachtas had legislated to permit repeated applications to court concerning ancillary relief so that finality could not be achieved. In a case where the relief sought is a decree of divorce, ultimately a "clean break" may be the most desired and appropriate outcome for the parties. Section 20(5) of the Divorce Act forbids the court from making any ancillary order (including a maintenance order) unless it is in the interests of justice to do so. However, this provision follows on from the long list of factors contained in section 20(2) which a court is required to consider before deciding what, if any, ancillary orders to make. Although section 20(5) does, theoretically, allow for no

[THE NEXT PAGE IS E55]

maintenance order to be made, the Act does not contain any reference, express or otherwise, in relation to the desirability of a clean break between the parties. There is almost an assumption that a clean break should be avoided, despite the very apparent division of the union of the parties.

In relation to the creation of a formula for the assessment of mainte- **E–117** nance by the Irish courts, three options could be adopted in the case of divorce. First, there is the viability of the "clean break" method where the property owned by the parties is sold and the proceeds divided. However, this option can be discounted because of its long-term unfairness in many cases as well as the lack of available assets for sale. Too often, the only asset available would be the family home, and the disposal of this would result in two homeless parties surviving on finances to the value of one home. Secondly, there is the concept of "rehabilitative maintenance". This would essentially involve the appropriate division of the marital assets with maintenance being paid on a short-term basis to the previously dependent spouse. This system would provide a short-term crutch for the dependent spouse thereby allowing him/her time to establish themselves in the working environment. This option amounts to a "clean break with a cushion". Clearly, the period in which the maintenance would be payable would vary with the facts of every case. However, this formula for division and survival is subject to criticism as too often spouses who have been dependent for all their married life will suffer in the workplace and most likely fail to ever realise their full earning capacity because of their long-term absence from the workplace. The "compensation model" is the final option and is also the most desirable option. This model allows for a spouse to be compensated for the losses and sacrifices made by him/her in favour of the other spouse during the course of the marriage. The formulation of amounts in this case would not be an arbitrary procedure but rather would be based upon actual events and spousal behaviour during the marriage. Support for this method can already be found in the judgment of McGuinness J. in *J.D. v. D.D.* [[1997] I.R. 64]. wherein the learned judge recognises that the notion of a clean break is not an option available to her in adjudicating on family law cases.

Social welfare payments

Many needy spouses rather than suing for arrears of maintenance, or **E–118** because of the simple inadequacies of the maintenance received, are choosing to rely on social welfare payments. Peter Ward [*Divorce in Ireland. Who should pay the cost?* p. 32] notes that:

". . . the difficulty of establishing an adequate and secure income from within the resources of the parties means that there can be little doubt but that social welfare payments will constitute the main source of income of a greater number of divorced women and children."

E55

This increasing reliance on social welfare payments has been facilitated by ongoing changes in the legislation governing State support for single parents. The hardship suffered by deserted wives and children was deemed to be sufficiently serious and widespread to warrant the introduction of the deserted wives allowance in 1970. However, to be entitled to receive this allowance, desertion had to be "firmly established and more or less permanent." [Social Welfare (Deserted Wives Allowance) Regulations 1970 (S.I. No. 227 of 1970), made pursuant to section 22 of the Social Welfare Act 1970]. Following on from this, the deserted wives benefit and social insurance payments were introduced in 1973 to provide long-term support for deserted wives. More recently, the area of marital breakdown has witnessed several important changes to the social welfare provisions applicable to it. The most important of these relating to maintenance payments, where a claimant is separated, was the introduction of a lone parents allowance and the change in the law concerning a claimant's liability to maintain relatives. Sections 12 to 16 of the Social Welfare Act 1990 provided for the introduction of a lone parent's allowance, which was brought into effect in November 1990. This is a means-tested payment and is payable to a lone parent of either gender who has at least one qualified child (under the age of 18 years, or under the age of 21 if in full-time education) residing with him or her. The introduction of this payment saw the abolition of, *inter alia*, the deserted husbands allowance and the deserted wives allowance. This allowance is now available to divorced parties who although no longer entitled to claim the status of "spouse", and thus prior to 1990 would not have been entitled to the deserted "wives" allowance, remain lone parents who continue to receive the support of the State. Thus, the transition from spouse to divorcee has no effect on the person's entitlements to this allowance.

E–119   Furthermore, following the introduction of the Social Welfare (Lone Parents Allowance and Other Analogous Payments) Regulations 1990 (S.I. No. 272 of 1990), the onus previously on a claimant to make "reasonable efforts" to trace and obtain maintenance from the deserting spouse was lessened somewhat, requiring the claimant to "make and continue to make appropriate efforts to the satisfaction of the Minister in the particular circumstances to obtain maintenance from his spouse" see article 5. This amendment reduces the level of obligation on the applicant spouse and allows for the hardship inclusion, making qualification for State support much easier. The introduction of section 12 of the Social Welfare Act 1989 allows the spouse to claim social welfare payments, despite the existence of a husband/father or wife/mother who is liable to contribute. Section 12 imposes liability on the paying spouse to make such payments to the Minister for Social, Community and Family Affairs or the health board where the claimant is in receipt of social welfare payments. Consequently, every person who is liable to support a claimant becomes liable to repay the Department of Social, Community and Family Affairs or the health board, such amount of the payment as that body may determine to be appropriate. If he/she fails to make that contribution, the relevant body may apply to the

E56

District Court for an order directing him/her to make such contribution, as per section 316 of the Social Welfare (Consolidation) Act 1981 as inserted by section 12 of the Social Welfare Act 1989.

When the claimant is already in receipt of support by virtue of a **E–120** maintenance order under the Family Law (Maintenance of Spouses and Children) Act 1976, and/or a periodical payments order under section 13 of the Divorce Act, payments made under any such order shall offset, in whole or in part any contributions due and the claimant will be liable to transfer the amount of that order to the Department of Social, Community and Family Affairs or to the health board. If a claimant fails to transfer the payments made under a maintenance order, the benefit or allowance paid to that person will be reduced by the amount which that person would have been liable to transfer. Although these provisions do not apply to maintenance paid by voluntary agreement or under a deed of separation, a claimant spouse will not be allowed to benefit twofold. In such a situation the Department of Social, Community and Family Affairs will require the maintenance debtor to make additional contributions directly to the Department in respect of any lone parent payments made to the claimant. Thus, a maintenance debtor is likely to cease voluntary payments or, alternatively, to seek to vary the maintenance agreement.

The clear advantage of this system of interaction between maintenance **E–121** and social welfare support is that the dependent spouse and children are more likely to be guaranteed a regular income. However, the onus to collect moneys appears to be placed on the Department of Social, Community and Family Affairs and the health boards. Should a liable spouse/parent fail to contribute to these bodies, the relevant board or Department must seek a court order. Thus, although payment to the dependent spouse is almost assured in some form, it is likely that too often the State and not the liable spouse/parent will provide the necessary financial support.

The duty of a spouse to maintain his/her dependent spouse and children is a long established obligation in law. The provisions of the Divorce Act present the court with a myriad of options which allow the courts to make the most appropriate order in every case. Thus, if a suitable application is made to the court by the dependent spouse, an order directing the payment of maintenance can now be made by the court before, during and after the hearing of an application for a decree of divorce.

SUCCESSION RIGHTS

INTRODUCTION

The Succession Act 1965 (hereafter referred to as the Succession Act) **E–122** has remained the principle authority in relation to all aspects of the law of succession. The Succession Act remains relatively unchanged since its enactment over 30 years ago. However, the ongoing effect of its provisions in the area of family law remains dependent on the introduction of any related legislation and the interpretations of such enactments by the judiciary. The introduction of judicial separation under the Judicial Separation and Family Law Reform Act 1989 and the subsequent provisions of the Family Law Act 1995 had a significant effect on the interpretation of the provisions of the Succession Act. More recently, the introduction of the remedy of divorce to our jurisdiction has again given rise to a restatement of the rules of succession resulting ultimately in the nullification of some of the basic effects of the Succession Act in the case of a divorced couple.

LEGISLATION

E–123 The Succession Act was described by the Supreme Court in *O'B. v. S.* [[1984] I.R. 316 at 335], as "a most important part" of family law. Prior to the coming into force of the Succession Act a testator had complete freedom of disposition and could distribute his estate amongst strangers whilst ignoring entirely the needs of his family. The relationship of husband and wife is given special priority by the legislature in the Succession Act. A widow/widower, by virtue of their status as a spouse, is granted an automatic share in the estate of their deceased spouse. Section 111(1) of the Succession Act provides that if a testator dies leaving a spouse and no children, the spouse is legally entitled to one-half of the estate. Section 111(2) states that if a testator dies leaving a spouse and children, the spouse has a legal right to one-third of the estate. Thus, the introduction of section 111, ensures that a testator's wife will be provided for out of the estate of her deceased spouse, irrespective of the contents of his will. The legislature in drafting the Divorce Act did not have to concern itself with granting the court the power to extinguish these spousal succession rights because once the decree of divorce is granted the parties are no longer spouses. What was provided for, however, was the right of the court under section 18(10) of the Divorce Act, to bar any application by either party on the death of the other for a share in the estate of the deceased. Such an application can be made by the surviving (divorced) party under section 18 within six months of the death.

E–124 The court, under section 18(1) of the Divorce Act, can, on the death of one spouse, make such provision for the surviving spouse as it considers appropriate having regard to the rights of any other person having an interest in the matter. In so doing, the court must be satisfied that proper provision in the circumstances was not made for the applicant during the lifetime of the deceased spouse under sections 13, 14, 15, 16 or 17 of the Divorce Act. Section 18(2) prohibits the court from making an order under section 18(1) in favour of a spouse who has remarried since the granting of the decree of divorce. The court is obliged under section 18(3) to have regard to all the circumstances of the case, including whether a lump sum payment was previously ordered under section 13(1)(c), any property adjustment order in favour of the applicant, or any devise or bequest made by the deceased spouse to the applicant.

If an order is made by the court under section 18(1), section 18(4) **E–125** prohibits the court from making an award to the applicant (including the value of any property adjustment order and/or lump sum payment) which exceeds the share in the estate which the applicant would have been legally entitled to under the Succession Act, if the marriage had not been dissolved. Sections 18(5) and 18(6) deal with the issue of notice requirements. The applicant is obliged under section 18(5) to give notice of the application to the surviving spouse (if any), of the deceased person, and to such other person(s) as the court may direct. Representations made by any notified party must be considered by the court when making an order under section 18. Section 18(6) places an obligation on the personal representative of the deceased spouse to "make a reasonable attempt to ensure that notice of his or her death is brought to the attention of the other spouse concerned". Where an application is made by the remaining (divorced) spouse under section 18(1), the personal representative is prohibited by section 18(6) from distributing any of the estate of the deceased until an order is made or refused by the court.

On receipt of notification, the surviving (divorced) spouse is required to **E–126** notify the personal representative within one month of his/her intention to make an application to court, of the existence of his/her current application to court, or of the existence of an order which has been made in his/her favour by the court under section 18, whatever the case may be. Failure to consult with the personal representative within one month, allows the personal representative to distribute the assets of the deceased's estate amongst those persons so entitled. No liability shall attach to the personal representative for this distribution of assets, unless at the time of distribution he/she had notice of the intention, pending application or order (section 18(8)). Despite the contents of section 18(7) and (8), section 18(9) provides that nothing shall prejudice the right of a spouse to follow assets into the hands of any person who may have received them. Finally, section 18(10) empowers the court, following the granting of a decree of divorce, upon application by either spouse, during the lifetime of the other spouse, to make an order if it considers it just to do so, barring either or both spouses on the death of either of them from making an application under section 18(1) of the Divorce Act.

GENERAL COMMENTARY AND JUDICIAL INTERPRETATION

The courts were granted the power under section 17(1) of the Judicial **E–127** Separation and Family Law Reform Act 1989, on the application of either spouse at any time after the granting of a decree of judicial separation, to consider making an order extinguishing the share that either spouse would otherwise be entitled to in the estate of the other spouse as a legal right or on intestacy. The provisions of section 17 were adopted and contained for the most part in section 14 of the Family Law Act 1995. No such provisions are contained in the Divorce Act, as upon the granting of a decree of divorce, a person ceases to be a "spouse" for the purpose of the Succession Act and is no longer automatically entitled to a share in the estate of his/ her deceased spouse. Although there is no specific provision in the Divorce Act which expressly states the effect of a decree of divorce on spousal succession rights, section 10(1) thereof provides as follows: "Where the court grants a decree of divorce, the marriage, the subject of the decree, is thereby dissolved and a party to that marriage may marry again." Therefore, it would appear reasonably clear that when a marriage is dissolved on foot of a decree of divorce, thereby permitting the parties to remarry, that the marriage is deemed to have ended and the former spouses no longer have that status. The Divorce Act does not have to give the court power to extinguish succession rights as this occurs automatically on the granting of a decree.

E–128   Although this may appear to finalise matters, the Divorce Act does not result in a clean break as regards inheritance rights. Section 18 of the Divorce Act confers jurisdiction on the courts to order provision for a divorced spouse out of the estate of a deceased former spouse in specific circumstances. Section 52(g) of the Divorce Act, which inserts a new section 15A into the Family Law Act 1995, extends this right to apply to a spouse whose succession rights were extinguished pursuant to an order made under section 14 of the Family Law Act 1995. However, this residual right of a spouse who has not remarried following the decree of divorce is subject to strict requirements as regards notice. Furthermore, the wording of section 18, suggests that an order making provision for the applicant spouse is only likely to be made in circumstances where the applicant was previously poorly provided for, and no third party rights are adversely affected. The legislature in drafting section 18, has effectively both empowered the court to deal with hardship situations and prevented a successful claim being made where a spouse has previously been adequately provided for.

E–129   An order under section 18(10) is, in practice, a standard ancillary order in proceedings for a decree of divorce. Most often this order is sought by both parties in an attempt to make a clean break from the marriage. Such an order will only be made if the court considers it just to do so. Thus, it is arguable that the court may refuse to make the order under section 18(10) where the extinction of that spouse's succession rights would jeopardise his/ her future financial security. However, an alternative in such circumstances would be for the court to order that the respondent take out a life assurance policy with the dependent spouse named as the beneficiary. The extinction of the right of the spouse to apply to the court for provision from the estate, would thus be replaced by the proceeds of the policy in the event of the death of the respondent spouse.

The effect of the terms of the Succession Act depends largely on the provisions and subsequent developments of other related areas of law. The Succession Act although largely unchanged from its original state, has been altered indirectly by the introduction and interpretation of subsequent related legislation. The introduction of the Divorce Act has had a dramatic effect on the operation of certain fundamental principles provided for in the Succession Act. The long-standing provisions in respect of the inheritance rights of a spouse on the death of his/her spouse can no longer apply on the granting of a decree of divorce. However, in order to prevent gross injustice, the inclusion of section 18 of the Divorce Act ensures that every facts scenario can be dealt with appropriately.

PROPERTY ADJUSTMENT ORDERS

INTRODUCTION

Section 14 of the Divorce Act empowers the court to make a property **E–130** adjustment order upon the granting of a decree of divorce. When used in the context of marital breakdown and divorce the term property is immediately associated with the family home. However, the property at issue in a divorce settlement/order can include businesses, commercial property, investments and savings. Section 14 of the Divorce Act can be used by the court, upon application to it by either of the spouses concerned, or by or on behalf of a dependent member of the family, in relation to such assets. The court is given broad discretionary powers under section 14 of the Divorce Act to make such property adjustment orders as it deems necessary. In so doing the court must take account of any separation agreement that may exist between the parties to the marriage. Although the parties to the agreement may be contractually bound by the terms of such an agreement, the court is empowered under section 14 to disregard or even set aside, any or all aspects of the agreement. The application by the courts of this aspect of the Divorce Act allows the courts to override fundamental principles of contract law and is likely to result in continuing comment and controversy. Because of the relative youth of the Divorce Act the attitude of the courts to date, in relation to the institution of proceedings for a decree of divorce by one party to a pre-existing separation agreement, has not yet been conclusively determined.

LEGISLATIVE PROVISIONS

Following the amendment of section 9 of the Family Law Act 1995 by **E–131** section 52(b) of the Divorce Act, the text of both the 1995 Act and the Divorce Act as they apply to property adjustment orders in the context of proceedings for the granting of a judicial separation/divorce are now the same. On granting a decree of divorce or at any time thereafter, the court can make a property adjustment order under section 14(1)(a). By such order the court may provide for one or more of the following:

"(a) the transfer by either of the spouses to the other spouse, to any dependent member of the family or to any other specified person for the benefit of such a member of specified property, being property to which the first-mentioned spouse is entitled either in possession or reversion;

(b) the settlement to the satisfaction of the court of specified property, being property to which either of the spouses is so entitled as aforesaid, for the benefit of the other spouse and of any dependent member of the family or of any or all of those persons;

(c) the variation for the benefit of either of the spouses and of any dependent member of the family, or of any, or all, of those persons of any ante-nuptial or post-nuptial settlement (including such a settlement made by will or codicil) made on the spouses;

(d) the extinction or reduction of the interest of either of the spouses under any such settlement."

E–132   Sections 14 and 15 of the Divorce Act do not attempt to limit the discretion exercisable by the court in this area. By declining to specify the assets to be governed by these sections, the legislature has left complete discretion to the courts to make an order in respect of any asset of either spouse. There exists a substantial lack of precedent, resulting in the absence of principles as to how and when such orders should be granted. This is due in the most part to the *in camera* proceedings as well as the relative youth of the divorce legislation. Such lack of clear and binding authority in respect of the manner and circumstances in which property adjustment orders ought to be made simply serves to exaggerate the powers of the judiciary and to increase the level of uncertainty in this sweeping area.

E–133   Although for the most part, the majority of orders governed by section 14 that are made by the court will be property transfer orders under section 14(1)(a), subsection (1)(b)–(d) of section 14 provides the court with alternative powers. Section 14(1)(b) empowers the court to order that property to which either spouse is entitled, either in possession or reversion, be settled for the benefit of the other spouse and/or any dependent member of the family. This power can be applied to award a life interest in the family home, by ordering a spouse to place the family home in trust for the benefit of the other spouse and dependent children, or equally to establish a trust to be funded by savings or investments of one or both spouses. This power is most often used, particularly in relation to the family home, where it would be inappropriate to transfer it into the sole name of one spouse because of a likely financial imbalance between the parties. Instead, a life interest can be awarded to him/her, resulting, for example, in the family home going by reversion to the children of the marriage.

FLP R.0: July 2000

Section 14(1)(c) essentially empowers the court to completely reconstruct **E–134** any ante-nuptial or post-nuptial settlement or agreement made by the spouses, provided it is in favour of either spouse and any dependent children. This means that the court can increase, reduce or extinguish a spouse's interest and may even confer an interest on a spouse, previously not provided for. Although not exclusive to the context of separation agreements, the primary focus to date of this subsection has been in this respect. The importance of separation agreements arises once more in section 20(3) of the Divorce Act where, in deciding whether to make an order for ancillary relief, the court is obliged to "have regard to the terms of any separation agreement which has been entered into by the spouses and is still in force."

GENERAL COMMENTARY AND JUDICIAL INTERPRETATION

Mary O' Toole in her assessment of the 1989 Act ["An Introduction to **E–135** the Judicial Separation and Family Law Reform Act 1989" [1990] 6 Fam. L.J. regards the powers of the court relating to property adjustment orders under section 15, as "by far the most radical provisions of the Act." Under section 15 of the 1989 Act, a property adjustment order could be made by the court on one occasion only, unless on that occasion a spouse wilfully concealed information of a nature relevant to the making of an order. However, the changes introduced by section 9 of the 1995 Act and repeated by section 14 of the Divorce Act serve to further extend this "radical power". A property adjustment order can now be made on the granting of a decree of divorce, or at any time thereafter, during the lifetime of the spouses. In relation to subsection (1)(b), (c) and (d) of section 14, which has no direct connection with the family home, a court will only make such an order at a stage later than the decree of divorce where there is a change in the circumstances of the parties as governed by section 22 of the Divorce Act, which deals with variation. In the High Court judicial separation case of *J.D. v. D.D.* [[1997] 3 I.R. 64], McGuinness J. regarded this lifetime right to apply to the court as "the most relevant change from the position under the 1989 Act." In this case the husband owned substantial assets, both proprietary and monetary. However, on the facts McGuinness J., in making proper provision for the applicant, favoured the making of a lump sum order and a periodical payments order, rather than making a property adjustment order. Although McGuinness J. made this order together with the direction to the respondent husband that he finance the purchase of the applicant's new dwelling, she nonetheless acknowledged the applicant's remaining right to return to the court in the future, a right which cannot be extinguished by the courts. Thus, a divorced spouse who does not remarry, has the capacity to bring an application under section 14 of the Divorce Act at any time during the lifetime of his/her former spouse, irrespective of the extent of the orders made at the time of the decree.

FLP R.0: July 2000

E–136   This wide level of discretion may serve to further increase the level of uncertainty in divorce proceedings. However, this far-reaching power was proven to be subject to certain limitations in the High Court. In *C.(C.) v. C.(J.)* [[1994] 1 Fam. L.J. 22], Barr J. declined to make an order in respect of the husband's business premises. He stated that the wife had never had any connection with her husband's business property and therefore was not entitled to any interest therein. It is likely that this "connection" requirement will be greatly welcomed by many wealthy potential divorcees. Furthermore, it is hoped that this decision indicates that a sensible approach will be taken by the courts in respect of property adjustment orders relating to non-marital property in divorce proceedings. Notwithstanding this decision by Barr J. in declining to make a property adjustment order, there are few reported judgments in this area, other than those relating to the family home. [See *S.(A.) v. S.(G.)* [1994] 1 Fam. L.J. 10; *C.(L.) v. C.(A.)* [1994] 1 Fam. L.J. 19 and *McA v. McA* [2000] 2 I.L.R.M. 48].

VALUATION OF COMPANIES

E–137   The valuation of family companies can sometimes be very artificial especially where the company will not be sold [see *Potter v. Potter* [1982] 1 W.L.R. 1255; *B. v. B.* (financial provision) [1989] 1 F.L.R. 241 and *P. v. P.* (financial provisions) [1989] 2 F.L.R. 241]. Private companies can be valued in a number of different ways. [See generally, Courtney T., *The Law of Private Companies* (Butterworths, 1994); *Attorney General v. Jameson*, [1904] 2 I.R. 644; *Re Clubman Shirts Ltd* [1991] I.L.R.M. 43; *Colgan v. Colgan*, unreported, High Court, Costello J., July 27, 1993; and *Irish Press Plc v. Ingersol Irish Publications Ltd*, unreported, High Court, Barron J., May 13, 1994]. Assessing the valuation of a spouse's shareholding is also a difficult task [see generally, Fox and Brown, *The Law of Private Companies* (Sweet & Maxwell, 1991) Chap. 14].

A PRE-EXISTING SEPARATION AGREEMENT AND DIVORCE

E–138   The term "post-nuptial settlement" was given a broad meaning in the 1995 Circuit Family Court case of *N.(C.) v. N.(R.)* [[1995] 1 Fam. L.J. 14], which facilitated a liberal application of section 14(c) to marital agreements. In this case the applicant wife sought a decree of judicial separation together with ancillary orders pursuant to both the Judicial Separation and Family Law Reform Act 1989 and the Family Law (Maintenance of Spouses and Children) Act 1976. Judge McGuinness (as she then was) agreed with submissions made by counsel for the applicant who sought to rely principally on English case law and commentary on the area of settlements. In the absence of an Irish authority on this matter she accepted the English position as being highly persuasive. In this regard the learned judge relied on Bromley's *"Family Law"* [(8th ed., Butterworths, 1992) p. 739] which states:

"The terms 'ante-nuptial' and 'post-nuptial' settlements are used in a sense much wider than that usually given to them by conveyances, the essential condition being that the benefit must be conferred on either or both of the spouses in the character of spouse or spouses ... A separation agreement comes within the section even if it is not in writing."

McGuinness J. also took note of the judgment in the early case of *Prinsep v.* **E–139** *Prinsep* [[1929] P. 225, *per* Hill J.], wherein it was stated that:

"... the particular form of [the settlement] does not matter ... what does matter is that it should provide for the financial benefit of one or other or both of the spouses ... The term 'settlement' thus appears to include a separation agreement whether made orally or in writing."[See also the dicta of Keane J. in *P.O'D. v. A.O'D.* [1998] 2 I.R. 225, where Keane J. held that a separation agreement was not a post-nuptial settlement, though it might incorporate one].

The express statement by McGuinness J. that separation agreements come within the ambit of section 15 of the Judicial Separation and Family Law Reform Act 1989 [this section has been repealed by section 14 of the Family Law Act 1995] has resulted in widespread debate as to the right of a party to a separation agreement to institute proceedings under the Judicial Separation and Family Law Reform Act 1989 .

The majority of case law to date on this issue has dealt with the validity **E–140** of an application for an order of judicial separation together with ancillary relief, where the applicant and respondent to the proceedings have at some earlier stage concluded a separation agreement. Two schools of thought emerged in this regard in the years pre-dating the enactment of the 1989 Act. These two contradictory approaches arose from applications made to the court for a decree of divorce *a mensa et thoro* where a separation agreement was already in place. The early case of *Courtney v. Courtney* [[1923] 2 I.R. 31], as determined by Dodd J., and the more recent decision of MacKenzie J. in *K. v. K.* [1988] I.R. 161, subscribe to the view that the existence of a separation agreement represents a bar to the applicant's petition for a decree of divorce *a mensa et thoro*. However, the opposite viewpoint was advocated by Walsh J. in *H.D. v. P.D.* [unreported, Supreme Court, May 8, 1978]. In this case, Walsh J. stated that "it is not possible to contract out of the Act by an agreement made after the Act came into force or by an agreement entered into before the legislation was enacted."

Despite the apparently contradictory nature of these decisions, it should **E–141** be highlighted that the applicant wife in the case of *H.D. v. P.D.* [unreported, Supreme Court, May 8, 1978] sought a variation in the maintenance provisions of the agreement. This was permitted by the Supreme Court and subsequent case law has proven that maintenance is always open to review by a court. Thus, it is submitted that it is wrong to

E65

interpret this Supreme Court ruling as giving the green light to an applicant who wishes to obtain a variety of ancillary reliefs under the Family Law Act 1995, irrespective of the existence of a separation agreement. Rather, this case should be limited to and distinguished on its own facts.

E–142   Recent case law includes *N.(C.) v. N.(R.)* [[1995] 1 Fam. L.J. 14], wherein the parties had entered into a separation agreement in 1986. McGuinness J. relied upon the express provisions of section 15(1)(c)–(d) and concluded that a separation agreement was not of itself a bar to the courts right to grant relief under the Judicial Separation and Family Law Reform Act 1989. She supported her decision by reference to English precedent and also by reference to necessity on the grounds of public policy. It is arguable that because of the real possibility of unequal bargaining positions it is essential that the court retains the right to review all such settlements. Despite representations by counsel for the respondent requesting finality, McGuinness J. noted that variability rather than finality is the general characteristic of family law matters. She stated that setting a matter out in a separation agreement cannot make it immune to this general policy of variability. McGuinness J. further strengthened her judgment by relying on the previously quoted unreported decision of Walsh J. in *H.D. v. P.D.* wherein it was emphatically stated [at p.7] that ". . . it is not possible to contract out of [the Family Law (Maintenance of Spouses and Children) Act 1976] by an agreement". In addition, it was submitted that following the enactment of the Family Law Act 1995, there now exists a greater number and variety of reliefs previously unavailable to the parties.

E–143   The decision of McGuinness J. in *N.(C.) v. N.(R.)* prompted family law practitioners, when advising a client in relation to the drafting of a separation agreement, to emphasise that once concluded, the separation agreement should not be regarded as final and that both parties retained the right to make an application under the Judicial Separation and Family Law Reform Act 1989, thereby permitting the court to review all matters contained in the separation agreement. This remained the position until the decision of Keane J. in *P.O'D. v. A.O'D.* [[1998] I.L.R.M. 543], a case stated to the Supreme Court from the Circuit Family Court by Her Honour Judge McGuinness (as she then was). The issue before the court was similar to that in *N.(C.) v. N.(R.)*. Counsel for the respondent wife brought a motion before the Circuit Family Court seeking an order for the proceedings brought by the husband under the Judicial Separation and Family Law Reform Act 1989 to be dismissed by reason of the deed of separation concluded between the parties in 1979. It was argued on behalf of the respondent wife that the husband was estopped from bringing proceedings. The questions posed by McGuinness J. in the case stated were as follows:

"(1) Whether I was correct in holding that I had jurisdiction to grant a decree of judicial separation where a deed of separation existed which relieved each of the duty to cohabit with the other and where the parties had lived apart since the conclusion of the agreement.

(2) Whether I was correct in holding that there was no estoppel by reason of the said [separation agreement] to prevent this court granting a decree of judicial separation pursuant to section 2 of [the 1989 Act]".

In delivering the judgment of the Supreme Court, Keane J. relied, *inter* **E–144** *alia*, on the decision of Blayney J. in *F. v. F.* [[1995] 2 I.R. 354]. The latter case decided that proceedings which had been compromised by a consent order [under the old regime a divorce *a mensa et thoro*] could not later be revisited in the context of proceedings under the new reformed regime. Two reasons were cited for this prohibition. First, the parties were already separated and did not need to apply again for a separation and, secondly, it would be unjust to allow one party to unilaterally repudiate that compromise of proceedings. The Supreme Court decided that litigants who obtained orders, or decided to compromise proceedings under the older and more restrictive regime, must live with those orders or compromise until they could apply again in the context of divorce. The case of *P.O'D. v. A.O'D.* applied this logic to the situation of people who entered into separation agreements. Keane J. quoted the following passage of Blayney J.'s judgment deeming its reasoning to be fully applicable to the position of the husband in the instant case:

> "I am satisfied that the applicant is not entitled to continue her proceedings under the (1989 Act) . . . .The applicant does not need a judicial separation. She has been lawfully separated from her husband for the last 7 years. The proceedings she has instituted are not for the purpose of obtaining a judicial separation but are an attempt on her part to get such an order so that she can ask the court to make various ancillary orders in her favour. So she is asking the court to give her relief she does not need with a view to being in a position to obtain such orders that she would like to have. It seems to me that this is not a form of proceeding to which the court could lend its support."

Essentially, the basis for this decision was to prevent the injustice that would invariably occur if one party could unilaterally repudiate a binding contract in the form of a separation agreement by instituting proceedings under the Judicial Separation and Family Law Reform Act 1989 whereby he/she would be applying for an order of separation that was effectively already in place.

The position in relation to an application for relief under the Divorce **E–145** Act where a separation agreement has previously been concluded, must, by the very nature of the relief available, be viewed in a different light by the courts. The new Article 41.3.2° of the Constitution arising from the referendum in November 1995 permits the court to grant the dissolution of a marriage where it is satisfied, *inter alia,* that:

> ". . . such provision as the court considers proper having regard to the circumstances exists or will be made for the spouses, any children of either or both of them and any other person prescribed by law".

Thus, in light of the existence of this constitutional obligation on the courts to ensure that proper provision exists prior to the granting of a dissolution of a marriage, the current position of the parties involved must be reviewed together with the adequacy of the provisions of any separation agreement previously concluded between the parties.

E–146   The decision of *P.O'D. v. A.O'D.*, together with earlier similar decisions, denies the applicant's right to seek relief under the 1989 Act where a separation agreement was already in existence, because the parties are already legally separated and the agreement provides for the parties to live separate and apart. Thus, in such circumstances, the granting of a decree of separation is deemed to be superfluous. The right to remarry, which is permitted once the decree of divorce is granted, results in a dramatic change in the circumstances of the parties and thus, it is contended that all issues must be open for review before the court.

E–147   Section 20(3) of the Divorce Act requires the court to "have regard to the terms of any separation agreement which has been entered into by the spouses and is still in force." It should be noted, first, that the obligation on the court is "to have regard to" which requires the court to take note of its existence and the contents therein, but permits the making of all orders deemed necessary by the court for the fulfilment of the court's obligations as set out in both the Constitution and the Divorce Act. The second interesting issue to arise from section 20(3) is the obvious lack of reference to the relevance of any existing order of judicial separation under the Judicial Separation and Family Law Reform Act 1989. Thus, it remains unclear as to how a court is to deal with a non-contentious divorce application which simply requires the court to make an order under the Divorce Act effectively echoing the terms of an order previously made under the 1989 legislation. In practice, the court is not investigating the terms of the order already in existence when it is once again placed before the court in an application for a consent divorce. The court in light of the proper provision requirement, may be failing to fulfil its constitutional and legislative obligations if it fails to review all aspects of the case before granting the new order sought.

E–148   The right to vary the terms of a separation agreement/order on the application for a decree of divorce together with ancillary orders has come before the courts recently and two greatly varying decisions have been made. First, the decision of a Circuit Court judge in the Cork Family Circuit Court, *Q. v. Q.*, denied the husband's application for the review of a property adjustment order previously agreed between the parties by way of separation agreement. The applicant in this case had previously concluded a separation agreement including a substantial property settlement with his wife pursuant to judicial separation proceedings issued by the wife. He sought a decree of divorce and asked the court to review the property issues in light of a dramatic change in the value of the relevant properties since the conclusion of the agreement. Clifford J. refused to review any aspect of the agreement. He believed the parties to be contractually bound by the provisions of the agreement and refused to consider reviewing the terms contained therein. Subsequently, however, White J. in the Western Circuit case of *B.S. v. J.S.* [Circuit Family Court, Western Circuit, February 5, 1999], ruled that the doctrine of *res judicata* does not apply to orders made following a decree of judicial separation and a court dealing with a divorce application can substitute new reliefs for the older ones. The parties in the instant case separated in January 1993 by order of judicial separation by Cassidy J. pursuant to section 2(1)(e) of the Judicial Separation and Family Law Reform Act 1989. In addition, the court made orders of ancillary relief by consent, including an order of joint ownership of the family home with the wife retaining a right of residence for life to the exclusion of the husband. In 1997, the wife filed proceedings for divorce and sought various ancillary reliefs including an order to transfer the family home into her sole name together with a pension adjustment order in respect of her husband's pension. In granting the decree and, more importantly, the ancillary reliefs sought, White J. relied on the policy as expressed in the statutes [and reiterated by McGuinness J. in *J.D. v. D.D.* [1997] 3 I.R. 64] which was against the concept of a clean break policy. What has occurred is a conflict in judicial interpretation of the relevant legislation. It is interesting to note that the earlier case of *Q. v. Q.* is under appeal to the High Court and it is hoped that the opportunity will be grasped by the High Court to make an authoritative and definitive statement on this important issue. Although ultimately each application under the Divorce Act will turn on its own facts a conclusive ruling is needed on the vital issue of whether new ancillary relief can be sought in a divorce application which follows an earlier decree of judicial separation or separation agreement. However, ultimately it is submitted that a court can not simply rubber stamp an application nor can it simply reiterate the terms of a separation agreement/order without examining the facts that exist at the time of the making of the divorce application.

One final aspect of the far-reaching power of the court under section 14 **E–149** relates to the variation of trusts. This discretionary power was recently discussed at length by McGuinness J. in *J.D. v. D.D.* [[1997] 3 I.R. 64]. Although the learned judge commented on the scarcity of authority in this area she noted that those traced by her indicated that the court can only deal with property to which the beneficiary is entitled in possession or in reversion. Her judgment is strengthened by the wording of section 14(c) which refers to any ante-nuptial settlement "made on the spouses". She refers specifically to the judgment of McKinnon L.J. in *Howard v. Howard* [[1945] 1 All E.R. 91 at 96] wherein he stated:

"A settlement by which the terms of which the trustees may at their discretion use the capital or income for the benefit of persons they may select would not seem to be such a settlement merely because the spouse or spouses is or are within the class of possible beneficiaries whom the trustees in their discretion are entitled to select".

E69

E–150   Applying this judgment to *J.D. v. D.D.*, McGuinness J. stated that an order could not be made in respect of the two discretionary family trusts because of the possibility of pressure being placed on the exercise of discretion by the trustees. However, the learned judge did take account of the trusts as well as the husband's beneficial status in respect of the trusts, when determining the value of the lump sum and periodical payments orders to be made.

The lifetime right of both spouses to apply to the court under section 14 of the Divorce Act means that finality in this area can never be guaranteed. The court has been granted extensive powers to rearrange the legal and beneficial ownership of property, irrespective of settlements or agreements previously made between the parties. It is possible that the introduction of divorce, as a more final solution than judicial separation, may result in a greater desire by the judiciary to achieve a sense of finality in the division of the assets. However, the ongoing right of the spouse to apply for a property adjustment order, coupled with the extensive powers of the court under section 14 of the Divorce Act, is likely to give rise to a complete lack of finality.

PENSIONS

INTRODUCTION

E–151   In many instances, pensions are the most valuable matrimonial asset after the family home. In the context of divorce, important and complex issues arise where one or both of the parties is a member of an occupational pension scheme. To ensure a complete understanding of the governing provisions it is proposed to analyse both the provisions and the process involved. The initial focus will be on the statutory provisions governing pensions and the schemes covered thereby. This will be followed by an examination of pension adjustment orders, who can apply for them and when, and the nature and effect of such an order. Other issues to be dealt with, will include the resulting obligations on trustees, the rights of persons other than the spouse and the criteria to be applied by the court before the making of a pension adjustment order.

LEGISLATIVE PROVISIONS

E–152   Section 17 of the Divorce Act is the primary provision governing the making of a pension adjustment order by the court when a decree of divorce is granted. It is an extensive provision comprising of some 26 subsections. The length of section 17 is in itself an indication of the complexity of the issue of pensions. However, despite the undeniable technicalities that exist within the area, section 17 by its very length deals admirably with all aspects of the making of a pension adjustment order in proceedings for an order of divorce. In addition, certain aspects of the Pensions Act 1990, particularly the area of definitions, are relied upon by section 17 of the Divorce Act, to be discussed below.

DEFINITIONS

Surprisingly, there is no express definition of a "pension" contained in **E–153** any of the relevant statutes. The provisions of the Divorce Act are framed entirely in terms of one or other spouse being a member of a "scheme". A scheme is defined by section 17(1) of the Divorce Act as a "pension scheme", which, in turn, is defined in section 2(1) of the Divorce Act. Clause (a) of the definition refers to occupational pension schemes within the meaning of the Pensions Act 1990. Section 2(1) of the Pensions Act 1990 defines an occupational pension scheme as "any scheme or arrangement which is comprised in one or more instrument or agreement which provides or is capable of providing benefits to employees in any description of employment." Clause (b) of the definition refers to certain annuity contracts, trust schemes and assurance policies, or contracts which would appear to govern schemes contributed to by self-employed persons or those working on a contract basis for different employers.

GENERAL COMMENTARY

Introduction

Following the breakdown of a marriage, the pension provisions of the **E–154** Divorce Act provide the courts with substantial powers to deal with the pension(s) held by one or both spouses. The other statutory provisions which regulate pensions and which are relevant to an ancillary order pursuant to a decree of divorce are contained in the Pensions Act 1990. This Act is expressly relied on by the Divorce Act for the definition of the concepts of "occupational pension scheme" and "relevant guidelines". The making of a pension adjustment order must be viewed simply as a further method of ensuring adequate and proper provision is made for the spouse and dependent children of the marriage. The decision to make such an order will depend upon the provision that can otherwise be made by the granting of periodical payments orders, lump sum orders, property adjustment orders or financial compensation orders.

Full disclosure

In deciding whether to make a pension adjustment order the court will **E–155** require full details of the pension scheme and the trustees thereof. The nature and extent of any such order will depend upon the value of the particular retirement benefit or contingent benefit in question. Gallagher

E71

suggests that this will necessitate a "trial within a trial" [Gallagher, "Pension Aspects of the Family Law Act 1995, Some Practical Implications." [1995] 3 Fam. L.J. 68]. Section 54 of the Pensions Act 1990 is specifically referred to in section 17(24) of the Divorce Act, and will apply to applications in respect of pensions during proceedings for the grant of a divorce decree. Section 54 requires trustees of occupational pension schemes to provide financial and other information about the scheme to, *inter alia*, members and their spouses. This section was, however, amended by section 28 of the Social Welfare Act 1998 to make it clear that a non-member spouse does not have the right to obtain specific information about the member's benefits from the schemes trustees. Thus, trustees will not release appropriate information to an applicant for a pension adjustment order without first obtaining the consent of the scheme member. Any necessary information, not obtained in this way, may be procured by discretion of the court pursuant to section 17(25) of the Divorce Act. Thereunder, the court may by its own motion, or at the request of either of the spouses, or any other person concerned, direct the trustees of the scheme to provide the spouses or that other person and the court with a calculation of the benefit payable under the scheme. Section 17(22)(a) provides that any costs incurred by the trustees of a scheme by reason of compliance with their statutory duties, must be borne by the member spouse or the other person concerned, or both of them in such proportion as may be determined by the court and in the absence of any such determination the costs shall be borne by them equally.

Defined contribution scheme v. defined benefit scheme

E–156   Occupational pension schemes can in turn be divided into two types: a "defined contribution scheme" and a "defined benefit scheme". Each scheme is treated differently under the provisions of section 17. A defined contribution scheme occurs where the employer and usually the employee pay a defined percentage of the employee's pay into the employee's pension account, which is then invested by the trustees of the scheme. The amount in the employee's pension account is then used at the date of retirement to purchase a pension scheme for the employee. Normally, there would exist an option under the scheme for members on retirement to take a lump sum, being a percentage of the amount accrued in the pension account. Self-employed arrangements are similar to a defined contribution scheme except that the contributions into the scheme are made by the self-employed person alone. A defined benefit scheme occurs where a specific level of pension is promised to the employee on retirement, usually by reference to the salary at or near retirement and to the amount of service completed. The level of benefit is defined in advance and the employer, and in most cases the employee, must make sufficient contributions to ensure that the promised benefit can be paid on retirement. Such a scheme usually operates on the basis that a person will get a particular fraction of the final pensionable salary for each year of reckonable service.

Retirement benefit v. contingent benefit

All benefits payable under a pension scheme can be the subject of a **E–157** pension adjustment order. For the purposes of the Divorce Act benefits are broken down into two categories: retirement benefit and contingent benefit. A contingent benefit is a benefit payable to a specified person or persons upon the occurrence of the stated contingency. For example, where the contingency is the death of the member, the scheme may provide for a payment to his/her widow or widower and any dependent members of the family if the spouse who is a member of the pension scheme dies while still in employment, and before attaining the normal pensionable age provided for under the rules of the scheme. Retirement benefit, in referring to all other benefits payable under a pension scheme, would, therefore, cover the pension paid to a person who retires or a pension payable to the widow or widower and any dependent member of the family on the death of a member after retirement. An application for a pension adjustment order in respect of a retirement benefit and a contingent benefit can be made under section 17(2) or section 17(3) respectively, by either spouse or by a person on behalf of a dependent member of the family. An order made in respect of a retirement benefit can only be made under section 17(2) in favour of the other spouse or for the benefit of a dependent member of the family, whereas an order made under section 17(3) in respect of a contingent benefit can be made in favour of both. Neither order, however, can be made in favour of the applicant spouse if he/she has remarried (section 17(23)(a)). Although an application for a pension adjustment order in respect of a retirement benefit can be made at the time of the making of the decree of divorce, or at any time thereafter during the lifetime of the member spouse, such an application in respect of a contingent benefit must be made not more than one year after the making of the decree of divorce (section 17(3)). In the case of *K. v. K.* [Circuit Family Court, Dublin Circuit, July 20, 1999], Buckley J. stated a case to the Supreme Court in an effort to determine whether a court can make an order pursuant to section 17(3) of the Divorce Act in relation to a contingent benefit payable to a spouse after retirement as opposed to before retirement. Contingent benefit is defined in section 17(1) of the Divorce Act as:

".... a benefit payable under a scheme, other than a payment under subsection (7) to or for one or more of the following, that is to say, the widow or the widower and any dependants of the member spouse concerned and the personal representatives of the member spouse, if the member spouse dies while in relevant employment and before attaining any normal pensionable age provided for under the rules of the scheme".

In view of the above definition, it is clearly arguable that a court cannot alter contingent benefits payable to a spouse if the death of the other spouse occurs after retirement. This issue will ultimately be decided by the Supreme Court.

Earmarking v. Pension splitting

E–158   The pension provisions of the Divorce Act permit a court by way of a pension adjustment order to attempt to secure the position of a spouse and/ or any dependent member(s) of the family. There are two basic concepts which are central to the operation of section 17 of the Divorce Act, namely "earmarking" and "pension splitting". Earmarking means that a percentage of the whole or part of a benefit should be paid directly to the other spouse or alternatively to another person for the benefit of a dependent member of the family. To facilitate the calculation of the part of the benefit to be earmarked for the benefit of the other spouse, the order must specify two things: the period of reckonable service to be taken into account and the percentage of the retirement benefit accrued to be paid to the spouse or other person. This view was advanced by Kevin Finucane of Coyle Hamilton Limited at a lecture entitled "Pension Implications of the Family Law Act 1995" given at the joint meeting of the Association of Pension Lawyers in Ireland and the Family Lawyers Association on December 6, 1995. The court determined the benefit that is to be earmarked for the spouse or other dependent member. However, the court can only adjust that part of the pension which relates to the member spouse's service that has accrued up to the date of the order (*i.e.* period of reckonable service). Future service cannot be taken into account. The court then decides what proportion of the benefit is to be paid to the spouse or other dependent member and what proportion remains payable to the member spouse. It should be noted that the position regarding contingent benefits (for example, lump sums) is somewhat simpler. The court can take the entire benefit into account and determine what percentage is payable. There is no requirement to take account of service accrued to the date of the order because the benefit is usually the same irrespective of the years of service completed by the member. Pension splitting on the other hand means that a percentage of a "retirement benefit" which has been earmarked for the other spouse is valued and is used to provide a separate pension for that spouse. Once a pension adjustment order has been made in respect of a retirement benefit, a spouse can apply to the trustees of the scheme to split the respondent's pension. The application can be made at any time from the date of such an order until the date of the commencement of the payment of the designated benefit. However, pension splitting is not applicable to a pension adjustment order made in respect of a contingent benefit.

E–159   The recent case of *J.C.N. v. R.T.N.* [unreported, High Court, McGuinness J., January 15, 1999], involved an applicant wife who sought a decree of divorce together with orders of ancillary relief, including an order under section 17(2) of the Divorce Act. The husband was retired and in receipt of a pension put in place by the Construction Industry Federation. It was an unusual situation in that following the completion of the deed of separation between the parties in 1975, the husband remarried (in 1978), the second purported marriage having no legal validity. In addition, all contributions to the scheme were made by the respondent after the deed of separation was completed. McGuinness J. felt that although all contributions were made after the signing of the separation agreement some provision had to be made for the applicant out of her husband's pension fund. As a result McGuinness J. ordered that should the respondent predecease the applicant the trustees of the pension fund were to divide the annual pension between the applicant and the respondent's second "wife". In the event that the applicant predecease the respondent it was ordered that the entire annual pension be paid to the second "wife".

While the decision in the case was a sensible one, there does not appear **E–160** to be any basis or grounding in the terms of the Divorce Act for it. There is nothing in the Divorce Act that specifically precludes this type of order either, and the order could be justified as a pension adjustment order whose operation turns on a condition precedent.

Whether this kind of order should be available is another matter. On the one hand, it may increase the already large uncertainty that flexible orders bring to the financial reordering of families. On the other hand, its availability might allow for "either/or" orders that obviate the need to return to court. In many ways the usefulness of this type of order will be determined by the clarity of the particular order and its use only in cases suited to such an order.

Significantly, McGuinness J. seemed to accept the second marriage in *J.C.N. v. R.T.N.* as valid for certain purposes and took it into account in making her order. It was noted that the second church wedding could not have been valid because of the prior subsisting marriage. That it had to be considered as part of the facts is clear; it was a long relationship that produced two children. In relation to the pension, however, McGuinness J. went further and appeared to recognise the second partner as a spouse, at least to some degree. It is clear that in making provisions for the second wife, McGuinness J. made a policy decision as opposed to one based on a statute, in an attempt to protect the interests of the respondent's two "spouses".

Role of the trustees

Section 2 of the Divorce Act gives a wide meaning to the term "trustees". **E–161** In the case of a scheme established under a trust, it means the trustees of the scheme. In relation to a pension scheme not so established, it means the persons who are responsible for the administration of the scheme. Various provisions of section 17 refer to the rights and duties of trustees. Section 17(18) states that the trustees must be notified by the person who makes an application for a pension adjustment order or an application in respect of an existing order. This section also entitles the trustees to make representations to the court and the court is obliged to have regard to these representations before deciding whether to make a pension adjustment order. As already stated, a spouse who has obtained a pension adjustment order from the court can apply to the trustees of the scheme for the pension to be split. On receipt of such an application, the trustees must value the percentage of the retirement benefit, which is earmarked under the order, for payment to the applicant spouse. This is likely to be an uncomplicated task in regard to a defined contribution scheme where the value of the member's contributions up to a particular date is readily ascertainable. However, such valuation is likely to be more difficult in respect of a designated benefit scheme where the value of the percentage to be earmarked for the applicant spouse is linked to the salary which the member will receive on retirement. Once the transfer amount, being the applicant's share of the pension, is ascertained the trustees have two options. They can hold the transfer amount within the original scheme, providing separate benefits on accrual (making the term "transfer amount" somewhat inappropriate) or, alternatively, the trustees can pay the transfer amount into another pension scheme. The decision will be made on the direction of the spouse who is seeking to split the pension.

E–162 When a court makes a pension adjustment order in respect of a defined contribution scheme and an application has not been brought by the other spouse for pension splitting, the trustees have in every case a discretion under section 17(6) to split the pension and to transfer the relevant amount into another pension fund. This discretion extends to permit the trustees to choose the second scheme. It should be noted, however, that the discretion cannot be exercised in regard to a designated benefit, payable under a pension adjustment order in respect of a defined benefit scheme.

E–163 When the pension adjustment order is made in respect of a retirement benefit, the death of the member spouse before the earmarked benefit commences to be paid obliges the trustees under section 17(7) within three months to transfer an amount equivalent to the transfer amount to the person in whose favour the order is made. Where a recipient spouse dies before the commencement of an earmarked benefit, obtained pursuant to a pension adjustment order in respect of a retirement benefit, the trustees are obliged under section 17(9) to pay, within three months of the death, an amount equivalent to the transfer amount to the personal representatives of the deceased. Interestingly, a pension adjustment order made in respect of a retirement benefit for the benefit of a dependent member of the family will cease to have effect upon the death of that person (section 17(11)). The death of the recipient spouse after the designated benefit obtained in respect of a retirement benefit commences to be paid also requires certain arrangements to take effect. The trustees must, within three months of the date of death, pay to the personal representatives of the deceased spouse, an amount equal to the actuarial value of the part of the designated benefit calculated in accordance with relevant guidelines [as defined in section 10(1), para. (c) of the Pensions Act 1990] which, but for the death of the (recipient) spouse, would have been payable to that spouse during the lifetime of the member spouse.

Finally, if the member spouse ceases to be a member of the scheme otherwise than on death, the trustees have a discretion to give effect to a pension adjustment order made in respect of a retirement benefit in a number of ways. As discussed previously, the designated benefit as valued can be retained within the original scheme or, alternatively, can be transferred to another scheme at the discretion of the recipient spouse.

Relevant factors to be considered

The factors which a court must have regard to in deciding whether to make a pension adjustment order under section 17 are set out in section 20 of the Divorce Act. This is not an exhaustive list, but contains several highly important and influential factors, including the property and income of the spouses, the duration of the marriage and the conduct of the spouses. [See also *M. v. M.*, unreported, High Court, McCracken J., May 23, 2000]. Section 17(23)(b) requires the court to examine in the first instance the possibility of making proper provision for the applicant spouse on foot of applications for maintenance, property adjustment and financial compensation orders, before considering whether a pension adjustment order should be made. Thus, although it may not be appropriate to make a pension adjustment order in every case, the potential to make such an order is likely to influence the division of non-pension assets. **E–164**

Varying a pension adjustment order

Section 22 of the Divorce Act empowers the court to vary or discharge any order, *inter alia,* made under section 17(2), if it considers it proper to do so having regard to any change in the circumstances of the case and to any new evidence. Section 17(2) refers only to orders made in relation to retirement benefit as opposed to contingent benefit under section 17(3). This inability to apply for a variation of an order made in respect of a contingent benefit, coincides with the limitation to one year after the granting of the decree of divorce for the making of an application for a pension adjustment order in respect of a contingent benefit. It should also be noted that as well as applications from either spouse or in the case of the death of either spouse a dependent member of the family, in the case of the remarriage of either of the spouses, his or her spouse can also apply under section 22(2)(c) for the variation of a pension adjustment order. Finally, section 17(26) allows the court to make an order restricting to a specific extent or excluding completely any application for variation made in respect of a pension adjustment order. **E–165**

An examination of the United Kingdom position

The positive approach of the Irish legislature to the division of pensions following a decree of divorce is to be commended as a triumphant avoidance of the unnecessary complications that its English counterpart has **E–166** been forced to continual address and amend. Section 25(2)(h) of the Matrimonial Causes Act 1973 requires the court to have regard to "the value to each of the parties to the marriage of any benefit which, by reason of the dissolution or annulment of the marriage, that party will lose the chance of acquiring." Hale J. in *B. v. B.* [unreported, Family Division, March 17, 1995] regarded the issue of financial provision for divorcing spouses who each have their own profession and provision for retirement as unquestionably relevant and governable by this subsection. The development of the court's powers in England in relation to the division of pensions as a form of ancillary relief has been slow and until recently, very unsatisfactory. Despite the fact that section 25(2)(h) of the Matrimonial Causes Act 1973 expressly directs the court to have regard to the value of any benefit which a spouse may lose on divorce, the English courts have lacked any definite power to make orders allocating pension rights to persons other than the pension scheme member. It was always assumed by the courts, as stated in *Milne v. Milne* [[1981] 2 F.L.R. 286] that pension funds fell outside the courts' statutory power to vary. The issue came to the fore in the case of *Brooks v. Brooks* [[1995] 3 All E.R. 257], a case that eventually reached the House of Lords. Lord Nicholls delivered judgment on behalf of the five judges in the House of Lords. The central issue to be considered in this case was whether the court had jurisdiction to make an order varying the terms of the pension scheme. The maintenance order, which was initially made by District Judge Plumstead, was to be secured by an attachment of earnings order against the appealing husband's pension entitlement under his pension scheme. Lord Nicholls noted [at 260–261 of his judgment] that the Law Commission had considered the topic of the treatment of pension rights on divorce in both 1969 and in 1977. In addition, several other bodies and organisations had also investigated this subject, resulting in a multitude of reports and articles. In spite of this he noted a general dissatisfaction with the state of the law in this area.

E–167   Although the aforementioned section 25(2)(h) would appear to allow the court to compensate for the loss of pension expectations, there was, in fact, no express power enabling the court to vary pension schemes, *e.g.* by splitting the pension rights between the parties. Thus, in order to ensure adequate provision could be made for the respondent wife, Lord Nicholls focused his attention on section 14(1)(c) of the Matrimonial Causes Act 1973. Paragraph (c) thereof empowers the court to make an order varying the terms of the marriage settlement, *i.e.*:

> ". . . an order varying for the benefit of the parties to the marriage and of the children of the family . . . any ante-nuptial or post-nuptial settlement (including such a settlement made by will or codicil) made on the parties to the marriage . . .".

Following a discussion by the learned judge about the term "settlement" and an examination of the pension scheme at issue, he declared that because rule 1(e) of Mr Brooks pension scheme allowed him to give part of the benefits to his wife, the natural inference to be drawn was that all the benefits payable to Mr Brooks formed part of the marriage settlement. Thus, on foot of rule 1(e) the court held that it was empowered under section 24(10)(c) to vary the scheme. However, Lord Nicholls distinguished his judgment by limiting it to the facts of Mr Brooks's pension scheme. He stressed that his decision should not be viewed as a solution to the overall problems relating to pensions and that facilitating legislation was still needed. Thus, the House of Lords decision in this case did not resolve the problem of pensions in the majority of cases. Thomas suggests that, rather than being based on clear legal reasoning, the decision in *Brooks v. Brooks* was a policy-based decision and reflects the view that the husband is not the sole owner of property acquired during the course of the marriage, including pension rights [[1997] 6 Conv. (N.S.) 52 at 57].

Both during and since this case, there have been ongoing attempts at **E–168** legislative intervention. In September 1993, the Pension Law Review Committee chaired by Professor Roy Goode Q.C. reported its findings on occupational pension schemes. In their paper "Pensions and Law Reform" the committee endorsed the recommendations of the Pensions Management Institute (U.K.). [These recommendations were published on May 19, 1993 in conjunction with the Law Society of England and Wales entitled "Pensions and Divorce".] Nevertheless in its White Paper the Government's response to the question of pension rights on divorce was to decline to act until a detailed research programme, undertaken to establish the extent of the problem, was completed. ["Security, Equality, Choice: The Future for Pensions" (June 1994)]. Despite lengthy debates in the House of Lords, the Pensions Bill introduced in January 1995 did not contain any reference to this issue. The pressure of the relevant House of Lords' debate resulted in amendments being made to the Bill, authorising the earmarking of pensions. Pension splitting, as noted by Hudson, continued to be regarded by the Government as too costly, complex and inherently inequitable [N.L.J. Practitioner July 14, 1985, 1059 "No Divorce for Pensions"]. As a result of an amendment made to the Family Law Bill during its passage through the House of Lords, the Family Law Act 1996 (U.K.) amended the Matrimonial Causes Act 1973, by inserting sections 25B–25D so as to allow for pension splitting. However, the Solicitors' Family Lawyers Association shortly thereafter produced a document "Family Law—Agenda for Change". It criticised this 1996 Act for only containing a commitment to pension splitting rather than any effective clause implementing it. More recently another White Paper, "Pension Rights on Divorce", was published in February 1997 by the Department of Social Security. It set out the Government proposals for the splitting of pension rights as part of a financial settlement on divorce. This followed on from the Green Paper, "The Treatment of Pension Rights on Divorce", issued in July 1996 which highlighted some of the issues which needed to be resolved before pension splitting could be implemented.

E–169 Finally, the legislature in England and Wales has recently introduced a Bill which provides for the splitting of a spouse's pension in family law proceedings. The Welfare Reform and Pensions Bill 1999 introduces pension sharing for divorcing couples. The English and Welsh courts will now have the discretion to divide a spouse's pension if it deems such an action to be necessary in the circumstances of the case. However, the Bill has already come under attack by Malcolm Wicks, a member of the Committee who launched the report "Pensions on Divorce", who pointed out that the Bill as introduced, fails to acknowledge the reality of the increased tendency of couples who choose to cohabit. It will be interesting to follow the lifetime of this Bill and discover what metamorphosis, if any, it undergoes before it is enacted by Parliament.

Conclusion

E–170 The importance of a pension as a distributable asset on the breakdown of marriage must not be underrated. The governing statutory provisions, while necessarily long and complex, should not be feared as overly technical and potentially expensive to both parties and thus preferably avoided. A patient and logical study of section 17 of the Divorce Act (and all other relevant statutory provisions) can only highlight the necessity for detail in order to guarantee that every possible scenario is properly catered for. Finally, in applauding the meticulous drafting of this lengthy section by the legislature, the significance of allowing the court the authority to decide whether to make a pension adjustment order, with the freedom to have regard to the overall circumstances which exist and whether proper provisions has otherwise been made for the spouse or the dependent family members involved, must also be acknowledged.

PRACTICE AND PROCEDURE IN DIVORCE APPLICATIONS

INTRODUCTION

E–171 Applications for divorce may be heard and determined by both the Circuit and the High Courts, which have concurrent jurisdiction pursuant to section 38(1) of the Divorce Act. This provision mirrors that set out in the Judicial Separation and Family Law Reform Act 1989 and the Family Law Act 1995 in relation to the jurisdiction of the courts to hear family law matters. Section 38(2) of the Divorce Act provides that in proceedings where the rateable valuation of lands concerned exceeds £200, the court shall, if an application is made to it in that regard, transfer the proceedings to the High Court. This application would appear to be unnecessary given the full concurrent jurisdiction, and also the wording of section 38(2) which envisages the Circuit Court hearing divorce applications where the rateable valuation of the lands exceeds £200 unless the parties themselves request a transfer to the High Court.

At present, most applications for divorce are made to the Circuit Court rather than to the High Court, the obvious advantages of the Circuit Court being lower costs and easier access to court lists. In addition, the provisions of the Civil Legal Aid Act 1996 dictate that proceedings be instituted in the court having the first level of jurisdiction to hear the matter and, in divorce applications, this is the Circuit Court. For the year ended December 1999, the High Court received 36 applications for divorce of which 13 were granted, in comparison with the Circuit Court which received 2,729 divorce applications of which 1,439 were granted.

The number of divorce applications granted by the courts increased **E–172** substantially during 1998 and 1999, and this would appear to reflect an initial hesitancy on the part of applicants and practitioners to make their applications until the provisions of the legislation, and the attitude of the courts thereto, had become more familiar. The development of practice and procedure in relation to family law applications in general, and divorce applications in particular, has not necessarily kept pace with the number of applications coming before the courts, and some confusion pertains in relation to procedures, particularly in relation to pension provisions. As with all court applications, there should be rigid adherence to, and implementation of, the rules of each court governing divorce applications, and this has been remarked upon as being desirable in a number of decisions. In the case of *L. (J.) v. L. (J.)* [[1996] 1 Fam L.J. 36], McGuinness J. commented that the financial evidence placed before the court was "of a most confusing and unsatisfactory nature", primarily because detailed information was not, as provided for in the Circuit Court rules, set out in the affidavits of means of the parties. [See also *E.P. v. C.P.,* unreported, High Court McGuinness J., November 27, 1998].

The procedure in the Circuit Court will be examined, followed by the procedure in the High Court.

THE RULES OF THE CIRCUIT COURT

Order 78, Rules of the Circuit Court (No.1) of 1997

Order 78 came into operation on the same day as the coming into **E–173** operation of the Family Law (Divorce) Act, 1996 on February 27, 1997. The rules set out in Order 78 are to be construed together with the Orders contained in the Circuit Rules, 1950, as amended. [Circuit Court Rules (No. 1) of 1989 (S.I. No. 289 of 1989), and the Circuit Court Rules (No. 1) of 1994 (S.I. No. 225 of 1994) are revoked by the 1997 Rules].

Order 78, rule 2 contains a transitional provision dealing with applications made or proceedings taken before February 27, 1997, but which were in accordance with the existing rules of court and court practice.

E–174   Order 78, rule 3 deals with the issue of venue, and states that proceedings may be instituted in the County where any party to the proceedings ordinarily resides or carries on any "profession, business or occupation." Theoretically, therefore, an applicant could have a number of venues available to him, and possibly a number of circuit court areas, depending on his geographical location.

Order 78, rule 3 does not specifically state that the either of the parties must be domiciled within the State at the date of the institution of proceedings for divorce, stating only that "[a]ny proceedings under this order shall be brought in the County where any party to the proceedings resides". Domicile is referred to in the provisions of section 39(1)(a) of the Divorce Act, which grants the court jurisdiction to grant a divorce if it is satisfied that "either of the spouses concerned was domiciled in the State on the date of the institution of the proceedings concerned . . .". However, section 39(1)(b) of the Divorce Act allows a court jurisdiction on the basis of one years residency in the State ending on the date of the institution of proceedings, either in addition to, or instead of, the requirement of domicile. Therefore, a situation could be envisaged whereby both parties are domiciled, but not resident in the State at the date of the institution of proceedings, thus failing to satisfy the rule 3 criterion of residency. The corrective measure would appear to involve an application for divorce to the High Court (if neither of the parties were carrying on a profession, business or occupation within the State), as the Circuit Court would not have jurisdiction to hear such an application. The Superior Court Rules are silent on this issue.

E–175   Section 39 subsections (2), (3) and (4) of the Divorce Act contain a useful power for a court, permitting it, in the context of any matrimonial application to grant an alternative relief. Section 39 (2) decrees that if an application for divorce is before the court, or an appeal against a determination of such an application is being heard, the court has jurisdiction to hear an application for a decree of nullity or judicial separation, should circumstances where this would become necessary arise.

Similarly, section 39(3) permits the granting of a decree of divorce on an application for a decree of nullity, and section 39(4) facilitates the granting of a decree of divorce on an application for judicial separation. This provision reflects that set out in section 39 of the Family Law Act 1995, wherein it was possible to have a court determine an application for judicial separation in the context of a nullity application.

The advantages of this provision are that if a Counterclaim for an alternative relief is before the court, the alternative relief may be granted without the necessity of separate proceedings.

FORM OF THE PROCEEDINGS IN THE CIRCUIT COURT

E–176   Proceedings in the Circuit Court are to be instituted by the issuing of a Family Law Civil Bill at the county Registrar's Office for the appropriate county. [Order 78, rule 7A]. The only exception to this is where an application is being made for relief after foreign divorce or separation outside the State and then the Family Law Civil Bill can only be issued after an *ex parte* application has been made.

The Family Law Civil Bill is the grounding document on foot of which every application for divorce will be set out. Order 78, rule 5 of the Circuit Court Rules sets out the contents to be included, and the format is supplied as a precedent in Division J.

The Civil Bill must contain the following information: **E–177**

   (i) the date and place of marriage of the parties;

  (ii) the length of time the parties have lived apart, including the date on which they commenced living apart and the addresses of both of the parties during that time, where known. (Where the applicant and respondent have been living apart from each other, whilst under the same roof, all relevant information to ground such a claim must be included in the Civil Bill. Details should be furnished, for example, as to how the house is being divided up and what are the arrangements for using kitchen and bathroom facilities.);

 (iii) details any previous matrimonial relief sought and/or obtained and details of any previous separation agreement entered into between the parties (with any relevant court orders or agreements annexed to the Civil Bill);

  (iv) the names and dates of birth of any dependant children of the marriage;

   (v) details of the family home(s) and /or other residences, of the parties, including all details of any former family home/residence to include details of the manner of occupation or ownership thereof. (It is recommended to set out in detail how the family home was disposed of or transferred or sold or purchased.);

  (vi) where reference is made in the Civil Bill to any immovable property, whether it is registered or unregistered land and a description of the land/premises so referred to. (Searches should be carried out prior to issuing the Civil Bill.);

 (vii) the basis of jurisdiction under the Divorce Act;

(viii) the occupation(s) of each party. (The ages of each party should also be inserted.);

  (ix) the grounds relied upon for the relief sought (*e.g.* that the parties have been living apart for at least four of the last five years, that there is no hope of reconciliation, that proper provision for the spouse and any dependent members of the family has been made and other relevant grounds);

   (x) each section of the Divorce Act under which relief is sought.

If relief pursuant to section 18 of the Divorce Act is being sought, after the death of one of the spouses, further information is required which is set out in Order 78, rule 5(g).

FLP R.0: July 2000

The Civil Bill must be dated and signed by either the Applicant or his Solicitor, and must contain the name, address and description of the Applicant together with an address for service of proceedings. The address of the Law Centre to which the Respondent could apply for legal aid should also be included.

When completed, the County Registrar issues the Civil Bill. The original Civil Bill is filed at the appropriate Circuit Court Office together with the section 5 or 6 certificate and an Affidavit of Means. In all cases where there are dependant children of the marriage, an Affidavit of Welfare must also be filed. The County Registrar enters the case and allocates a Record Number which will be used at all stages in the court process.

Section 6 and section 7 certificates

E–178   Sections 6 and 7 of the Divorce Act set out the obligations and responsibilities on Solicitors who represent either Applicants or Respondents in matrimonial cases, and are very similar to the provisions of Sections 5 and 6 of the Judicial Separation and Family Law Reform Act 1989.

Compliance by a solicitor with the requirements set out by sections 6 and 7 of the Divorce Act is mandatory. Prior to the institution of proceedings, the solicitor for the applicant is obliged to:

(i) discuss the issue of a possible reconciliation with the applicant and supply him or her with names and addresses of appropriately qualified persons in that regard;

(ii) discuss, similarly, the possibility of mediation with a view to effecting the terms of a separation or divorce on an agreed basis, and provide appropriate names and addresses in that regard;

(iii) discuss if appropriate the possibility of separation by deed of separation;

(iv) ensure that the applicant is aware of judicial separation as an alternative to divorce.

The duties on a solicitor acting for a respondent are identical and are set out in section 7 of the Divorce Act. In all cases where the solicitor has complied with these requirements prior to filing a Civil Bill or Defence and Counterclaim, a certificate signed by the solicitor in the formats set out in Forms 9 and 10 of the Circuit Court rules must be filed with the originating documentation and served on the relevant person [see precedents in Division J]. If this has not been done the proceedings may be adjourned for that purpose [sections 64(a) and 74(a) of the Divorce Act].

The affidavit of means

E–179   In every case "where financial relief under the Acts is sought" the parties must file an Affidavit of Means. Order 78, rule 18 and Form 2 of the Circuit Court Rules set out the contents and format of the Affidavit of Means. The

Affidavit of Means contains five schedules. [See Division J]. The following details are to be contained in the affidavit which is to be sworn by each party to the proceedings in any case where financial relief is being sought:

(i) details of the party's income [from whatever source. State the income on a gross and net basis. Detail all deductions made from the gross income on a regular basis.] Assets [all assets, including those in which the applicant or respondent may have only an equitable interest, should be mentioned], debts [List institutions to whom monies are owed], expenditure [list the outgoings of the applicant and respondent on either a weekly, monthly or annual basis] and other liabilities wherever situated and from whatever source;

(ii) similar details relating to any dependant member of the family;

(iii) if a pension adjustment order is sought, the affidavit should wherever possible include the nature of the scheme, the benefits payable thereunder, the normal pensionable age and the period of reckonable service of the member spouse. In this regard, Order 78, rule 18 only deals with these details insofar as they relate to an order being sought under section 12 of the Family Law Act 1995 but presumably the same criteria apply.

It is clear from the case law that Affidavits of Means are not a mere formality in advance of discovery. In *L.(J.) v. L.(J.)* [[1996] 1 Fam.L.J. (Circ. Ct.)], McGuinness J. reminded the solicitors involved in the case that the swearing of Affidavits of Means was mandatory under the Rules of the Circuit Court. An Affidavit of Means should be based on full and frank discovery of all of the assets, income, benefits—in-kind and emoluments of the person swearing the Affidavit, and should also comprehensively disclose all liabilities, outgoings and pension information. Information on income should be full and not merely relate for example to basic salary, which would only provide a distorted picture of the averring party's real position, but should also include details of overtime, expenses and all forms of emoluments which the deponent is entitled to receive. Outgoings should be fully documented and based on actual payments calculated rather than round estimates. These should be vouched when requested. In *A.K. v. P.K.* [unreported, High Court, March 13, 2000], Murphy J. criticised the Applicant's Affidavit of Means. Murphy J. noted that none of the items were vouched, no evidence was adduced as to cheques paid in relation to the weekly outgoings and the roundness of the figures of the outgoings seemed to suggest some exaggeration rather than an accurate analysis of the sums paid. Moreover, it appeared to the Court that there could have been some element of double counting. Ultimately, the Court awarded maintenance below that claimed by the wife. In *F. v. F.* [unreported, High Court, December 2, 1999], O'Neill J. awarded the wife a sum of £550 net maintenance per week, together with all reasonable and necessary medical and educational expenses. Her husband had proposed a sum of £450 gross maintenance, which would yield a net of £320 together with educational and medical expenses. However, O'Neill J. noted that the figure given for the husband's income was somewhat stale in that the husband's accounts were two years out of date. Moreover, the Court considered that there was a certain amount of cash transaction in the business, which was not indicated in the figure provided. A more extreme case of non-disclosure arose in *P. O'D. v. J. O'D.* [unreported, High Court, March 31, 2000]. The Respondent in that case had significant assets than he had not disclosed in his Affidavit. He had concealed his ownership of various properties both in Ireland and abroad, through the use of fictitious names. Budd J. ultimately made an Order transferring to the Applicant all of the properties in Ireland in which the husband had a legal or beneficial interest. While the Respondent argued that he was left with nothing, Budd J. concluded that in all probability, he still retained substantial assets. Budd J. also made an Order for solicitor and client costs in favour of the Applicant. He noted that it took meticulous detective work on the part of the Applicant and her legal advisers to piece together the jigsaw to expose the web of deception, which had been woven by the Respondent and that many consultations, more than the usual number, would have been required due to the "devious dissembling by the Respondent".

It is important that practitioners advise clients as to the significance of the Affidavit of Means and the consequences of failing to make disclosure. Also, where there is evidence of social welfare fraud and tax evasion, clients should be advised of the possible consequences in terms of 'whistle blowing'. [See further, *A. v. A., B. v. B.* [2000] 1 F.L.R. 701].

What is a claim for financial relief?

E–180   This question arises particularly when considering whether financial relief includes an application for an order under section 18(10) of the Divorce Act [an order blocking an application for provision out of the estate of a deceased spouse]. This arises frequently in circumstances where parties have been separated for a considerable period of time and where the intention is to sever all ties completely. The answer would seem to be that an Affidavit of Means need not be filed in such circumstances as the application is not a claim for financial relief.

The Affidavit of Welfare

E–181   In any case where there are dependant children involved, an Affidavit of Welfare must be filed, again at the same time as the Family Law Civil Bill. The Affidavit of Welfare requires information on the children born to the applicant and respondent or adopted by them and also should include details of other children of the family or to which either of the parties stand *in loco parentis*. The format of the affidavit is set out at Form No. 3 of the Rules [See Division J], and includes details of living arrangements, educational arrangements, childcare details, maintenance details, access arrangements, the number of rooms in the house and care or any other previous court proceedings relating to the children. The purpose of the affidavit is to ensure that all details relating to the children are before the court in order that they would be accorded proper importance. In the event that the Respondent is in agreement with the contents of the Applicant affidavit of welfare, they may file an affidavit to that effect, or if not so in agreement, they may file an alternative affidavit of welfare.

Service of proceedings

Rule 8(a) deals with service of Family Law Civil Bills. Service may be **E–182** effected on the respondent either by registered post or personally [by any person over the age of 18 years], and an affidavit of service is to be sworn by the server and filed in the relevant Circuit Court office within fourteen days of service having taken place. The Respondent is to be served at his last known address, and if difficulties arise in relation to service out of the jurisdiction, or in any other way, an application may be made to the County Registrar pursuant to the Court and Court Officers Act 1995. It is important to note that if a claim is being made for a Pension Adjustment Order, then notice must be served [see Draft Notice in Division K] on the Trustees of the Pension Scheme by registered post at their registered office and an Affidavit of Service of such notice should be sworn and filed. [See also Division B].

Appearance

If a respondent, having been served with the Family Law Civil Bill and **E–183** supporting documentation, intends to contest or in any way participate in the proceedings, he must enter an Appearance in the Circuit Court office within ten days of receipt of same. The appearance is to be served on the Applicant or his solicitor, if one is on record [rule 9]. In practice, this time limit is not always strictly adhered to and may be "cured" by the provision by the Applicant or his solicitor of a letter consenting to the late filing of the appearance.

Defence

Rule 10(a) provides the respondent with a further ten days within which **E–184** to file a defence, if it has not been filed at the same time as the appearance. In this instance, rule 10(a), concerning defences, specifies that further time

[THE NEXT PAGE IS E87]

for the filing of the defence may be agreed between the parties or allowed by the court. If a defence is not filed in the stipulated ten day period, a letter consenting to the late filing of a defence should be procured and filed, together with the Solicitors Certificate pursuant to Section 7 of the 1996 Act and the Affidavits of Means and Welfare if appropriate.

Counterclaims

Any counterclaim forms part of the defence. The rules are identical to **E–185** those pertaining to the Endorsement of Claim in a Family Civil Law Bill.

Interim applications

Interim applications are by way of Notice of Motion and Affidavit [rule **E–186** 24(a)], save for a Motion for Discovery where no Affidavit is needed.

Motions for judgment

If a respondent fails to enter an appearance or defence within the **E–187** allotted timescale, the applicant may issue and serve a Notice of Motion seeking Judgment in Default of Appearance/Defence on the Respondent and, in cases where a pension adjustment order is sought, on the trustees of the pension scheme concerned. This can only be done when notification of the applicant's intention to do so has been served in writing on the respondent together with a letter consenting to the late filing of the appropriate document. If the respondent defaults again at that time, the Notice of Motion may be issued returnable to a date which is not less than fourteen days before the hearing and the Notice of Motion shall not be returnable to a date less than fourteen days from the date of service of the Notice [Rule 11(c)]. The Notice of Motion must be filed in the Circuit Court Office. Rule 11(d) provides that if the appropriate Appearance of Defence is delivered to the applicant within seven days after the service of such Notice of Motion, and a copy is file in court not less than six days before the return date of the Motion, then the Motion or Judgment will not be put into the Judges' List will be struck out. Rule 11(d), however, provides that costs will be borne by the respondent for the Motion for Judgment.

If there is a matter of urgency, Rule 11(e) provides for an *ex parte* application to either the court or the County Registrar for leave to serve and have heard a notice of motion on four clear days service on the respondent.

When the matter comes on for hearing in the absence of an Appearance or Defence, the court may give judgment in the terms of the Family Law Civil Bill, or in the terms required by the applicant, provided all matters are in order. It may, in the alternative, grant leave to the respondent to defend part or all of the proceedings. The issue of costs will be decided "as the Court considers just". [Rule 11(g) and (j)].

This system is an improvement to that which existed prior to the coming into operation of the 1997 rules, which did not facilitate in any way the movement forward of cases where there was no appearance or response from the respondent.

Fast track divorce

E–188   In circumstances where there is agreement between both parties as to the terms of the orders to be sought from the court, the matter can be brought before the court as an uncontested divorce, pursuant to the provisions of Rule 11(h). The Family Law Civil Bill, together with the Affidavit of Means and Affidavit of Welfare, is issued and served. The respondent then files a form of "Consent Defence". A notice is then served by the applicant by way of Notice of Motion for Judgment by Defence.

Notice of trial

E–189   Rules 12, 13 and 14 deal with this issue. There is a difference between the bringing on for trial matrimonial matters in Dublin and elsewhere. In Dublin, a Notice to Fix a Date for a Trial is issued and served and on that date the court will fix the hearing date. If the applicant fails to do this, the respondent may do so. Elsewhere, a Notice for Trial shall be served and listed for the next sittings after the time mentioned in the Notice, pursuant to rules 12 and 13. Other than the Family Law Civil Bill, service of which we have seen must be effected personally or by registered post together with the associated documents, service of all other pleadings may be by ordinary pre-paid post.

The hearing

E–190   All applications for divorce are to be heard *in camera*, on oral evidence unless the court directs otherwise There is a degree of informality to the hearing, with no wigs or gowns being worn by the judges, barristers or solicitors. Family law matters are to be heard at different times to ordinary court matters, as *per* section 32 of the Judicial Separation and Family Law Reform Act 1989.

Judgments on consent

E–191   Regularly, applications for divorce come before the Courts where the terms of ancillary relief orders to be made have been agreed between the parties, as has the fact that a divorce would be granted in the first place. This is particularly the case where parties have been separated for a long time, and where satisfactory arrangements have been operating between them for some time. In practice, what usually happens in such cases is that terms are finalised and reduced to writing to be signed by both parties, and then handed into court to be ruled on. It should be noted that the court must be satisfied that a decree of divorce should be granted. Evidence must be given by the applicant as to the length of the separation and the impossibility of reconciliation, and also, as to whether or not proper provision has been made for the parties. It is important not to assume that the courts will automatically "rubber stamp" terms agreed between the parties purporting to endow proper provision on the spouse and or dependent family members. The court has a duty, in every case, to satisfy itself that proper provision has been made for the appropriate parties. The courts are most vigilant in exercising this duty. It is not unusual for terms of consent to be refused by the courts and the parties sent back to review the financial position. This may be difficult to accept for both participants and for their legal advisors who may have had protracted and difficult settlement negotiations about the terms of the divorce, but it is a duty imposed on the court by the provisions of the Divorce Act.

Costs

As with all matrimonial matters, the issue of costs is one to be decided at **E–192** the conclusion of each case at the discretion of the Court. Rule 35 of the Circuit Court Rules directs that the costs may be measured by the Judge, and if not so measured are to be taxed, in default of agreement by the County Registrar according to the appropriate scale. It is open to any party dissatisfied by taxation to appeal to the court for a review. The usual practice of costs following the event is not as established in family law matters as in other cases, and it is more common for a court to direct that each party bear their own costs. In cases where either or both of the parties are legally aided, the same situation pertains. The issue of costs is discussed further at paragraph E–200 in the context of discovery.

PRACTICE AND PROCEDURE IN THE HIGH COURT

The rules governing an application for divorce in the High Court came **E–193** into operation on September 1, 1997, and are referred to as the Rules of the Superior Courts (No. 3) of 1997, being construed together with the Rules of the Superior Courts 1986.

A new order 70A refers to all family law proceedings including divorce, separation, applications for declarations as to marital status, applications for relief subsequent to a foreign divorce, and a wide variety of other applications.

Proceedings for divorce are commenced by a special summons, which is to be a family law summons and which is to contain a "Special Endorsement of Claim" specifying all necessary particulars, the relief sought and

E89

the section of the Divorce Act on which such reliefs are grounded. An accompanying affidavit either verifying the proceedings, or in response to them, is to be filed pursuant to Rule 4, and is to contain the following details:

(i) the date and place of the marriage of the parties;

(ii) the length of time the parties have lived apart and their addresses during that time, where known;

(iii) full particulars of children, whether any of them are dependent, and what provision has been made for them;

(iv) whether any possibility of reconciliation exists and of the basis on which this might take place;

(v) details of any separation agreement or previous matrimonial relief sought or obtained, and copies of all relevant documentation are to be exhibited in a separate affidavit;

(vi) the domicile of each party at the date of commencing the proceedings, or where each party has been ordinarily resident for the year prior to the commencement of the proceedings;

(vii) details of the family home and any other residences of the parties, together with details of their ownership and occupation;

(viii) details of whether property is registered or unregistered land and any other details.

E–194 Order 70A, rule 4 (b), (c), (d), and (e) set out additional details required in applications for relief after a foreign divorce, for a declaration as to marital status, for determination of property issues between spouses or engaged persons, and for relief out of the estate of a deceased spouse. Any affidavit filed under rule 4 is to exhibit the section 6 or 7 certificate.

Order 70A, Rule 6 deals with the issue of the Affidavit of Means, which is to be filed with the verifying or replying affidavit in each case, and the format of which is provided in Rule 5 of the rules. The affidavit of means is only to be filed where financial relief is being sought, and is filed without prejudice to the right of either party to seek particulars of any matter from the other side, or to seek discovery. Order 70A, rule 6(3) specifies that either party may be requested to vouch items set out in the Affidavit of Means within 21 days of a request to do so, and in default of so doing, an application for discovery may be made by Notice of Motion which could result in an order for discovery being made, as in the Circuit Court Rules. Order 70A, Rule 7 deals with the Affidavit of Welfare.

E–195 Order 70A, rule 11 provides a mechanism for seeking directions from the court, a provision not provided for in the Circuit Court Rules. At any stage in High Court proceedings, either party to the proceedings may bring a motion for directions before the court, such motion to be grounded on an affidavit. Directions may be sought in relation to the following matters:

(i) where there are dependent children who are *sui juris* and whose welfare may be effected by the determination of the proceedings;

(ii) where an order is sought concerning the sale of any property in respect of which either of the parties may have an interest;

(iii) where an order is sought which will affect the rules of a pension scheme or require non-compliance therewith;

(iv) where an application is brought seeking provision out of the estate of a deceased spouse; or

(v) in any other case in which it is appropriate.

This is a useful provision, particularly as divorce applications of any complexity are usually instituted in the High Court and a motion for directions could be used to clarify matters prior to the hearing, thus saving time.

E–196 Order 70A, rule 12 permits the court to direct that the parties exchange pleadings in relation to any or all of the issues arising, either between themselves or with a third party, again useful in circumstances where further information is required. There is no such provision in the Circuit Court Rules.

The provisions of section 38(2) of the Divorce Act permit the transfer of proceedings from the Circuit Court to the High Court where the rateable valuation of land the subject matter of the proceedings exceeds £200. Otherwise, the jurisdiction of the High Court and the Circuit Court to hear divorces is concurrent as per section 38(1) of the Divorce Act.

Subsequent to the granting of the decree of divorce, any application for ancillary relief may be made by Notice of Motion, grounded on the application of the moving party.

DISCOVERY AND FINANCIAL DISCLOSURE

E–197 From the point of view of practitioners, it is impossible to advise clients or to predict the outcome of their case with any degree of accuracy in the absence of complete financial disclosure. Accordingly, discovery is a pre-trial procedure which is designed to make available to both the applicant and the respondent all documents which exist and which may impact on the particular divorce case or the particular reliefs sought. Barron J.'s comments on the issue of discovery in the recent case of *M.W. v. D.W.*, unreported, Supreme Court, November 25, 1999, are particularly instructive. He stated as follows:

"In general where the issues are financial there are two basic rules:

(a) What assets do the parties own?
(b) What provisions should be made for the parties and their children if any?

FLP R.0: July 2000

Discovery of documents is not the most efficient way of dealing with the first issue while the second issue cannot be resolved until the Court is satisfied that all relevant financial details have been disclosed.

Too often in matrimonial cases where there are such issues there are lengthy interlocutory proceedings whereby each party seeks discovery of documents from the other. In the course of such applications there are as a general rule allegations that assets are being hidden by one or other party. This results in applications for further and better discovery. Too often the financial situation of the parties is never totally clarified. In matrimonial proceedings time is really of the essence and after months if not years of wrangling in this fashion the party, still dissatisfied as to the information supplied is nevertheless anxious to get on with the matter and too often the hearing is held before there has been total clarification of the appropriate assets."

E–198   Discovery is an area which, in the context of any matrimonial proceedings can be fraught with difficulty, but particularly so in divorce cases, where the expectation of at least one of the spouses is generally that the financial relationship between them would be severed on the granting of the decree. The fact also, that by the time the decree is applied for, the parties will have been living apart from each other for a period in excess of four years, can lead to a reluctance on the part of certain participants to divulge all financial details of their new lives.

Discovery is, however, usually seen as a necessary adjunct to cases where one of the parties is a non-PAYE income earner. Discovery is also usually necessitated where one of the spouses is of the firm belief that assets are not being disclosed and where they may in fact be secreted or hidden from the proceedings.

Incomplete discovery impedes the smooth running of a matrimonial case. The judge in matrimonial proceedings is therefore considerably assisted by the provision of properly structured and easily accessible financial information, particularly in cases of financial complexity. In the case of *L.(J.) v. L.(J.)* [1996] 1 Fam L.J. 36, the court provided an insight into the difficulties faced by it in an effort to make comprehensive orders for financial relief when provided with incomplete discovery:

"Although the financial issues are of prime importance in this case, the financial evidence before the court was of a most confusing and unsatisfactory nature . . . During the trial a great deal of time was spent in detailed cross-examination of both parties arising out of the discovery of documents. Finally the entire documents were handed into court . . . However what was entirely lacking was a clear and systematic picture of the present financial position of each parties assets and liabilities, resources and needs."

McGuinness J. in *O.L. v. O.L.* [[1996] 2 Fam. L.J. 66 (Circ. Ct.)] addressed the wife's failure to make proper discovery. [In the course of the trial, a number of matters came to light which suggested that the wife had additional monies in various accounts which she had not disclosed]. The learned judge, at the end of the case, indicated that she had intended to direct that the husband should make a contribution towards the wife's costs. However, in view of the wife's failure to make proper discovery, she decided not to do so. More recently, in *P. O'D. v. J. O'D.* [unreported, High Court, March 31, 2000], Budd J. made an Order for solicitor and client costs in favour of the Applicant in a case where the Respondent had deliberately concealed his ownership of various properties both in Ireland and abroad, through the use of fictitious names. Budd J. noted that it took meticulous detective work on the part of the Applicant and her legal advisers to piece together the jigsaw to expose the web of deception, which had been woven by the Respondent and that many consultations, more than the usual number, would have been required due to the "devious dissembling by the Respondent".

The starting point for proper and adequate discovery should be the **E–199** Affidavit of Means, which if comprehensively completed by both parties and vouching documentation provided, should set out the preponderance of information required, particularly where the financial position of the parties is uncomplicated. In the case of *L.(J.) v. L.(J.)*, this point was raised:

"(If) the financial framework of the affidavits is missing, the process of examination and cross-examination based on the discovery materials can be both confusing and unproductive as indeed was the position in this case."

It should be noted that either party may request the other party to vouch any or all items referred to in the Affidavit of Means pursuant to rule 18(a) of the Circuit Court Rules [S.I. No. 84 of 1997]. It can also be the case that despite the provision of a completed Affidavit of Means, the instructions of the client will be that further information is required. In that event, it should be sought on a voluntary basis where either party may request the other, in writing, to make voluntary discovery of all relevant documents within a reasonable period of time.

If an exchange of voluntary discovery can be agreed, the rules direct that the format of such discovery is to be by way of properly completed affidavits of discovery. Any agreement for voluntary discovery has the same effect as though ordered by the court, and failure of either party to fulfil their requirements as agreed can be brought to the attention of the court in any subsequent application for discovery. It is not possible to bring a Motion for Discovery unless voluntary discovery has first been requested. In particular, a letter seeking voluntary discovery should precede the initial application for discovery [see Rules of the Superior Court: S.I. No. 233 of 1999 and Circuit Court Rules: S.I. No. 84 of 1997. Also, D–090.]

Applications to the court

Where voluntary discovery is not forthcoming, or where an application to **E–200** the court is necessitated, same is made pursuant to the provisions of section 38(6) and (7) of the Divorce Act. Section 38(6) states that in proceedings seeking ancillary relief under Part III of the Divorce Act, each of the spouses concerned shall give to the other such particulars of his or her property and income as "may reasonably be required for the purposes of the proceedings". Section 38(7) provides the court with the power to direct a person who has not complied with the provisions of section 38(6) to so comply, but no other sanctions are set out in that section.

The word "reasonably" is intended to indicate the intention of the legislature to ensure that parties and their legal advisors do not over-use the pre-hearing procedure of discovery incurring inflated costs in the process. This point was made in the case of *E.P. v. C.P.*, [unreported, High Court, McGuinness J., November 27, 1998 (*ex tempore*)], a case in which there had been repeated adjournments on the grounds that discovery was not complete, and a number of applications for attachment and commital for failure by the respondent to comply with orders made in that regard. McGuinness J. commented:

> ". . . I should say that in this type of family law case (and I and other judges have said it before) discovery can sometimes be, to put it in plain language, more trouble than it is worth . . . it should be borne in mind that long delays for extra discovery may well be counterproductive in these cases."

The court went on to comment that "prolonged proceedings do considerable harm to both parties and also add to the legal costs", while noting that the Applicant had reason for taking the steps that were taken in relation to discovery. In the Circuit Court case of *F.R. v. F.J.* [[1996] 1 F.L.R. 12 (Circ. Ct.)], McGuinness J. criticised the applicant wife who was convinced that her husband had significant hidden assets and cash. The learned judge was critical of the manner in which disovery was pursued and refused to grant an order for costs when she would otherwise have done so. There is a balance to be struck by practitioners in advising on discovery, on the possible results of such applications against the likely costs of same. In England, there have been a number of cases in which orders for "wasted costs" have been made, effectively punishing parties for dissipating monies on costs and it can only be a matter of time before a similar order is made in this jurisdiction. In this regard, it should be noted that in *M.W. v. D.W.* [2000] 1 I.L.R.M. 416, Barron J. stated *obiter* that while obviously neither party can be prevented from making interlocutory applications, if they do and if the trial judge whether on the application or the ultimate hearing regards such application as unnecessary, unreasonable or worse, the costs wasted should be taken out of the share of the party responsible. Barron J. also stated that solicitors should advise their clients as to their obligations in relation to making full disclosure and, if necessary, the Court should not be slow to make a solicitor personally liable for costs thrown away by unnecessary and unreasonable recalcitrant behaviour apparently on behalf of their clients. This would apply equally to a solicitor whose client was seeking the information as to the solicitor whose client was refusing it.

Discovery can, of course, be sought in relation to issues other than financial issues and depending on the relevance of the information being sought, orders may be made in relation to same.

Discovery must be made in the format provided for in the Rules of the **E–201**
Circuit Court and of the Superior Courts. Order 29 of the Circuit Court
Rules [S.I. No. 84 of 1997] states that application is made to the court by
way of Notice of Motion. No grounding Affidavit is required. The new rules
governing discovery applications in the High Court came into operation on
August 3, 1999 and are to be found in S.I. No. 233 of 1999. Their main aim
is to reduce the number of unnecessary discovery applications in the High
Court. Every Notice of Motion must now specify the precise categories of
documents in respect of which discovery is sought and is to be grounded on
affidavit. This affidavit must verify that the discovery of documents sought
is necessary and should also detail the reasons why each category of
documents is required. [See *dicta* of Barron J. on the new discovery rules in
M.W. v. D.W. [2000] 1 I.L.R.M. 416.] Once the affidavits are sworn and
exchanged and filed, the documentation referred to may be inspected by
the other side, and copies of same requested. The affidavit must set out all
documents in the power, possession or procurement of each party, with
explanations as to why certain documents are not being provided, if that is
the case. The documentation should be provided in easily accessible form,
with efforts made to ensure ease of reference by all parties, including the
court.

Legal professional privilege may be claimed in respect of certain **E–202**
documentation, and disputes in relation to this documentation should be
referred to the court for guidance, as occurred in the case of *L.(T.) v. L.(V)*
[[1995] 1 Fam.L.J. 7]. Therein, McGuinness J. referred to advices given by
legal advisors to their clients to make notes in preparation for trial. It was
held that these notes were not admissible and were covered by privilege,
but reference was made to the power of the court to override legal
professional privilege in circumstances where the welfare of a child is at
issue. In the event that a client is dissatisfied with what discovery yields, an
application for further and better discovery may be made to the court, but
the client must demonstrate good reason for seeking further discovery
before the court will make the order.

Third party discovery

Discovery may be sought against a third party if they have documentation **E–203**
in their power, possession or procurement which is relevant to the issues
between the parties. The onus to prove such relevance is on the party
seeking the third party discovery. Order 29 of the Rules of the Superior
Courts provides that the court may make such an order at its discretion.
The application is brought by way of Notice of Motion grounded on
affidavit, both of which must be served on the other party and on the
relevant third party. Any such application must include an undertaking to
the third party in respect of all costs which that third party may reasonably
incur in their compliance with the order made. These costs may ultimately
be claimed by the party who obtained third party discovery at the end of the
case, provided they are successful in their application for costs.

Bankers books evidence

E–204   The provisions of the Bankers Books Evidence Acts 1879 and 1959 permit an order to be made by the court directing that a party and their legal advisor may travel to named banks or building societies to examine any accounts which may be held there by the other spouse. The application is made on an *ex parte* basis and the order then served on the relevant financial institutions. Care should be taken to ensure that the order records the possibility of copies being taken of any relevant documentation, as otherwise this may not be possible. It is likely that these orders will only be made in exceptional cases.

Anti-avoidance provisions

E–205   Section 37 of the Divorce Act sets out the powers which the court has, in relation to transactions carried out by a party to the proceedings, which are intended to prevent or to defeat an application by the other party for financial relief. Section 37(2) provides that, in circumstances where proceedings have been instituted for the grant of relief, but not been determined, and where the court is satisfied that the other spouse, or any other person, proposes to make any disposition or transfer out of the jurisdiction or otherwise deal with any property, with a view to preventing that relief, then the court may make an order restraining the other spouse from so doing. The purpose of this section is to prevent the reduction of assets by either of the spouses with a view to reducing the amount of assets available for the making of an order for ancillary relief. The section also applies to preventing relief being granted by the court in the first instance or restricting or interfering with existing orders.

E–206   Section 37(2)(a)(ii) of the Divorce Act allows the court to set aside any "reviewable disposition" which has been made by one of the spouses with the intent of depleting the assets available for the making of an order for ancillary relief. The most important element of such a disposition is that it must have been made by the defaulting spouse with an intention to defeat the other spouse's application for relief. Orders which are made by the court with a view to preventing dispositions are frequently referred to as "freezing orders".

As section 37(2)(a) of the Divorce Act refers to the applicant "who has instituted proceedings", application for relief under this section does not apply in the absence of proceedings being issued. However, the applicant who does not wish to issue proceedings for divorce could seek relief in the form of a Mareva injunction.

The issue of intention could be difficult to prove, if it cannot be established that the Respondent did not intend any of the three outcomes set out in section 37. [See Division D for the discussion of the case of *Tesco Ireland Limited v. Patrick J. (Otherwise P.J.) McGrath and Thomas McGrath*, unreported, High Court, June 14, 1999.] Matters are eased somewhat by the provisions of section 37(4) of the Divorce Act which provides that if the disposition was made within three years of the application for relief, or in relation to a disposition yet to take place, and where the court is satisfied that the consequence of such disposition would be the prevention or restriction of relief which could be granted, or that that has already been the consequence, then the intention of the respondent to so prevent or defeat relief will be presumed. The effect of this provision is to place the burden of proving that a party had no intention to defeat relief on the defendant as opposed to the applicant.

It is not unusual for applications under section 37 to be made on an *ex parte* basis, because of fears that property will be lost or disposed of. If not so urgent, for example in the case of a possible disposition of redundancy monies which have yet to be received, the application should be made by Notice of Motion grounded on affidavit.

EXPERT WITNESSES

Analysis of information provided by either party in preparation for trial **E–207** may necessitate the employment of expert witnesses such as a forensic accountant, valuer or pensions or insurance advisor. The rules provide that evidence of experts in relation to pensions and certain other matters may be by way of affidavit. In addition to this, practitioners should be careful to carry out other enquiries such as Land Registry and Registry of Deeds searches, and judgment searches.

SETTLEMENTS

Many practitioners are putting 'full and final settlement' clauses into **E–207A** Consent Ancillary Relief Orders in the hope that the Courts will apply a *PDD v. AOD* [1998] 2 I.R. 225; [1998] I.L.R.M. 543] rationale to any future applications and value 'certainty and finality' over flexibility and the power of the Court to vary under section 22 [See E—093]. The value of a 'full and final settlement' clause in consent Separation/ Divorce ancillary relief proceedings will no doubt be the subject of future litigation, however in the meantime most practitioners include such clauses and simply hope for the best. In respect of maintenance however, it is very clearly not possible to achieve a clean break. Even so practitioners are in some cases capitalizing the periodical maintenance into a lump sum and taking a risk on the willingness of the Court to bind the parties to the settlement unless there is a fairly significant change in circumstances. While this may work in many cases, it is important to warn the client both verbally and in writing that the Court may alter the settlement on an application by the other spouse.

Where there is lack of full and complete disclosure in the negotiation of **E–207B** a Consent Order of a capital nature, there is a considerable danger that the Court could set the Consent Order aside for material non-disclosure. This occurred in the English case of *Livesey (Formerly Jenkins) v. Jenkins* [1985] F.L.R. 813. It is therefore wise to ensure the exchange of full Affidavits of Means in advance of executing a Consent Order or Separation Agreement. Clients should be advised of the need to make full and complete disclosure and the consequences of failing to do so.

E–207C   Another point to note regarding settlements is that they can often be complicated by practical issues, which were not considered on the day the agreement was negotiated. Frequently, they are hand-written under pressure. On occasion, one of the parties may subsequently seek to distance himself or herself in some way from the agreement reached. Attempts to enforce settlements can be complicated by drafting errors or loose drafting of the original Terms of Consent. As a general rule, a Consent Order should stick to the terms of the pleadings and should not contain 'orders' outside those terms. If it is necessary to go outside the terms of the pleadings, then agreements should be expressed in terms of 'undertakings'. In drafting Consent Orders, practitioners should be mindful of the difficulties, which might subsequently arise in relation to enforcement and accordingly, take care to ensure that the 'orders' are ones, which the Court has jurisdiction to make. Orders for periodical maintenance or secured periodical maintenance, and pension adjustment orders should contain all the necessary technical information to make them enforceable. There have been many complaints in relation to Pension Adjustment Orders and the Department of Finance has produced a Draft Pension Adjustment Order for practitioners in relation to State pensions.

E–207D   It is also vitally important for practitioners to be aware of the tax implications of the Orders in advance of ruling. In particular, it is prudent to 'tax proof' settlements as they may have hidden tax implications which could dramatically alter the financial cost of the settlement to the client. It is also important to ensure that in advance of a settlement, all searches are completed with regard to property (*i.e.* for judgment mortgages/encumbrances). Where it is proposed that one spouse takes over a mortgage, it is important to indicate that this is subject to the necessary consent to transfer being obtained from the relevant lending institution and to the other spouse being released from the obligations of the mortgage. If such a provision is not included, the property may be transferred leaving the transferring spouse bound by the mortgage and unable to raise a new mortgage.

E–207E   When an agreement is reached following negotiations, it is normal for the clients and counsel and or solicitors to sign the heads of an agreement, leaving the formal terms of settlement to be typed up containing all the necessary formal orders. Clients should be advised that the settlement is binding even when waiting for a formal order to be drawn up. If an 'agreement' on all the issues has not been reached but negotiations have merely sought to narrow the issues, this should be indicated clearly at the start of the negotiations. [See *Xydhias v. Xydhias* [1999] 1 F.L.R. 683 and *G. v. G. (Financial Provision: Separation Agreement)* [2000] 2 F.L.R. 18].

E98

Finally, it is important to ensure that the client does not feel that he has been pressured into the settlement 'on the steps of the court' as such settlements invariably cause problems later on for all parties including the practitioners. The client must be fully informed of the nature and legal consequences of the consent in every respect. There are always some 'downsides' to Consent Orders. Indeed, unless such Orders represent a compromise in respect of both parties' expectations, they are less successful. The client should be fully and completely advised about all aspects of the consent and about any misgivings, which the legal advisors have in relation to it. These should be fully noted on file. In acrimonious cases, the Consent Order is unlikely to see an end to hostilities. On the other hand, clients who have engaged fully in the decision-making process frequently feel much better about the decision and are happy to have saved the time and costs of a Trial.

Finally, now that the Supreme Court has addressed the issue of 'wasted costs', 'Calderbank offers' in advance of the hearing should be given serious consideration in order to save or reduce costs in the event of the case going to Trial.

PRACTICAL PROBLEMS IN RELATION TO ANCILLARY RELIEF PROCEEDINGS

Practitioners are often faced with the problem of what to do with information obtained through improper means. In the family law arena, spouses in dispute are often aware of much of each other's business transactions. In particular, where the couple is residing in the same home pending the hearing of the proceedings, there may be a tendency to 'snoop' in order to obtain more information regarding the financial position of the other spouse. In *P. O'D. v. J. O'D.* [unreported, High Court, March 31, 2000], it was alleged that the husband had stolen his wife's legal bag, which contained all the documentation she had collected in connection with the family law proceedings. It was also alleged that the wife had breached her husband's constitutional right to privacy by intercepting his telephone messages. In the course of the proceedings, the wife had sought an Order pursuant to Order 39, Rule 5 of the Rules of the Superior Courts for the taking of evidence outside the jurisdiction. She alleged that her husband had concealed the existence of funds and property in London and elsewhere. It was clear from her Affidavit however, that she had obtained much of her information by listening to her husband's voicemail and intercepting telephone messages left for him. Counsel for the Respondent alleged that such evidence was inadmissible. That said, no decision was taken on the issue as the Respondent subsequently opted to give his explanation for the telephone messages. In the course of his judgment, Budd J. criticised the behaviour of the Respondent, noting that a considerable amount of Court time had been taken up with arguments about the inadmissibility of the telephone messages, which would have been quite unnecessary if the Respondent had given a totally innocent explanation of

E–207F

the messages. Ultimately, Budd J. made an Order for the taking of evidence outside the jurisdiction, having heard the evidence of two bank officials that the Respondent was involved in financial transactions both in the Isle of Man and in England. Regarding the allegation that the husband had stolen the Applicant's legal bag, Budd J. noted that there was much to support the reality of this suggestion. Earlier in his judgment, he observed that in the course of cross-examination of the Applicant regarding the interception of the husband's telephone messages, certain accounts were put to her, which she alleged had been in her stolen bag. It appears from the judgment, that this line of cross-examination was abandoned on behalf of the husband. Although no statements of principle regarding the inadmissibility of illegally obtained evidence emerge from the decision in *P. O'D. v. J. O'D*, it is clear from the earlier decision of McMahon J. in *O.C. v T.C.* [unreported, High Court, December 12, 1981] that evidence must be obtained lawfully and not as a result of the deliberate violation of the constitutional rights of the Respondent.

E–207G   Quite apart from the question of admissibility of evidence, difficulties can also arise for practitioners where the information given by the client discloses the existence of social welfare fraud or tax evasion. In a recent English case, *A. v. A., B. v. B.* [2000] 1 F.L.R. 701, Charles J. considered the approach, which Courts should take in such cases. The case involved a claim for financial relief in two separate divorces. The claims were heard together as the two Respondent husbands were in business together and there was a considerable overlap between the two cases in relation to determining the assets of the Respondents. By the time of the hearing, the Respondents had admitted that they were the beneficial owners of a series of linked companies under a tax scheme fronted by a professional trust company in the Isle of Man. The Respondents had lied for a number of years about their interests in these companies, maintaining that they were mere employees. Ultimately however, the persistent effort of the wives to unravel the web paid off, and the tax manager in the trust company admitted that the reality was that the husbands owned the companies. Agreement was reached between the parties at the end of the first day of the hearing and the Court made an Order approving the terms of the settlement. Before the Orders were drawn up however, Charles J. indicated that he intended to disclose the papers to the Revenue, the DPP and the prosecuting authorities in the Isle of Man. In reaching this conclusion, he stated that in ancillary relief proceedings, in assessing the available assets the court had to consider liabilities to the Revenue and if it was satisfied that such liabilities existed, it would be wrong for it to ignore them, or to proceed on the basis that such liabilities would not be, or were unlikely to be, met because the Revenue would not be made aware of the relevant information, unless, there was a compelling public interest, which led to the conclusion that to take this course would be in the overall public interest. Regarding the approach to be taken by practitioners, he noted that they, together with the Courts, should be alert to warning parties of their privilege against self-incrimination.

REFORM

During the divorce campaign, much assistance was pledged by the **E–208** government of the day to "protect from attack" the institution of marriage by way of increased financial resources for such services as marriage guidance counselling, mediation and improved court facilities. The government-run Family Mediation Service expanded throughout the country, and the newly established Courts Service embarked on a program of providing improved court facilities. Progress in providing support services, however, has been slow. It is now four years since the publication of the Law Reform Commission *Report on Family Courts* [L.R.C. Report 52, Dublin 1996.] Indeed, many of its recommendations were approved by the Denham Commission in its final report published in November 1998. [*Working Group on a Courts Commission*, Sixth Report, November 1998, PN 6533, Government Publications, Dublin.] Among the recommendations made in the latter report with specific reference to Family Law are the following:

1. Family Law Divisions should be set up in the High, Circuit and District Courts and improved staff and other services resources made available.

2. Venues for court hearings should be centrally located in both District and Circuit Court areas, with good consultation, information and waiting facilities;

3. Staff operating in the Family Law Division should have proper training, experience and suitable temperament for this area, and resources in this regard should be made available.

4. A basic system of case management should be commenced, with administrative functions in this regard carried out in Dublin by a Family Case Management Registrar, and in other areas by the County Registrars.

5. Support services in the form of a family law section of the Court Probation and Welfare Service are needed as is a panel of suitably qualified psychiatrists and psychologists to provide expert reports should the need arise.

6. In the longer term, a system of Regional Family Law Courts should be set up.

A considerable number of other recommendations were made, including improvements to be made in the collection of statistics, and a "one-stop shop" to be made available in court areas to facilitate ease of information on all aspects of the family law "system" for participants. It would appear that steps have been taken towards a number of these ends, but there is little doubt that the system requires nothing less than a major overhaul if it is to meet the increasing demands placed on it.

THE RECOGNITION OF FOREIGN DIVORCES

INTRODUCTION

E–209   From the time it was first mooted in legal and social circles, it was a considerable time before the right to apply for a decree of divorce was introduced into Irish law. In 1997 legislation was enacted to allow for an application to be brought for a decree of divorce to be obtained. Not surprisingly, therefore, the Irish courts did not readily recognise divorces granted in foreign jurisdictions. Various issues have been discussed since foreign divorces were first considered for recognition under Irish law. This section examines, *inter alia,* the current position and traces the varying requirements for recognition by referring to the common law, legislative and judicial positions. Ultimately, the introduction of divorce to this jurisdiction will be seen to have lessened the requirements that need to be fulfilled to satisfy the Irish court.

EARLY VIEWS

E–210   Whether a decree of divorce obtained in another jurisdiction was recognised under Irish law before the introduction of the Constitution in 1937 was dependent upon the domicile of the parties. In the matter of *Sinclair v. Sinclair* [[1896] I.R. 603], the court was willing to recognise a foreign divorce where the parties to the divorce were domiciled in the country granting the divorce at the time the proceedings were issued. In 1937 the Constitution was enacted and Article 41.3.3° thereof deals with the issue of divorce and provides that where a marriage has been dissolved under the civil law of another state but remains a subsisting and valid marriage under the law of Ireland, this "divorce" cannot be recognised under Irish law. Article 41.3.3° of the Constitution states:

> "No person whose marriage has been dissolved under the civil law of any other State but is a subsisting valid marriage under the law for the time being in force within the jurisdiction of the Government and Parliament established by this Constitution shall be capable of contracting a valid marriage within that jurisdiction during the lifetime of the other party to the marriage so dissolved."

The obvious question arising from this subsection of the Constitution is when is a marriage no longer regarded as valid under Irish law? This question was to a degree dealt with by the Supreme Court in *Mayo-Perrott v. Mayo-Perrott* [[1958] I.R. 336]. In that case, although the reason for the application by the wife was the enforcement of the order for costs made in her favour by the English court, the Supreme Court wisely used the case as an opportunity to interpret Article 41.3.3° and to establish the requirements under Irish law for the recognition of a foreign divorce. The applicant spouse who was domiciled in England was granted a divorce *a vinculo matrimonii* by the English court from her husband who was also domiciled in England. The Supreme Court held that Article 41.3.3° did not expressly preclude the recognition of foreign divorce. It did not, however, permit the Oireachtas to enact legislation refusing to recognise foreign divorces. As the Oireachtas had not enacted any such legislation, the basis for the recognition of foreign divorces was that recognised at common law, *i.e.* a foreign divorce would be recognised in Ireland once the divorcing spouses were both domiciled in the jurisdiction that granted the divorce at the time it was granted.

The issue of the spouses' domicile was, therefore, deemed to be the **E–211** central issue for consideration. [In summary, domicile is the place where a person has his permanent home.] In dealing with the concept of domicile the court continued to rely upon the old idea of dependent domicile whereby the wife always shares the domicile of her husband. Thus, it was noted by the court that both before and since the enactment of the Constitution a divorce decree granted by a foreign court would be recognised under Irish law where the court making the decree of divorce is also the country of common domicile of the parties. So long as both parties to the divorce are deemed to both be domiciled in the country granting the decree of divorce, the Irish courts at this time were satisfied to recognise the decree to be valid. Considering the court's position regarding the dependent domicile of a wife, the reality was that if the husband was deemed to be domiciled in the country where the decree was granted, that decree was then recognisable by the Irish courts. This view was endorsed by Walsh J. in *Gaffney v. Gaffney* [[1975] I.R. 133 at 150]:

> "The Courts here do not recognise decrees of dissolution of marriage pronounced by foreign courts unless the parties were domiciled within the jurisdiction of the foreign court in question." [See also *Bank of Ireland v. Caffin* [1971] I.R. 123].

DOMICILE AND RECOGNITION OF FOREIGN DIVORCES ACT 1986

The decisions of the courts followed this domicile-based logic until the **E–212** enactment of the Domicile and Recognition of Foreign Divorces Act 1986 (hereafter referred to as the 1986 Act) which came into force from October 2, 1986. The Dáil debates show that the primary purpose of the 1986 Act was to rid our law of what Lord Denning once called the last vestiges of a wife's servitude. This Act lessened the domicile requirements of the parties for the foreign divorce to be recognised by the Irish courts. Section 5 of the 1986 Act empowers the Irish courts to recognise a divorce granted in a country where either spouse is domiciled at the date of the institution of the proceedings:

"For the rule of law that a divorce is recognised if granted in a country where both spouses are domiciled, there is hereby substituted a rule that a divorce shall be recognised if granted in the country where either spouse is domiciled."

E–213   Thus, from October 2, 1986 a wife was deemed capable of having a domicile independent of her husband. Section 5 of the Domicile and Recognition of Foreign Divorces Act 1986 was considered most recently in *R.B. v. A.S. (Orse A.B.)* [unreported, High Court, Lavan J., February 28, 2001]. The respondent, A.S., in this case was a German national who emigrated to Ireland with her family in 1962. [The parents of A.S. established a business and permanently settled in Ireland]. In 1975 A.S. married W.S., a German national who had lived in Ireland since 1955. [W.S. had spent little time in Germany during his adult life and did not own property there]. The parties sought and were granted a divorce by a German District Court in 1986, which assumed jurisdiction on the basis of the nationality/citizenship of the parties. The petitioner, R.B., subsequently married A.S. in Germany, in 1996. R.B., pleading section 5 of the Domicile and Recognition of Foreign Divorces Act 1986, claimed that this marriage was null and void as the respondent, A.S., was a party to a prior subsisting marriage. The issue arose as to whether the 1986 German divorce was entitled to recognition in Ireland.

The High Court, in considering the validity of the 1986 German divorce, held that the divorce would be recognised if either A.S. or W.S. were domiciled in Germany at the relevant time. Lavan J., in refusing to recognise the validity in Irish law of the 1986 German divorce, held that the parents of A.S. and W.S. had abandoned their domicile of origin in Germany and had acquired a domicile of choice in Ireland when they moved here. Therefore, as minors both A.S. and W.S. had acquired an Irish domicile of dependency. As there was no evidence by either W.S. or A.S. of an intention to reside in Germany permanently or indefinitely before the 1986 divorce, the German divorce was not entitled to recognition in Ireland.

An equally fundamental change introduced by the 1986 Act related to the issue of dependent domicile. Section 1 thereof, abolished the notion that upon marriage a woman acquired the domicile of her husband and provided that the domicile of a married woman would be an independent domicile, to be determined by the same factors as were previously applied to a married man. The 1986 Act was not retrospective in operation and thus foreign divorces granted before October 2 of that year continued to be recognised on the unmodified common law rules, with the dependent domicile of a wife still operating. Despite the absence of a statute on the matter, there has been significant development in the common law recognition rules as they operate outside the statute.

E–214   The first such development came in *C.M. v. T.M. (No.2)* [1990] 2 I.R. 52], where Barr J. questioned the constitutionality of the dependent domicile rule in the context of a pre-1986 divorce. The issue of a married woman's dependent domicile arose again in the case of *W. v. W.* [[1993] 2 I.R. 476]. This case dealt with a decree of divorce granted by the English courts in 1972 and thus the provisions of the 1986 Act could not be invoked by the court. However, despite their inability to apply the provisions of the 1986 Act, the Supreme Court ruled that the concept of dependent domicile was contrary to Article 40.1 of the Irish Constitution. By invoking the personal rights of a married woman as guaranteed by the Constitution the Supreme Court was able to recognise the divorce decree without needing to rely upon the 1986 Act. It was stated by Egan J. that a more acceptable basis for the recognition of a foreign divorce:

> ". . . which would be consistent both with the Constitution and with the general principles of international law, would be a recognition of divorce if granted by the courts of a country in which either party to a marriage was domiciled at the time of the proceedings for divorce."

The Supreme Court, in declaring the law relating to dependent domicile to be unconstitutional, made it possible for divorces granted before October 2, 1986 to be recognised where, allowing the wife an independent domicile, would validate the decree under Irish law.

CURRENT POSITION

The rules governing the recognition of foreign divorces by the Irish courts were examined and updated once more in the case of *G. McG. v. D.W.; A. R. notice party* [[2000] 1 I.R. 96]. The previously vital issue of domicile was replaced with the notion of ordinary residence, which is now regarded as the pertinent issue in these matters. The parties were married in 1967 in Ireland, which was their country of domicile. In the late 1970s their marriage ended and subsequently they both formed new relationships. The applicant issued divorce proceedings in England in 1984 against his first wife (hereinafter the notice party). The petition based the jurisdiction of the English court on either the notice party having an English domicile at that time or, alternatively, on her having ordinarily resided in England for one year prior to the petition. The divorce was granted in 1985. In November 1995 the applicant married the respondent. The marriage subsequently broke down. The applicant brought nullity proceedings on the basis that the divorce was not recognised in the State and therefore his second marriage was void because at the time of obtaining the divorce, the notice party was not domiciled in England and thus did not satisfy the Irish court's requirement as stated in *W. v. W.*. The real purpose of the petition was to ascertain the marital status of the applicant and that being the case, McGuinness J. treated the case as being an application under section 29 (1)(d) or (e) of the Family Law Act 1995 regarding the validity or invalidity of the foreign divorce.

E–215

E–216   It was not seriously argued that the notice party was domiciled in England at the time of the divorce proceedings there. It was accepted that the divorce was valid in English law on the basis of the notice party's ordinary residence.

The High Court, in granting a declaration that the 1985 divorce was entitled to recognition in Ireland, stated that the common law rules for the recognition of foreign divorces should be extended to cover cases where foreign jurisdictions base their jurisdiction on similar grounds to those used by courts in the State. [The common law rules were based on judge-made law, and it was therefore open to the courts to develop such rules according to the policy of the carers.] McGuinness J. noted that since the enactment of the Divorce Act, Ireland can grant a divorce based upon a party's domicile within the State or upon ordinary residence within the State for one year prior to the institution of proceedings. Accordingly, she held that this demonstrates a clear policy that the modern matrimonial jurisdiction of the State is not limited to a party's domicile. In this case, the court held that the jurisdiction of the English courts having been based on one year's ordinary residence entitled a decree granted there to recognition here. McGuinness J. also cited the doctrine of the comity of the courts in support of her decision. She stated the position as follows:

> "It would seem to me both logical and reasonable that the Irish common law recognition rule should similarly be extended to cover cases where under the statute law, the Irish courts claim entitlement not alone to dissolve marriages but also to annul them and to make far-reaching declarations as to marital status. The well-known policy of the comity of courts alone would support such an extension of recognition". [[2000] 1 I.R. 96].

It would appear that the decision could only apply to pre-1986 divorces, as those granted after that date fall for recognition under the 1986 Act. The decision has as its consequence a situation that more flexible rules apply to recognition of a pre-1986 foreign divorce than to a post-1986 foreign divorce. This seems unusual given the fact that the intent of the 1986 Act was to liberalise the recognition rules.

E–217   In summary, McGuinness J. in *G. McG. v. D.W.* [P. 96], was essentially invited to extend the recognition rules to one of mutuality. There is ample United Kingdom authority for such an approach. [See *Travers v. Holley* [1953] (C.A.) 246]. The central idea is that since our courts allow a divorce to a spouse ordinarliy resident here, our courts should recognise those granted by foreign courts on a similar basis. [Such an approach is only possible in Ireland since the introduction of divorce; *K.D.C. v. M.C.* [[1985] I.R. 697]. McGuinness J. was satisfied that this should be done and accordingly recognised the divorce. In her judgment, McGuinness J. creates a new formula for the recognition of foreign divorces where the more onerous requirement of domicile is replaced with the concept of ordinary residence. [The decisions of Buckley J. in *Trustees of the Blood Transfusion*

Services Board Superannuation Fund v. H. L. [1999] 3 I.J.F.L. 19 and *B.B. v. T.B.* [1999] 3 I.J.F.L. 20 provide some insight as to the application of the *G. McG. v. D.W.* decision in the Circuit Family Court].

It should be noted that some months after the delivery of the High Court **E–218** judgment in *G.McG. v. D.W.*, the Attorney General sought to be joined as a notice party to the proceedings [See *G.McG. v. D.W. (No. 2) (Joinder of the Attorney General)* [2000] 4 I.R. 1]. The Attorney General had only become aware of the proceedings after judgment had been delivered and had concerns relating to the state of the common law in relation to the recognition of foreign divorces and as to the effect to be given to the judgment of the High Court. It was his intention, if joined, to apply to the Supreme Court to extend the time within which to appeal the decision of the High Court. His application was dismissed by the High Court and this decision was upheld on appeal. The Supreme Court held that while the Family Law Act, 1995 provided for the joining of the Attorney General to proceedings relating to the validity of a marriage, the proceedings before McGuinness J. were no longer in being. Accordingly, it had no jurisdiction under the Act to re-open the proceedings. The Court also held that the inherent jurisdiction of the Courts to amend a final order was only exercised in special and unusual circumstances, which did not arise in the case before the Court.

Another interesting point, which arose in the course of the appeal was as to the effect of section 29(8) of the 1995 Act pursuant to which a declaration under section 29 is only binding on the State where the Attorney General is a party to the proceedings. In the course of his judgment, Murphy J. noted that Counsel for the Attorney General had expressed concern as to the consequences, which might result from such an Order, in particular, in relation to the registration of particulars of marriage, the acquisition of passports and other dealings with agents of the State. While Murphy J. did not consider it necessary to deal with the issue since the parties to the proceedings did not wish to pursue it, he expressed doubt as to whether the problems envisaged by counsel for the Attorney General could be the consequences of the statutory exemption. Murray J., for his part, noted that it was by no means clear, which organs or authorities of the State are envisaged by the notion "the State" as used in section 29. He considered that this lack of clarity in the Act was unsatisfactory. However, it was not an issue, which arose in the application before the Court.

The first occasion the High Court had to consider the far reaching effects **E–219** of the decision of McGuinness J. in *G.McG. v. D.W.* [[2000] 1 I.R. 96] was in *M.E.C. v. J.A.C.; J.O.C. and by order the Attorney General (notice parties); And J.O.C. v. J.A.C.; the Attorney General (notice party)* [unreported, High Court, Kinlen J., March 9, 2001]. In the first set of proceedings the parties married in Sligo in 1968. They moved to London later that year. The respondent, J.A.C., resided there until 1974, and the applicant, M.E.C., resided there until 1979, when they separated. J.A.C. and M.E.C. were granted a divorce in England in 1980. In 1989 J.A.C. married the applicant in the second set of proceedings, J.O.C. The applicant in the first set of proceedings, M.E.C., applied for a declaration that the 1980 English divorce was not entitled to recognition in Ireland. The issue for consideration was whether a pre-1986 foreign divorce was entitled to recognition in Ireland on the basis of residence. The High Court (in March 2000) directed that the Attorney General be joined in both sets of proceedings, so as to argue, if the point arose, that the decision in *G.McG. v. D.W.* was wrongly decided and should not be followed. It should be noted that as a preliminary issue it was held that neither of the parties to the first set of proceedings were domiciled in England at the time of the granting of the divorce decree. Therefore the divorce was not entitled to recognition under the common law. [See *W. v. W.* [1993] 2 I.R. 476 and E—214].

Kinlen J., in refusing to recognise the validity of the English 1980 divorce, cited the uncertainty a retrospective extension of the grounds of recognition (to include the residence of either party to a divorce) would produce for those couples who were party to pre-1986 foreign divorces and were advised that such divorces were not entitled to recognition in Ireland. A further argument advanced by the learned judge against the extended basis of recognition was that it was not for the courts to so extend the grounds of recognition. This was properly a matter for the legislature. This most recent judgment will serve to create uncertainty as to whether a pre-1986 foreign divorce is entitled to recognition on the basis of residence. The judgment does not address the merits of the formula for the recognition of pre-1986 divorces established in *G.McG. v. D.W.*, which is a matter of concern as that decision must be seen as a binding precedent on later High Court cases. Clarification from the Supreme Court is urgently needed on the point.

BRUSSELS II CONVENTION

E–220   The Brussels II Convention, signed on May 28, 1998, is arguably the most dramatic development in the field of family law since the introduction of divorce in Ireland. [[1998] O.J. C-221/1. See generally Kennett, "Current Developments: Private International Law", (1999) 48 (2) I.C.L.Q. 465 at 467, Shannon, "The Convention on Jurisdiction and the Recognition and Enforcement of Judgments in Matrimonial Matters" (1999) 93 *Law Society Gazette,* 47 and Shannon, "Cut to the Quick" (2001) 95 (3) *Law Society Gazette,* 14]. The impact of the Convention has been further increased by its recent adoption as a Regulation of the European Community. [Council Reg. 1347/00 on jurisdiction and the recognition and enforcement in matrimonial matters and in matters of parental responsibility for the children of both spouses]. Both build upon the groundwork laid by the Brussels I Convention of 1968, which was designed to improve co-operation in relation to the enforcement of judgments in civil matters generally. [Convention on the Jurisdiction and Enforcement of Judgments in Civil and Commercial Matters, 1968]. That Convention dealt in particular with the mutual recognition and enforcement of Maintenance orders, [see Article 5(2)], although other family matters were excluded from the remit of the 1968 Convention. [Article 1]

The Brussels II Convention is designed to fill that lacuna. As between **E–221** European Union countries, it aims to standardise rules relating to the recognition of foreign divorces and family law judgments. In theory, this sounds relatively innocuous. Yet in its detailed workings, the Brussels Convention would appear to alter in the most radical fashion the basis on which certain family law judgments, (and in particular decrees of divorce) will be recognised in this jurisdiction. The overriding concern is that the restrictive divorce regime laid down in the Constitution may ultimately be undermined, with the prospect of divorces obtained abroad being more easily recognised in this jurisdiction. [See O'Doherty, "Quickie EU divorces bypass wait rule", *Examiner,* July 13, 2001].

The basic aim of the Convention, and the Regulation that followed it, is twofold: first, to standardise the rules regarding the jurisdiction of courts in divorce, marital separation and annulment proceedings, and second, to give priority among courts with jurisdiction to the court first hearing the case. In other words, where more than one State may potentially claim jurisdiction in a case, it is the court *in which proceedings are first issued that retains exclusive jurisdiction.* All similar proceedings subsequently commenced in another state in relation to the same parties must be stayed pending the decision of the court in which proceedings were first issued.

The concern behind this convention and legislation is to obviate the **E–222** incidence of what are sometimes called "limping marriages", marriages that are recognised in some jurisdictions but not others. [See *R.B. v. A.S. (orse A.B.),* unreported, High Court, Lavan J., February 28, 2001]. Interjurisdictional divergence in treatment in relation to the acquisition and loss of marital status has led at least one commentator, Professor Anton, to describe the "treatment of divorce in private international law" as "anarchic". Professor Anton continues to describe the "quite serious social consequences" that arise from such "anarchy":

"The validity of second marriages, the legitimacy of the children of such marriage and rights deriving from the law of matrimonial property or of succession may all depend on whether, from system to system, recognition is accorded to a divorce". [Anton, "The Recognition of Divorces and Legal Separations" (1969) 18 I.C.L.Q. 620 at 620].

The aim of the Convention, thus, is to minimise the incidence of such 'limping marriages' by providing a single framework for the determination of marital validity. Once the courts of one EU country (with proper jurisdiction) have determined a matter with which the Convention is concerned, the courts and other authorities in every other contracting party are obliged to enforce and recognise such judgment, subject to certain exceptions to be outlined below.

The nature of the legislative framework

E–223   The Brussels Convention, in its original form, took the guise of an international convention between EU members. As such, at least initially, it remained independent of the corpus of European Union Law. Its applicability in Irish law, thus, initially depended on the enactment of an Act of the Oireachtas. Article 29.6 of the Irish Constitution, after all, stipulates that no international convention will have the force of law in Ireland without the approval of Parliament.

E–224   In 2000, however, this situation changed dramatically when the European Union transposed the Convention into a binding Regulation of the European Union. [Council Reg. 1347/00 on jurisdiction and the recognition and enforcement in matrimonial matters and in matters of parental responsibility for the children of both spouses]. A regulation is the EU legislative measure of the most binding nature. Once it has been duly enacted and promulgated, it normally is directly applicable throughout the European Union. This means that it automatically has the full force of law in every member state without the need for *any* action by that member state. Moreover, as EU law is superior to national law, any national law that conflicts with the Regulation in any member state is deemed (in national as well as EU law) to be unenforceable to the extent of such conflict. [See C-6/64 *Costa v. ENEL* [1964] E.C.R. 585, C-106/77 *Simmenthal* [1978] E.C.R. 629, *Campus Oil v. Minister for Industry and Energy* [1982] I.R. 82]. A judge who comes across such a conflict must always enforce the EU measure over the Irish measure, even if neither the *Oireachtas* nor the Superior Courts have yet invalidated the Irish measure.

E–225   The Regulation came into force in Ireland on March 1, 2001. The impact of this metamorphosis from Convention to Regulation is highly significant in several respects.

- It brings the convention directly into the corpus of European Union law. As such it enjoys the status of supremacy accorded to all binding EU laws. [See C-6/64 *Costa v. ENEL* [1964] E.C.R. 585, C-106/77 *Simmenthal* [1978] E.C.R. 629, *Campus Oil v. Minister for Industry and Energy* [1982] I.R. 82].

- It renders the measure directly applicable as a matter of European Union and Irish law alike. In other words, the measure becomes part of the national law of the various member states *without the need for incorporation* by the individual states. *As such, the Brussels Convention is now directly a part of Irish law, binding on the courts and citizens of this State as fully as if it was part of our own Constitution.*

Application of the Regulation.   The Regulation only applies to the Member States of the European Union (excluding Denmark). Thus, the States to which the Regulation applies are as follows: Austria, Belgium, Finland, France, Germany, Greece, Ireland, Italy, Luxembourg, the Netherlands,

E110

Portugal, Spain, Sweden and the United Kingdom. Denmark successfully obtained a derogation from the Regulation such that it does not apply to judgments issued in that jurisdiction. [See Article 1(3) of the Regulation]. Nor does the Regulation apply to either the Channel Islands or the Isle of Man, although Gibraltar is covered by its terms.

Scope of the Convention/Regulation

The Convention applies to all civil proceedings seeking the following: **E–227**

- a divorce, legal separation and an annulment of marriage; and

- a declaration or other order concerning parental responsibility in respect of the children of both spouses, which declaration is sought in connection with proceedings for a divorce, legal separation and an annulment of marriage.

This portion of the text focuses only on the former of these two categories. The issue of parental responsibility will be dealt with in a future release when the pending Commission initiative in relation to children is finalised.

It is important to note that pre-nuptial agreements do not fall within the scope of the convention. As will be seen below, it is also unlikely that a party could seek, under this Convention, to enforce orders ancillary to any of the above proceedings, such as an order for the sale of a family home.

Jurisdiction under the Convention/Regulation

Article 2 of the Regulation governs the issue of jurisdiction. A court will **E–228**
have the power or jurisdiction to litigate a matter relating to divorce, legal separation or marriage annulment in the following cases:

- Where the spouses, at the time of the application, are "habitually resident" in the territory over which the Court has jurisdiction, or

- Where the spouses were last "habitually resident" together in the territory over which the Court has jurisdiction, provided that one of the parties remains "habitually resident" there, or

- Where the respondent to the action is "habitually resident" in the territory over which the Court has jurisdiction, or

- If both parties make a joint application, where either spouse is 'habitually resident' in the jurisdiction, or

- Where the applicant has been "habitually resident" in the territory for at least one year immediately prior to the application being made.

Each of the above-mentioned grounds is broadly based on the "habitual residence" of one or both parties. There is however, an additional

FLP R.2: October 2001

alternative avenue based on either the nationality or domicile of the parties. In the case of all States except Ireland and the United Kingdom, nationality is the relevant criterion. In the case of the jurisdictions of Ireland, Northern Ireland, England and Wales, and Scotland however, the concept of domicile is used for these purposes. In these cases a court will have jurisdiction:

- where the applicant is a *national* of a member state (or in the case of the United Kingdom and Ireland, *domiciled* within the jurisdiction) and has resided in the relevant state for at least 6 months immediately prior to the application being made.

Parental responsibility (custody). The forum exercising jurisdiction in respect of matrimonial proceedings has jurisdiction in custody issues where the child is habitually resident in the same State. Where the child is habitually resident in a Member State other than the Member State exercising jurisdiction in respect of matrimonial proceedings, the courts of the State exercising jurisdiction in the matrimonial proceedings will also have jurisdiction subject to one of the spouses having parental responsibility in relation to the child. In this regard, that jurisdiction must be accepted by the spouses and be in the best interests of the child.

The jurisdiction of a State over parental responsibility under this Regulation is linked with the substantive application and thus will cease when the judgment allowing or refusing the application for divorce, separation or annulment has become final. Where those proceedings have finished but where proceedings in relation to parental responsibility are still pending, the State retains jurisdiction until they also end. One notable feature of the new Regulation is the non-availability of the principle of *forum non conveniens*. This will impact significantly on the custody issue and may result in this sensitive issue being considered in a jurisdiction other than that in which the children reside. The Commission initiative in relation to parental responsibility, currently being considered by the Department of Justice, Equality and Law Reform, will have significant implications for custody and access issues linked to matrimonial proceedings arising under Brussels II.

E–229 **The impact of the Convention in Ireland.** The private international law test normally used in this State in relation to the recognition of such matrimonial proceedings is one solely based on the domicile of the parties. A foreign divorce, for instance, would be recognised only if either or both parties was domiciled in the jurisdiction granting the divorce, and not otherwise. [Domicile and Recognition of Foreign Divorces Act 1986 and *W. v. W* [1993] 2 I.R. 476. See also E—211—E—214.] In *G.McG. v. D.W.* [[2000] 1 I.R. 96, (1999) 1 I.J.F.L. 26 and E—215—E—217] however, McGuinness J. (then a High Court judge) ruled that a foreign divorce could be recognised where either party was 'ordinarily resident' in the relevant jurisdiction for one full year immediately preceding the institution of divorce proceedings. This, she argued, would be in line with the jurisdictional rules laid out in the Family Law (Divorce) Act 1996 in relation to the granting of Irish divorces. The provisions of that Act allow a divorce to be sought in Ireland, where at least one of the parties is either domiciled in the State or ordinarily resident therein at the time of the institution of proceedings. McGuinness J. thus felt it appropriate that the common law regarding the recognition of foreign divorces be extended to mirror these changes.

This represented a dramatic change to the traditional position on this **E–230** island, and led to some considerable uncertainty on this matter in the courts. In *M.E.C. v. J.A.C.* [unreported, High Court, Kinlen J., March 9, 2001 and E—218], for instance, Kinlen J. declined to accept the extension of recognition to situations where the parties were 'resident' in the jurisdiction granting the divorce, basing his decision instead solely on the parties' lack of domicile in that jurisdiction. Similarly in *R.B. v. A.S. (orse A.B.),* [unreported, High Court, Lavan J., February 28, 2001 and E—213], Lavan J. refused to recognise a German divorce on the grounds that the parties were not domiciled there at the relevant time. It remains to be seen which of these two rival perspectives will ultimately be accepted. It may indeed be the case that the conflict will not be resolved until the matter comes before the Supreme Court.

It is arguable, however, that at least insofar as European Union **E–231** (excluding Danish) decisions are concerned, this question may be largely otiose. With effect from the beginning of March, 2001, the new jurisdiction rules in the Regulation require that a divorce be recognised on grounds based on the 'habitual residence' of the parties, or either of them. With respect to decisions handed down by EU courts, then, the Irish courts will be obliged to recognise and enforce such rulings provided that the criteria for jurisdiction in the Convention (which include grounds based on 'habitual residence') have been met. The conflict over *McG.,* thus, remains relevant only in the context of the recognition of Danish and non-EU matrimonial proceedings, such as those of the courts of the United States. [See Article 42 of the Regulation in relation to transitional provisions. While the Regulation is generally prospective, it may, in certain circumstances, apply to judgments given after it has entered into force which stem from proceedings initiated before that date.]

Multiple legal systems. Several Member States of the European Union **E–232** consist of more than one territorial unit. In such a case a State may be comprised of more than one 'jurisdiction' with different systems of law. The United Kingdom for instance consists of three: (1) Scotland, (2) England and Wales and (3) Northern Ireland. In such cases any reference to 'habitual residence', 'nationality' or domicile' shall be taken to refer to the relevant territorial unit.

Contractual Choice and Brussels II. Brussels II would appear to preclude **E–233** the prospect of parties to a pre-nuptial contract (if such an agreement is even legal in this State) assigning a jurisdiction to hear any future divorce between the parties. Unlike Brussels I, which did permit the parties to determine the jurisdiction by agreement, Brussels II forecloses the possibility of a pre-selection of jurisdiction.

"Same Cause of Action"

E–234   The question of what constitutes the 'same cause of action' in any particular scenario is one of fact in each case. In C-144/86 *Gubisch Maschinenfabrik v. Palumbo* [[1987] E.C.R. 4861] such a situation arose in the context of the Brussels Convention. A German vendor had agreed to sell a machine to an Italian buyer. Following on a dispute between the parties, the seller commenced proceedings in the German courts seeking payment for the machine. The buyer, meanwhile, commenced proceedings in the Italian courts seeking the rescission of the contract. The European Court of Justice ruled that although the relief sought in each court was different, the proceedings involved substantially the same cause of action. While the court did not establish any firm principle regarding the meaning of the 'same cause of action', it did note that the matter was a question of European Law only, and not one to be determined by reference to national rules.

E–235   **Where two or more States satisfy the jurisdiction requirements.**   Where a case might potentially be taken in either or any of two or more States, Article 11 of the Regulation must be considered. Article 11 requires that when proceedings have already been commenced in the courts of one member state, a court in a different member state cannot subsequently hear proceedings in the same cause of action. The Court 'second seised' of the cause of action (in other words all courts but the court in which proceedings were first commenced) must "stay its proceedings until such time as the jurisdiction of the court first seised is established". [Article 11(1)]. Should the jurisdiction of the first court be established, the second and subsequent courts must decline jurisdiction in such a case.

Similar principles apply where different and potentially conflicting causes of action are brought in different courts between the same parties. If for instance, a petitioner applied for an annulment in an Irish court, while divorce proceedings were already under way in respect of the same parties in an English court, the Irish court would be obliged to decline jurisdiction in favour of the English court.

E–236   **Meaning of "Habitual Residence".**   For these purposes, one must determine the meaning of the term "habitual residence". While there is some considerable case law on the meaning of the term "resident", it has generally arisen in the context of tax law. [In which context it is, moreover, now no longer relevant as section 819 of the Taxes Consolidation Act 1997 now provides a statutory definition of "residence" for tax purposes]. It is not clear then that these cases are applicable or even helpful, thus, in the context of Family law. Nor is it clear whether the addition of the word "habitual" in any material sense modifies the established meaning of the term "residence".

What is clear from these cases, however, is that the term 'residence' denotes a physical presence in the State over a relatively prolonged period of time. The question of residence is [according to Lord Buckmaster in *I.R.C. v. Lysaght* [[1928] A.C. 234 at 248] "essentially a question of fact" in each case. In *Levene v. I.R.C.* [[1928] A.C. 217 at 222] Viscount Cave L.C., nevertheless, referred with approval to an Oxford English dictionary definition of residence as "to dwell permanently, or for a considerable time, to have one's settled usual abode, to live in or at a particular place". To be resident, however, one need not occupy a particular dwelling. [See the comments of the English and Welsh Court of Appeal in *Levene v. I.R.C.* [1927] 2 K.B. 38]. Indeed even a homeless person could be "resident" in Ireland for a relevant year. The term "residence" thus denotes a physical presence in the State and not in any particular place or building therein.

That said, occupation of a dwelling within the territory formerly provided some evidence of "residence" for tax purposes. In *Cooper (I.R.C.) v. Cadwallader* [(1904) 15 T.C. 101] for instance a New York resident who kept a shooting lodge in Scotland, visiting it only on holidays, was nonetheless deemed to be resident in Scotland for tax purposes. [See also *Hewson v. Kealy* (1945) Ir.T.C. 286]. Similarly in *Rogers v. I.R.C.* [(1879) 1 T.C. 225] a master mariner who had spent a full tax year on the high seas (and thus physically outside the U.K.) was quite remarkably deemed to be resident in Scotland for that year, as his family and home were situated there. [See also *Re Young* (1875) 1 T.C. 57. Although see *contra, Turnbull v. Foster* (1904) 6 T.C. 206 where it was said that a "pretty strong case indeed" would be required to establish residence where a person had not been physically in the State for the relevant tax year].

A person may build up a pattern of residence over several years. In **E–237** *Levene v. I.R.C.* [[1928] A.C. 217] for instance, a gentleman was deemed to be resident in England and Wales. Although he ordinarily lived in France, he spent at least four months in each of five consecutive years in England attending to family business, his religious obligations and other matters. While he had no fixed abode in the U.K., and his visits in any one-year would not have been sufficient on their own to deem him a resident, the cumulative pattern suggested a 'settled habit' of residence. [On regularity of visits see also *I.R.C. v. Kinloch* (1929) 14 T.C. 736].

The basic former rule in tax law was that physical presence in the State lasting six calendar months (counted as 183 days) in aggregate in any one year would make one a resident of the State. At present, modern Irish tax law defines a resident generally as a person who has spent 183 days or more in the State in any one year, or an aggregate of 280 days or more over two consecutive years. [Taxes Consolidation Act 1997, section 819(1) and (2)]. For the purposes of the aforementioned aggregate, the individual must have remained in the State for at least 30 days in aggregate in each of the consecutive years.

The Brussels Convention and Regulation 1347/00, by contrast, contain no **E–238** such numerical definition although the addition of the term "habitual" would appear to suggest that the residence so required should not be either temporary or transient in nature. It is nonetheless somewhat difficult to see what the term "habitual" adds to the term "residence" as defined by Viscount Cave in *Levene*. It may best be contrasted with the phrase 'occasional residence' denoting residence ". . .taken up or happening as passing opportunity requires. . .or admits". [L.P. Clyde, in *I.R.C. v. Combe* (1932) 17 T.C. 405].

The term 'habitual' thus may suggest that the residence required should form part of a pattern of living that is inconsistent with any temporary or short-term arrangement. In *Levene v. I.R.C.* [[1928] A.C. 217 at 232] Lord Warrington defined a somewhat similar phrase 'ordinary residence' as "the way in which a [person's] life is usually ordered", Viscount Cave adding that it connoted "some degree of continuity". [*Ibid.* at 225]. Similarly in *Shah v. Barnet London B.C.* [[1983] 1 All E.R. 226 at 235] Lord Scarman defined 'ordinary residence' as being one's 'abode' "adopted for settled purposes as part of the regular order of his life for the time being".

E–239 **The meaning of "domicile".** A court in Ireland or the United Kingdom may acquire jurisdiction where one of the parties to the case is domiciled in the jurisdiction in which the case is taken. For these purposes, each of the separate legal jurisdictions of the United Kingdom (1) England and Wales, (2) Scotland and (3) Northern Ireland are treated separately from each other. Thus, a Scottish court, for instance, might decline jurisdiction on the grounds that a litigant is domiciled and habitually resident in Northern Ireland.

The term "domicile" is not easily defined nor is the domicile of certain persons always easy to identify. [On domicile generally see Corrigan, *Revenue Law, Volume I,* (Dublin: Round Hall, 2000), at para. 4–154 to para. 4–170, pp. 315–321, and McAteer, Reddin and Deegan, *Income Tax,* (13th ed. Dublin: Institute of Taxation in Ireland, 2000) at pp. 396–398]. Broadly however one might say that a person is said to be "domiciled in the country in which he is considered by the law to have his *permanent home"*. [Corrigan, *Revenue Law, Volume I,* (Dublin: Round Hall, 2000), p. 315 citing Binchy, *Conflicts of Law,* (Butterworth's, 1988), Chapter 6. Emphasis added by present author]. One's domicile then is the jurisdiction with which one is connected most profoundly. Usually, a person will retain a domicile of origin (one's domicile at birth) throughout life although it is possible, though remarkably difficult, to acquire a "domicile of choice". This can only occur where a person has physically and intentionally abandoned on a permanent basis his or her domicile of origin in favour of another jurisdiction. This task is far from easy. As Whiteman and Wheatcroft comment "a domicile of origin has amazing qualities of adherence". [Whiteman and Wheatcroft (with Milne), *Income Tax* (2nd ed. London/ Edinburgh: Sweet and Maxwell/W. Green & Son, 1976), p. 70. See also *R.B. v. A.S. (orse A.B.)*, unreported, High Court, Lavan J., February 28, 2001.]

Examples of the Jurisdictional rules in operation

E–240 Some brief case studies may help to explain the impact of the Convention/Regulation.

1. Pedro wishes to obtain a divorce from his wife Maria. Maria still lives in her native Seville, Spain. Pedro now resides in Portugal and has been so resident for two years. As such there are three options open to the parties:

   - If they are willing to make a joint application they may do so in either Spain or Portugal.
   - Pedro may apply for a divorce in Spain, as his wife, the respondent, would be habitually resident in that jurisdiction.
   - He could alternatively apply for the divorce in Portugal, as he has been habitually resident there for at least a year.

2. Marie and Pierre are Belgian nationals. They resided together in France for 3 years. Pierre has returned to Belgium and has been resident there for 7 months. Marie has moved to Germany and has resided there for 7 months also. The options open to the parties are:

   - Pierre, as a Belgian national can invoke the jurisdiction of the Belgian courts as he has resided there for more than 6 months.
   - Marie cannot invoke the jurisdiction of the German Courts (as she is not a national) for another 5 months, unless Pierre and Marie make a joint application.
   - Pierre, as applicant, could invoke the jurisdiction of the German courts, if he can establish that Marie is habitually resident there.

3. Peadar and Máire were both Irish resident for at least 30 years prior to their marriage. After one year of marriage Peadar moves to Birmingham. One year later he may apply (as he has been habitually resident in England for one year) for an English divorce.

The last example exposes the potential for the Brussels Convention to subvert the Irish divorce regime. It holds out the prospect of Irish parties obtaining a divorce after only one year of 'living apart' (subject of course to satisfying English and Welsh legal requirements) instead of the four out of five years required under the Irish regime. The prospect of this happening, of course, is contingent upon the mobility (and ultimately the wealth) of the parties. Not everyone has the resources, economic or otherwise, simply to move to another jurisdiction. For dual nationality spouses, and for the mobile, however, the Brussels Convention holds out the prospect of 'forum-shopping', whereby a party may 'choose' the jurisdiction most inclined to be favourable to his perspective. Thus, the parties or either of them, may quite easily give jurisdiction to the court of their choice by simply residing in that jurisdiction for what is a relatively brief period of time. In example 3 above for instance, Peadar, by moving to England can obtain a divorce in almost half the time it would have taken him in Ireland.

The Consequences of Acquiring Jurisdiction

When, in a matter with which the Convention is concerned, a court's **E–241** jurisdiction has been invoked, it is generally not open to that court to deny a hearing on the grounds that another forum may be more appropriate.

Provided that that court has lawful jurisdiction under the above-mentioned rules to hear the case, it must proceed with the hearing. Even where a court in another State may fall under the rules of jurisdiction, it must decline to hear the case if it is already pending before a court in another competent jurisdiction.

This would appear to foreclose the possibility of what is called the *forum non conveniens* doctrine. This common law doctrine allows a court, at its discretion, to refuse to hear a case on the grounds that a hearing in the courts of another country would be more appropriate. This might happen for instance where the parties had strong ties to another jurisdiction and correspondingly few to Ireland. Under the Convention however, it would appear that a court has no power to exercise this discretion to refuse jurisdiction, even if it feels that another jurisdiction would be a more suitable venue for the case.

E–242   This obviously makes speed of the essence in such applications. Where the courts of more than one State could potentially claim jurisdiction in a case, the court whose jurisdiction is invoked first must hear the case. The danger then is that the parties to a transnational marital breakdown will be lured into a 'race' to see who can get to court first. Article 11(1) of the Regulation provides that where the same action is taken in the courts of two or more different countries, all but the first court to be seised of the case must stay proceedings pending that first court's decision. That first court thus has exclusive jurisdiction in the case. The Regulation is quite inflexible in this regard. Neither the parties to the case nor the court first obtaining jurisdiction can opt for a hearing in another court, by agreement or otherwise.

In short the absence of the *forum non conveniens* doctrine will:

> "prompt parties to litigate earlier in an attempt to secure jurisdiction in their home state. This militates against the recent statutory provisions encouraging parties to engage in mediation and other forms of alternative dispute resolution". [Shannon, "Cut to the Quick", *op. cit.*, at p. 19].

Certain difficulties may also arise owing to the different civil procedures and rules in common law as opposed to civil law states. In common law States (primarily England and Wales, Northern Ireland and Ireland) a court is said to be seised of a matter when proceedings are issued by the plaintiff. In most civil law jurisdictions, by contrast, the court is said to be seised only when the defendant is served with notice of the plaintiff's proposed action. The difference is perhaps too slight to matter in most cases, though this divergence may yet lead to specific jurisdictional conflicts between the courts of different states.

Recognition of Foreign Judgments

E–243   The Convention and Regulation both broadly require that where any EU court has jurisdiction in a matter, its judgment must be afforded formal recognition in all EU States. This means for instance that where a party has obtained a divorce in another jurisdiction, an Irish court must generally treat the relevant marriage bond to have been dissolved. Similar considerations apply where a foreign annulment or judicial separation has been obtained. The judgment of the foreign court, in other words, is deemed to be sufficient for the purposes of determining the marital status of the individual.

The status of any orders *ancillary* to the dissolution, however, is unclear. Article 14 of the Regulation requires only that the divorce, annulment or judicial separation (that is the principal relief) be recognised. It is not at all certain that where the court has ordered that, for instance, maintenance be paid consequent upon divorce, that an Irish court would be obliged to recognise or indeed enforce this portion of the judgment. Technically speaking decisions as to maintenance, property adjustments and other orders that normally follow a divorce are ancillary to the divorce decree and may not thus be covered by the Regulation. Therefore Brussels II may not require the enforcement of ancillary orders.

It is worth noting, however, that the Maintenance Act 1994 provides for **E–244** the reciprocal enforcement of maintenance orders within the European Union. As such, it would appear that at least in so far as maintenance is concerned, this potential lacuna in the Regulation may be largely irrelevant. In fact it is likely that the Contracting Parties intended that matters of maintenance would continue to be governed by Brussels I, (the Brussels Convention on Jurisdiction and Enforcement in Civil and Commercial Matters, 1968) which concerned the mutual recognition of maintenance orders.

This raises the possibility that jurisdiction might be 'split' between the **E–245** principal relief and ancillary relief in an appropriate case. In *D. v. P. (forum conveniens)* [1998] 2 F.L.R. 25, an English judge stayed proceedings in a divorce case pending the decision of an Italian court in proceedings for maintenance. Although an English divorce decree had already been granted, Connell J. felt that he should allow the Italian court to consider the matter of maintenance notwithstanding the fact that this effectively split the jurisdiction in the case. It is thus quite possible that although a foreign court may be forced to hear a case for principal relief, it might nonetheless be perfectly within its rights to decline an application for ancillary orders in favour of a more convenient forum.

Example. Mary and Pat are Irish domiciled persons who have been habitually resident in England and Wales for one year. Although an English Court would be obliged to hear an application for their divorce, it would be perfectly possible for the Court to decline to grant any ancillary orders on the grounds that an Irish court would be the more appropriate venue for the determination of such matters.

Reasons for Non-Recognition

It is well-established in the conflicts of law jurisprudence that even where **E–246** a court in one State has jurisdiction, a court in another state is not required to recognise such judgments in certain limited circumstances. The most obvious example is where the judgment of a court in one State is 'clearly contrary to the public policy' of another State. In such a case, a court in the latter State is not required to recognise such a judgment. In *Vervaeke v. Smith* [[1983] 1 A.C. 145], for instance, a marriage annulment was obtained in Belgium under false pretences. The British House of Lords ruled that because of the fraud that had been perpetrated in obtaining such a judgment, no British Court could recognise the Belgian decision.

E–247   There are four broad grounds upon which a judgment relating to a divorce, legal separation or marriage annulment shall not be recognised. All but one of these grounds are outlined in Article 15 of the Regulation.

1. **Lack of Jurisdiction.** Although this is not mentioned in Article 15, it is worth repeating that a Court in one State should not recognise the decision of a Court that did not have jurisdiction in such a case. Take the following example. An English court grants a divorce to two Irish parties. The parties falsely declared that they were resident in England and Wales for the requisite period. In fact, neither party has ever spent more than a month in that jurisdiction. An Irish court should refuse to recognise such a decision for want of jurisdiction.

2. **Contrary to Public Policy.** A court in one State shall not recognise any decision that is "manifestly contrary to the public policy" of that Member State. [Article 15(1)]. Such a conflict of policy must be extremely profound in order to justify refusal. It is not enough for instance, simply to say that the decision is one that the courts of Ireland could not make or would not have made. Nor is it sufficient to refuse recognition on the grounds of legislative differences alone.

    Vervaeke v. Smith [[1983] 1 A.C. 145; [1982] 1 All E.R. 144] is perhaps the best example of a case involving public policy grounds. There, the British House of Lords refused to recognise a Belgian annulment decree on the grounds that the decree had been obtained using falsified evidence. That said, the European Court of Justice has made it clear in *Hoffman v. Krieg* [Case 145/86 [1988] E.C.R. 645] that the public policy ground is to be used sparingly and only in exceptional cases. It is likely however, that "the sensitivities inherent in family law cases may result in a wider interpretation being taken of this defence". [Shannon, "Cut to the Quick" *op. cit.* at p. 17].

3. **Natural Justice.** Where a judgment was given in default of appearance of one of the parties certain special considerations apply. A court may refuse to recognise such a judgment where the respondent was

    > "not served with the document which instituted the proceedings or with an equivalent document in sufficient time and in such a way as to enable the respondent to arrange for his or her defence". [Article 15(1)(b)].

    The reasoning here is that such failure may constitute a breach of natural justice, a failure to give all parties to the case an opportunity to be heard in the case. A court cannot refuse such recognition, however, where the respondent has clearly indicated that he or she has accepted the judgment of the court without any conditions or complaint ("unequivocally").

4. **Irreconcilable Judgments**. In some cases, a judgment will not be recognised where it conflicts with a judgment given in proceedings between the same parties in the Member State in which recognition is sought. In such a case, priority is taken by the judgment of the recognising court. A court, for instance, would obviously not be required to recognise a foreign divorce in respect of parties whose marriage has already been annulled by the courts of the jurisdiction in which recognition is sought.

In cases where a judgment is irreconcilable with an earlier judgment of the courts of another Member State or a non-member state involving the same parties, a similar principle applies. [Article 15(1)(d)]. In such a case, the earlier judgment is to be enforced in preference to the later on condition that the earlier judgment meets the conditions necessary for recognition in the Member State in which recognition is sought.

The substance of the decision cannot be questioned

Proceedings to obtain recognition however may not question the decision **E–248** of a court on the basis of the substance of that decision. [Article 19.] In this respect the recognition process is somewhat like judicial review. Once the Court has established that none of the criteria for non-recognition set out above have been satisfied, it must recognise the judgment in question. It cannot query the decision on the basis, for instance, that the domestic judge would not have reached the same decision on the facts. Indeed, the domestic court cannot challenge the decision on the basis that such a judgment would have been unobtainable in this State. Article 18 makes it clear that differences in the applicable laws cannot be invoked as a ground for non-recognition. The fact that the law of the Member State in which recognition is sought would not have permitted a divorce, legal separation or annulment in such a case is irrelevant.

Enforcing Judgments. The enforcement provisions are limited to judgments relating to parental responsibility. For judgments relating to matrimonial matters, recognition procedures are sufficient. [Article 14]. The procedure for enforcement is similar to that in the Brussels Convention. Article 20 provides that an enforceable judgment from one Member State can be declared enforceable in another Member State on the application of an interested party. [An "interested party" includes spouses, children and in some states a relevant public authority, and need not be resident in the jurisdiction. See Borras Report (1998) O.J. C221/27, para. 80.]

E121

Procedure for Enforcing Judgments

E–249   Article 23 provides that the procedure for making an application for recognition is to be governed by the law of the Member State in which recognition is sought. In each case, however, Articles 32 and 33 require that certain documents accompany the application. These documents are:

- A copy of the judgment in question. The person seeking to rely on the judgment must be able to satisfy the court of the document's authenticity.

- The Certificate referred to in Article 33 and outlined in Annex IV to the Regulation.

Annex IV requires that the following information be supplied:

- The name of the country in which the judgment was obtained.

- The name, address and contact details of the court issuing the certificate.

- The full name, place of birth and date of birth of both parties.

- The country, place and date of the relevant marriage.

- The name and location of the court that issued the judgment.

- The date and reference number of the judgment.

- The nature of the judgment (divorce, annulment or separation).

- Whether the judgment was issued in default of appearance of one of the parties.

- Whether either of the parties received legal aid.

- Whether the judgment is subject to further appeal in the relevant Member State.

- The date on which the divorce or legal separation came into legal effect.

The certificate must be signed and/or stamped by the relevant authorised officer.

- Where judgment has been obtained in default of appearance, an original or certified true document must be produced. That document must establish that the defaulting party was issued with documents instituting the relevant proceedings or with an equivalent document. Alternatively, a document may be produced showing that the defendant/respondent accepted the judgment without condition or complaint.

Where the documents are in a language other than that known to the court, a translation should be furnished. [Article 34(2)]. Such translation should be certified by a person qualified to do so in one of the Member States.

Absence of documents

In certain cases even where the documents specified under Article 32 **E–250** cannot or are not produced the court can take certain actions. It may require that they be produced by a specific date. It may, in the alternative, accept in their absence equivalent documents. It may, finally, and only if the court believes that it has sufficient information to do so, dispense entirely with the requirement that the relevant documents be produced and proceed to judgment. It is suggested, however, that this should only be done in exceptional cases where the court is otherwise convinced of the *bona fides* of the parties and the veracity of their claim.

Commentary

Considering the thorough debate that accompanied the introduction of **E–251** divorce in 1995, it appears strange that these new developments have attracted so little attention. The Brussels II Convention, after all, introduces a new and comparatively easy way of obtaining a divorce or legal separation outside the jurisdiction. A married person no longer has to wait the four years required by Irish law for a divorce to be granted. [See E—033]. He or she may use the alternative route of the Brussels II Convention to obtain a legally recognised divorce in as short a time as a year. It is hard to escape the conclusion, thus, that the Convention and the Regulation that followed it have introduced 'quickie' divorces by the backdoor, at least for those who are able to afford to reside abroad for a year. This is at best ironic considering the Government's insistence in 1995 on imposing a four-year 'living apart' requirement for the obtaining of a divorce. Indeed, it seems remarkable, considering the sensitivity of the issue in this jurisdiction, that the Irish Government did not seek to retain its initial derogation from some of the terms of the convention, especially when it was transposed into a Regulation.

The fear is that Brussels II will effectively lead to the creation of a two **E–252** tier system of divorce in Ireland between those who are able to afford to go abroad for a 'quick' divorce, and those who will have to resign themselves to waiting it out in Ireland. While there is certainly good grounds for the retention of some rules on the mutual recognition of marital judgments, it is arguable that Brussels II goes too far in this regard. It is suggested, in particular, that the rules for acquiring jurisdiction place a premium on ease of access to the courts of other countries at the expense of other important considerations, in particular as to whether the court with first jurisdiction is the most appropriate venue for the parties' case.

RELIEF AFTER DIVORCE OR SEPARATION OUTSIDE STATE

E–253   Where a foreign divorce or legal separation is recognised in this jurisdiction, section 23 of the Family Law Act 1995 allows the court, on the application of either the spouse or a person on behalf of a dependent member of the family, to make any of the ancillary orders under Part II of the 1995 Act (other than an order under section 6 or a maintenance pending suit order), subject to some modifications, following a decree of judicial separation. It should be noted that a spouse who has remarried following a foreign divorce cannot apply for relief under section 23. Section 25 of the Family Law Act 1995 is significant in that it allows the court to make provision for a spouse out of the estate of the other spouse after a foreign divorce. The application must be made by the surviving spouse to the court within six months of the issue of a grant or representation to the estate of the deceased spouse. As with section 23 of the Family Law Act 1995, provision cannot be made for a spouse who has remarried following the grant of the foreign divorce. In summary, the factors to be taken into account before making an order under section 25 are broadly similar to those pertaining to orders making provision for an applicant spouse out of the estate of the deceased spouse following a decree of divorce under section 18 of the Divorce Act.

Order 70A

[As enacted by Rules of the Superior Courts (No. 3) 1997, S.I. No. 343 of 1997, which came into operation on September 1, 1997.]

1. (1) In this Order family law proceedings shall include:　　　**J–400**

  (a) Any proceeding pursuant to section 36 of the Family Law Act, 1995 or to that section as applied by section 44 of the Family Law (Divorce) Act, 1996.

  (b) An application pursuant to section 3 of the Adoption Act, 1974 or pursuant to section 3 of the Adoption Act, 1988.

  (c) An application pursuant to section 3(8), 4, 5 or 9 of the Family Home Protection Act, 1976.

  (d) Any application pursuant to section 6 or 7 of the Family Law Act, 1981.

  (e) Any proceeding pursuant to the Guardianship of Infants Act, 1964, the Family Law (Maintenance of Spouses and Children) Act, 1976 or pursuant to the Domestic Violence Act, 1996 which has been instituted and maintained in the High Court pursuant to Article 34.3.1° of the Constitution.

  (f) An application for a decree of judicial separation pursuant to section 3 of the Judicial Separation and Family Law Reform Act, 1989 and any preliminary or ancillary application relating thereto under Part II of the Family Law Act, 1995.

  (g) Any proceeding transferred to the High Court pursuant to section 31(3) of the Judicial Separation and Family Law Reform Act, 1989.

  (h) An application for a decree of divorce pursuant to section 5 of the Family Law (Divorce) Act, 1996 and any preliminary or ancillary application relating thereto under Part III thereof.

  (i) An application to institute proceedings for relief subsequent to a divorce or separation outside the State pursuant to section 23 of the Family Law Act, 1995.

  (j) An application pursuant to section 15(A) or section 25 of the Family Law Act, 1995 or pursuant to section 18 of the Family Law (Divorce) Act, 1996.

  (k) An application for a declaration as to marital status under Part IV of the Family Law Act, 1995.

Definitions

1. (2) In this Order　　　**J–401**

"the 1989 Act" means the Judicial Separation and Family Law Reform Act, 1989,
"the 1995 Act" means the Family Law Act, 1995,

"the 1996 Act" means the Family Law (Divorce) Act, 1996,
"the Acts" means all or any of the Acts referred to in rule 1(1).

Commencement

J–402   2. All family law proceedings other than an application under rule 27 of this Order shall be commenced by a special summons which shall be a family law summons and shall be entitled:

"The High Court
Family Law

In the matter of the . . . . .Act,   19 . . . .(as the case may be)
Between/

A.B. the Applicant
- and -
C.B. the Respondent"

3. The endorsement of claim shall be entitled "Special Endorsement of Claim" and shall state specifically, with all necessary particulars, the relief sought and each section of the Act or Acts under which the relief is sought and the grounds upon which it is sought.

4. In any proceeding pursuant to rule 1(1) above an affidavit verifying such proceeding or in reply thereto shall contain the following, where applicable:—

(a) In the case of an application for a judicial separation or a decree of divorce

(1) The date and place of the marriage of the parties.
(2) The length of time the parties have lived apart and the address of both of the parties during that time, where known.
(3) Full particulars of any children of the applicant or respondent stating whether each or any of them is or are a dependent child of the family and stating whether and if so what provision has been made for each and any such dependent child of the applicant or respondent as the case may be.
(4) Whether any possibility of a reconciliation between the applicant and respondent exists and if so on what basis the same might take place.
(5) Details of any previous matrimonial relief sought and/or obtained and details of any previous separation agreement entered into between the parties. (Where appropriate a certified copy of any relevant Court order and/or Deed of Separation/Separation Agreement should be exhibited with the affidavit).
(6) Where each party is domiciled at the date of the application commencing the proceeding or where each party has been ordinarily resident for the year preceding the date of such application.
(7) Details of the family home/s and/or other residences of the parties including, if relevant, details of any former family

J754

homes/residences which should include details of the manner of occupation and ownership thereof.

(8) Where reference is made in the summons to any immovable property whether it is registered or unregistered land and a description of the lands/premises so referred to.

(b) In the case of an application for relief after a foreign divorce or separation outside the State, such of the particulars at (a) above as are appropriate and

(1) The date and place of marriage and divorce/ separation of the parties. (Where appropriate, a certified copy of the decree absolute or final decree of divorce/separation, (together with, where appropriate, an authenticated translation thereof) should be exhibited with the affidavit).

(2) Particulars of the financial, property and custodial/access arrangements operating ancillary to the said decree, and whether such arrangements were made by agreement or by order of the Court or otherwise, and whether such agreements were made contemporaneously with the decree or at another time and the extent of compliance therewith.

(3) The present marital status and occupation of each party.

(4) All details relevant to the matters referred to in section 26 of the 1995 Act.

(c) In the case of an application for a declaration as to marital status, such of the particulars at (a) above as are appropriate together with

(1) The nature of the applicant's reason for seeking such a declaration.

(2) Full details of the marriage/divorce/annulment/legal separation in respect of which the declaration is sought including the date and place of such a marriage/divorce/annulment/legal separa-tion. (Where appropriate a certified copy of the marriage certificate/decree of divorce/annulment/legal separation should be exhibited with the affidavit).

(3) The manner in which the jurisdictional requirements of section 29(2) of the 1995 Act are satisfied.

(4) Particulars of any previous or pending proceeding in relation to any marriage concerned or relating to the matrimonial status of a party to any such marriage in accordance with section 30 of the 1995 Act.

(d) In the case of an application for the determination of property issues between spouses pursuant to section 36 of the 1995 Act or that section as applied by section 44 of the 1996 Act to engaged persons, such particulars of (a) above as are appropriate and

(1) The description, nature and extent of the disputed property or monies.

(2) The state of knowledge of the applicant's spouse in relation to possession or control of the disputed properties or monies at all relevant times.

(3) The nature and extent of the interest being claimed by the applicant in the property or monies and the basis upon which such claim is made.

J755

(4) The nature and extent of any claim for relief being made and the basis upon which any such claim is made.

(5) The manner in which it is claimed that the respondent has failed, neglected or refused to make to the applicant such appropriate payment or disposition in all of the circumstances and details of any payment or disposition actually made.

(6) Sufficient particulars to show that the time limits referred to at section 36(7) of the 1995 Act have been complied with.

(e) In the case of an application for relief out of the estate of a deceased spouse pursuant to section 15(A) or section 25 of the 1995 Act or section 18 of the 1996 Act, such of the particulars at (a) above as are appropriate and

(1) The date and place of the marriage and date of any decree of divorce/judicial separation. (The marriage certificate and a certified copy of the decree of divorce/separation shall be exhibited with the affidavit (with authenticated translations where appropriate)).

(2) Details of any previous matrimonial reliefs obtained by the applicant and in particular lump sum maintenance orders and property adjustment orders, if any.

(3) Details of any benefits received from or on behalf of the deceased spouse whether by way of agreement or otherwise and details of any benefits accruing to the applicant under the terms of the will of the deceased spouse or otherwise.

(4) The date of death of the deceased spouse, the date upon which representation was first granted in respect of the estate of the said spouse and, if applicable, the date upon which notice of the death of the deceased spouse was given to the applicant spouse and the date upon which the applicant spouse notified the personal representative of an intention to apply for relief pursuant to section 18(7) of the 1996 Act and section 15(A)(7) of the 1995 Act, as the case may be.

(5) The marital status of the deceased spouse at the date of death and the marital status of the applicant at the date of the application and whether the applicant has remarried since the dissolution of the marriage between the applicant and the deceased spouse.

(6) Details of the dependants of the deceased spouse at the date of death and of all the dependants of the applicant at the date of the application together with details of any other interested persons.

(7) An averment as to whether any order pursuant to section 18(10) of the 1996 Act or section 15(A)(10) of the 1995 Act has previously been made.

(8) Details of the value of the estate of the deceased spouse where known.

5. Any such affidavit filed under rule 4 shall, where appropriate, also exhibit the certificate required under section 5 or, as the case may be, section 6 of the 1989 Act or under section 6, or as the case may be, section 7 of the 1996 Act which shall be in Form Nos. 1, 2, 3 or 4 respectively as set out in the Schedule hereto.

Affidavit of Means

6. (1) Without prejudice to the right of any party to seek particulars of **J–403** any matter from the other party to any proceeding or to the right of such party to make application to the Court for an order of discovery and without prejudice to the jurisdiction of the Court pursuant to section 12(25) of the 1995 Act or section 17(25) of the 1996 Act, in any case where financial relief under either of the Acts is sought each party shall file and serve an Affidavit of Means in the proceeding.

(2) The Affidavit of Means shall be in Form No. 5 as set out in the Schedule hereto.

(3) An Affidavit of Means of the applicant shall be served with the verifying affidavit grounding such proceeding and the Affidavit of Means of any respondent or any other party shall be served with the replying affidavit in the proceeding unless otherwise ordered by the Master or the Court. Subsequent to the service of an Affidavit of Means either party may request the other party to vouch all or any of the items referred to therein within 21 days of the said request.

(4) In the event of a party failing properly to comply with the provisions in relation to the filing and serving of an Affidavit of Means as herein-before provided for or failing properly to vouch the matters set out therein, the Court may, on application by notice of motion, grant an order for discovery and/or make any such order as the Court deems appropriate and necessary, including an order that such party shall not be entitled to pursue or defend as appropriate such claim for any ancillary relief under the Act save as permitted by the Court and upon such terms as the Court may determine are appropriate or the Court may adjourn the proceeding for a specified period of time to enable compliance with any such previous request or order of the Court.

Affidavit of Welfare

7. In any case in which there is a dependant child or children of the **J–404** spouses or either of them an Affidavit of Welfare shall be filed and served on behalf of the applicant and shall be in Form No. 6 as set out in the Schedule hereto. In a case in which the respondent agrees with the facts as averred to in the Affidavit of Welfare filed and served by the applicant, the respondent may file and serve an Affidavit of Welfare in the alternative form provided in Form No. 3 of the Schedule hereto. In a case in which the respondent disagrees with all or any of the Affidavit of Welfare served and filed by an applicant, a separate Affidavit of Welfare in the said Form No. 6 herein shall be sworn, filed and served by the respondent within 21 days from the date of service of the applicant's Affidavit of Welfare.

Ex parte application to seek relief under section 23 of the 1995 Act

8. (1) An applicant for relief under section 23 of the 1995 Act may issue **J–405** but not serve a special summons and shall as soon as may be after the issue of such summons apply ex parte to the Court for leave to make the application for the relief claimed in the summons.

(2) The applicant shall by affidavit verify the requirements specified in section 27 of the 1995 Act and shall set forth the substantial grounds relied upon for seeking relief.

(3) The Court may upon such application, if appropriate, grant or refuse such application or may, in circumstances which seem appropriate, adjourn the application to allow the applicant to put further evidence before the Court on any relevant matter.

(4) If upon application made to it the Court shall grant leave to make the application for the relief claimed in the summons, the applicant may thereupon proceed to serve the summons in the manner provided for by these rules and the matter shall thereupon proceed in accordance with the provisions of this Order.

Interim and Interlocutory Relief

J–406   9. (1) An application for:

(a) a preliminary order pursuant to section 6 of the 1995 Act; or

(b) a preliminary order pursuant to section 11 of the 1996 Act; or

(c) maintenance pending suit pursuant to section 7 of the 1995 Act; or

(d) maintenance pending relief pursuant to section 24 of the 1995 Act; or

(e) maintenance pending suit pursuant to section 12 of the 1996 Act; or

(f) calculations pursuant to section 12(25) of the 1995 Act; or

(g) calculations pursuant to section 17(25) of the 1996 Act; or

(h) relief pursuant to section 35 of the 1995 Act; or

(i) relief pursuant to section 37 of the 1996 Act; or

(j) relief pursuant to section 38(8) of the 1995 Act: or

(k) relief pursuant to section 38(7) of the 1996 Act; or

(l) a report pursuant to section 47 of the 1995 Act: or

(m) a report pursuant to section 42 of the 1996 Act; or

for any other interlocutory relief, shall be by notice of motion to the Court. Such notice shall be served upon the other party or parties to the proceeding 14 clear days before the return date and shall, where appropriate, be grounded upon the affidavit or affidavits of the parties concerned.

(2) An application may be made ex parte to the Court in any case in which interim relief of an urgent and immediate nature is required by the applicant and the Court may in any case, where it is satisfied that it is appropriate, grant such relief or make such order as appears proper in the circumstances.

(3) Any interim or interlocutory application shall be heard on affidavit unless the Court otherwise directs. Where any oral evidence is heard by the Court in the course of any such application ex parte, a note of such evidence shall be prepared by the applicant or the applicant's solicitor and approved by the Court and shall be served upon the respondent forthwith together with a copy of the order made, if any, unless otherwise directed by the Court.

Notice to Trustees

10. An applicant who seeks an order under Part II of the 1995 Act or **J–407** under Part III of the 1996 Act affecting a pension in any way shall give notice to the trustees thereof in the Form No. 7 as set out in the Schedule hereto informing them of the application and of the right to make representations in relation thereto to the Court.

Motion for Directions

11. (1) An applicant or respondent may, at any stage, bring a motion for **J–408** directions to the Court:

(a) Where there are any dependant children who are sui juris and whose welfare or position is or is likely to be affected by the determination of the proceeding or of any issue in the proceeding;

(b) Where an order is sought concerning the sale of any property in respect of which any other party has or may have an interest;

(c) Where an order of any type is sought which will affect the rules of a pension scheme or require non-compliance therewith; or

(d) Where an application is brought seeking provision out of the estate of a deceased spouse,

or in any other case in which it is appropriate. Such notice of motion shall be grounded upon the affidavit of the applicant which shall, in particular, identify the party or parties whose interests are or are likely to be affected by the determination of the proceeding or any issue in the proceeding and who ought to be put on notice of the said proceeding and given an opportunity of being heard.

(2) The Court may, upon such motion or of its own motion, make such order or give such direction pursuant to section 40 of the 1995 Act or section 40 of the 1996 Act as appears appropriate and may, where any order affecting the rules of a pension scheme is sought, direct that further notice be given to the trustees of such pension scheme in accordance with the Form No. 7 set out in the Schedule hereto or in such variation thereof as the Court may direct, as appropriate.

(3) Save where the Court shall otherwise direct, a notice party who wishes to make representations to the Court shall make such representations by affidavit which shall be filed and served on all parties to the proceeding within 28 days of service upon them of the notice of application for relief or within such further time as the Court may direct.

12. The Court may, at any stage, direct that the parties to any proceeding exchange pleadings in relation to all or any of the issues arising in the proceeding between the parties or between the parties or any of them and any third party on such terms as appear appropriate and may give such directions in relation to the matter as appear necessary.

Hearing

13. (1) Save where the Court otherwise directs, the hearing of any **J–409** interim or interlocutory application brought under the Acts shall be on the affidavits of the parties subject to the right of the parties to seek to cross

examine the opposing party on their affidavit. Any party may serve a notice to cross examine in relation to the deponent of any affidavit served on him.

(2) Save where the Court otherwise directs the hearing of any application under the Acts shall be on the oral evidence of the parties.

(3) Where relief is sought by the applicant or the respondent pursuant to section 12 of the 1995 Act or section 17 of the 1996 Act, evidence of the actuarial value of the benefit under the scheme shall be by affidavit filed on behalf of the applicant or respondent as the case may be. Such affidavit on behalf of an applicant shall be sworn and served on all parties to the proceeding and filed at least 28 days in advance of the hearing and subject to the right to serve notice of cross examination in relation to the affidavit. When one of the parties has adduced evidence of the actuarial value of the benefit by such affidavit as provided herein which the other party intends to dispute, he shall do so by affidavit which shall be filed at least 14 days in advance of the hearing, subject to the right to serve notice of cross examination in relation to same.

14. Where any relief is sought which has not been specifically claimed, the Court may adjourn the proceeding to allow such amendments to the Family Law Summons as may be necessary and upon such terms and conditions as it seems fit.

15. (1) Where any action or proceeding is pending in the High Court which might have been commenced in the Circuit Court or the District Court any party to such action or proceeding may apply to the High Court that the action be remitted or transferred to the Circuit Court or the District Court (as the case may be) and if the High Court should, in the exercise of its discretion, consider such an order to be in the interests of justice it shall remit or transfer such action or proceeding to the Circuit Court or the District Court (as the case may be) to be prosecuted before the Judge assigned to such Circuit or (as the case may require) the Judge assigned to such District as may appear to the Court suitable and convenient, upon such terms and subject to such conditions as to costs or otherwise as may appear just.

(2) An application under this rule to remit or transfer an action or proceeding may be made at any time after an appearance has been entered.

16. The provisions of Order 49, rules 1, 2, 3 and 6 shall apply to any proceeding commenced under rule 2 above.

17. Any respondent in family law proceedings may counterclaim by way of a replying affidavit and such affidavit shall clearly set out the relief claimed and the grounds upon which it is claimed in like manner as if he were an applicant and subject to the provisions of this order.

18. In any proceeding which has been transferred to the High Court pursuant to section 31(3) of the 1989 Act, the applicant and the respondent shall each within fourteen days from the making of the order or such further time as the Master may allow, file in the Central Office an affidavit or supplemental affidavits as shall appear necessary to conform to the requirements of this order as if the proceeding had commenced in the High Court, together with a certified copy of the order transferring the same and the proceeding shall thereupon be listed for hearing.

19. An application by either spouse or on behalf of a dependent member pursuant to section 18 of the 1995 Act or section 22 of the 1996 Act shall be made to the Court by motion in the proceeding on notice to the party concerned and shall be supported by an affidavit verifying the same and shall set out fully how, when and in what respect circumstances have changed or what new evidence exists as a result of which the Court should vary or discharge or otherwise modify in any respect an order to which the section applies.

20. An application pursuant to section 35 of the 1995 Act or pursuant to section 37 of the 1996 Act may, at any time, be made to the Court by motion on notice in the proceeding to the party concerned and shall be supported by an affidavit verifying the facts alleged in relation to the disposition complained of and shall specify the relief claimed and the way in which the disposition is said to be intended to defeat the relief claimed or to affect it in any way and the Court may make such order upon such motion as appears proper in the circumstances and may, if necessary, adjourn the motion in order to give notice of the application to any party affected by the disposition complained of or the disposal of the property concerned.

21. An application pursuant to section 8 [of] the 1989 Act, for the rescission of a grant of a decree of judicial separation shall be preceded by a notice of re-entry which shall have been given at least one month before the date of the application and shall be grounded on an affidavit sworn by each of the spouses seeking such rescission which shall specify the nature and extent of the reconciliation including whether they have resumed cohabiting as husband and wife and shall also specify such necessary ancillary orders (if any) as they require the Court to make or to consider making in the circumstances.

Subsequent Ancillary Relief

22. Subsequent to the grant of a decree of judicial separation or of a decree of divorce any party who seeks any or any further ancillary relief under Part II of the 1995 Act or under Part III of the 1996 Act shall do so by notice of motion in the proceeding. Such notice shall be served on any party concerned and shall be grounded on the affidavit of the moving party. **J–410**

Service of Orders

23. In all cases in which the Registrar of the Court is required to serve or lodge a copy of an order upon any person or persons or body such service or lodgement may be effected by the service of a certified copy of the said order by registered post to the said person or persons or body. **J–411**

Adoption

24. (1) In any proceeding pursuant to section 3 of the Adoption Act, 1974 and upon the service of a summons on An Bord Uchtala, the Board shall take the following steps: **J–412**

(a) It shall cause the person who has agreed to the placing of the child, the subject matter of the application for adoption, to be informed of the following matters:-

   (i) the fact of the institution of the proceeding under section 3 of the Adoption Act, 1974 without revealing to such person the name or identity of the applicants;

  (ii) the fact that such person is entitled to be heard and represented upon the hearing of the summons.

(b) It shall ascertain from such person the following information:-

   (i) whether such person wishes to be heard and to be represented at the hearing of such summons;

  (ii) whether such person has available to him/her advice and is in a position from his/her own resources to be represented by solicitor or solicitor and counsel at the hearing of such summons;

 (iii) the address at which such person may be informed of the proceeding and in particular of the date of any hearing at which such person will be heard and represented.

(2) Upon the completion of the steps provided for in subrule (1) the Board shall apply by Motion on Notice to the applicants to the Court for directions. Such application shall, in the first instance, be made on affidavit and in the event that it has been possible to communicate with the person involved such affidavits shall include an affidavit by the servant or officer of the Board who has actually spoken to and had communication with such person. Such person shall not be identified in the body of the affidavit but the name and address present and future of such person shall be set out in a sealed envelope exhibited in such affidavit. Such exhibit shall be opened by the Judge only and unless by special direction of the Court the name, address and identity of such person shall not be revealed to any of the other parties in the suit.

(3) Upon the hearing of such motion for directions the Court may give such direction as it shall think fit for the hearing of the action and in particular may:-

(a) provide, if necessary, for the representation of such person;

(b) fix a date for the hearing *in camera* of the evidence and submissions on behalf of the applicants in the absence of such person but in the presence of the solicitor or solicitor and counsel representing such person;

(c) fix a separate date for the hearing *in camera* of the evidence and submissions by and on behalf of such person in the absence of the applicants but in the presence of the solicitor or solicitor and counsel for the applicants.

(4) If it is satisfied upon the affidavits supporting such motion or upon such further evidence, oral or otherwise, as may be adduced on behalf of the Board that it is not possible to ascertain the whereabouts of the person who has placed the child for adoption and that it is not possible to

J762

communicate with such person the Court may proceed to hear and determine the application without further notice to such person.

25. (1) In an application brought pursuant to section 3(1)(a) of the Adoption Act, 1988, the Health Board shall serve a copy of the summons on the applicants and shall verify by affidavit the reasons why it considers it proper to make the application.

(2) In any proceeding brought pursuant to section 3(1)(b) of the Adoption Act, 1988 the applicants shall serve a copy of the summons on the relevant Health Board and thereupon the Health Board shall verify by affidavit its reasons for (as the case may be):-

(i) declining to apply to the Court, or

(ii) failing to apply to the Court and failing to serve the notice required by section 3(1)(b)(i) of the Act.

Such affidavit shall be sworn by the Chief Executive Officer or by a Deputy Chief Executive Officer of the Board.

(3) In an application brought under subrule (1) or (2) above, the provisions of rule 24 relating to the steps to be taken by An Bord Uchtala shall apply *mutatis mutandis* to a Health Board in relation to the parents alleged to have failed in their duty to the child or children concerned.

26. (1) In an application to Court pursuant to section 6A or section 11(4) of the Guardianship of Infants Act, 1964 (as inserted by sections 12 and 13 of the Status of Children Act, 1987, respectively) where an infant is in the care of prospective adoptive parents under the Adoption Acts, 1952 and 1988, the following procedure shall be followed:

(1) Upon the service of a summons on An Bord Uchtala, the Board shall take the following steps:-

(a) It shall cause the prospective adoptive parents to be informed of the following matters:-

(i) the fact of the institution of the proceeding under section 6A or section 11(4) of the Guardianship of Infants Act, 1964 without revealing to such parents the name or identity of the applicant or of the natural mother;

(ii) the fact that such parents are entitled to be heard and represented upon the hearing of the summons.

(b) It shall ascertain from such parents the following information:-

(i) whether they wish to be heard and to be represented at the hearing of such summons;

(ii) whether they have available to them advice and are in a position from their own resources to be represented by solicitor or solicitor and counsel at the hearing of such summons;

(iii) the address at which they may be informed of the proceeding and in particular of the date of any hearing at which they will be heard and represented.

J763

(2) Upon the completion of the steps provided for in subrule (1) the Board shall apply by Motion on Notice to the father to the Court for directions. Such application shall, in the first instance, be made on affidavit and such affidavits shall include an affidavit by the person who has actually spoken to and had communication with such parents. Such parents shall not be identified in the body of the affidavit but their names and addressees present and future shall be set out in a sealed envelope exhibited in such affidavit. Such exhibit shall be opened by the Judge only, and unless by special direction of the Court the name, address and identity of such person shall not be revealed to any of the other parties in the suit.

(3) Upon the hearing of such motion for directions the Court may give such directions as it shall think fit for the trial of the action and in particular may:

(a) provide, if necessary, for the representation of such parents and of the father and mother of the child;

(b) fix a date for the hearing *in camera* of the evidence and submissions on behalf of the applicant and the natural mother in the absence of such parents but in the presence of the solicitor or solicitor and counsel representing such parents;

(c) fix a separate date for the hearing *in camera* of the evidence and submissions by and on behalf of such parents in the absence of the applicant and the natural mother but in the presence of the solicitor or the solicitor and counsel for the applicant and the natural mother.

27. An application to Court pursuant to section 6A(3) of the Guardianship of Infants Act, 1964 (as inserted by section 12 of the Status of Children Act, 1987) shall be by Motion on Notice to the mother and not by summons and shall be entitled in a similar manner as in rule 2 and shall be grounded on the affidavit of the father seeking to be appointed guardian. Such affidavit shall afford proof of the paternity of the said infant and shall exhibit the written consent of the mother to the appointment of the father as guardian (such consent having been witnessed by a registered medical practitioner or a solicitor) and a true copy of the Birth Certificate of the infant in respect of whom the father wishes to be appointed guardian. The Court may require such proof of paternity of an infant as it thinks fit.

28. The provisions of Order 119 rules 2 and 3 shall not apply to any cause, action or proceeding under Order 70 or Order 70A.

SCHEDULE OF FORMS

FORM NO. 1   **J–430**

THE HIGH COURT
FAMILY LAW

IN THE MATTER OF THE JUDICIAL SEPARATION AND FAMILY LAW REFORM ACT, 1989 AND IN THE MATTER OF THE FAMILY LAW ACT, 1995

BETWEEN/

A.B.

Applicant

-and-

C.D.

Respondent

CERTIFICATE PURSUANT TO SECTION 5 OF THE
JUDICIAL SEPARATION AND FAMILY LAW REFORM ACT, 1989

I,   , the Solicitor acting for the above Applicant do hereby certify as follows:-

1. I have discussed with the Applicant the possibility of reconciliation with the Respondent and I have given the Applicant the names and addresses of persons qualified to help effect a reconciliation between spouses who have become estranged.

2. I have discussed with the Applicant the possibility of engaging in mediation to help effect a separation on an agreed basis with the Respondent and I have given the Applicant the names and addresses of persons and organisations qualified to provide a mediation service.

3. I have discussed with the Applicant the possibility of effecting a separation by the negotiation and conclusion of a Separation Deed or written Separation Agreement with the Respondent.

Dated the   day of   , 19 .

Signed: . . . .
        Solicitor

Address:

J–431

FORM NO. 2

THE HIGH COURT
FAMILY LAW

IN THE MATTER OF THE JUDICIAL SEPARATION AND FAMILY LAW REFORM ACT, 1989 AND IN THE MATTER OF THE FAMILY LAW ACT, 1995

BETWEEN/

A.B.

Applicant

-and-

C.D.

Respondent

CERTIFICATE PURSUANT TO SECTION 6 OF THE
JUDICIAL SEPARATION AND FAMILY LAW REFORM ACT, 1989

I,   , the Solicitor acting for the above Respondent do hereby certify as follows:-

1. I have discussed with the Respondent the possibility of reconciliation with the Applicant and I have given the Respondent the names and addresses of persons qualified to help effect a reconciliation between spouses who have become estranged.

2. I have discussed with the Respondent the possibility of engaging in mediation to help effect a separation on an agreed basis with the Applicant and I have given the Respondent the names and addresses of persons and organisations qualified to provide a mediation service.

3. I have discussed with the Respondent the possibility of effecting a separation by the negotiation and conclusion of a Separation Deed or written Separation Agreement with the Applicant.

Dated the   day of   , 19   .

Signed: ....
        Solicitor

Address:

FORM NO. 3   J–432

THE HIGH COURT
FAMILY LAW

IN THE MATTER OF THE FAMILY LAW (DIVORCE) ACT, 1996

BETWEEN/

A.B.

Applicant

-and-

C.D.

Respondent

CERTIFICATE PURSUANT TO SECTION 6 OF THE
FAMILY LAW (DIVORCE) ACT, 1996

I,   , the Solicitor acting for the above Applicant do hereby certify as follows:-

1. I have discussed with the Applicant the possibility of reconciliation with the Respondent and I have given the Applicant the names and addresses of persons qualified to help effect a reconciliation between spouses who have become estranged.

[The following paragraphs to be inserted where appropriate].

2. I have discussed with the Applicant the possibility of engaging in mediation to help effect a separation on an agreed basis (the spouses the parties hereto not being separated) or a divorce on the basis agreed between the Applicant with the Respondent and I have given the Applicant the names and addresses of persons and organisations qualified to provide a mediation service for spouses who have become estranged.

3. I have discussed with the Applicant the possibility of effecting a separation by the negotiation and conclusion of a Separation Deed or written Separation Agreement with the Respondent.

4. I have ensured that the Applicant is aware of judicial separation as an alternative to divorce, no decree of judicial separation in relation to the Applicant and the Respondent being in force.

Dated the   day of   , 19 .

Signed: . . . .
        Solicitor

Address:

J–433

FORM NO. 4

THE HIGH COURT
FAMILY LAW

IN THE MATTER OF THE FAMILY LAW (DIVORCE) ACT, 1996

BETWEEN/

A.B.

Applicant

-and-

C.D.

Respondent

CERTIFICATE PURSUANT TO SECTION 7 OF THE
FAMILY LAW (DIVORCE) ACT, 1996

I,   , the Solicitor acting for the above Respondent
do hereby certify as follows:—

1. I have discussed with the Respondent the possibility of reconciliation with
the Applicant and I have given the Respondent the names and addresses of
persons qualified to help effect a reconciliation between spouses who have
become estranged.

[The following paragraphs to be inserted where appropriate].

2. I have discussed with the Respondent the possibility of engaging in
mediation to help effect a separation on an agreed basis (the spouses the
parties hereto not being separated) or a divorce on the basis agreed between
the Respondent with the Applicant and I have given the Respondent the names
and addresses of persons and organisations qualified to provide a mediation
service for spouses who have become estranged.

3. I have discussed with the Respondent the possibility of effecting a separation
by the negotiation and conclusion of a Separation Deed or written Separation
Agreement with the Applicant.

4. I have ensured that the Respondent is aware of judicial separation as an
alternative to divorce, no decree of judicial separation in relation to the
Respondent and the Applicant being in force.

Dated the   day of   , 19 .

Signed: . . . .
        Solicitor

Address:

FORM NO. 5   **J–434**

THE HIGH COURT
FAMILY LAW

[Insert as appropriate]

IN THE MATTER OF THE JUDICIAL SEPARATION AND FAMILY LAW
REFORM ACT, 1989
IN THE MATTER OF THE FAMILY LAW ACT, 1995
IN THE MATTER OF THE FAMILY LAW (DIVORCE) ACT, 1996

BETWEEN/

A.B.
Applicant

-and-

C.D.
Respondent

AFFIDAVIT OF MEANS

I,   , [insert occupation],
of   , aged 18 years and upwards MAKE OATH
and say as follows:-

1. I say that I am the Applicant/Respondent [DELETE AS APPROPRIATE] in the above entitled proceedings and I make this Affidavit from facts within my own knowledge save where otherwise appears and where so appearing I believe the same to be true.

2. I say that I have set out in the First Schedule hereto all the assets to which I am legally or beneficially entitled and the manner in which such property is held.

3. I say that I have set out in the Second Schedule hereto all income which I receive and the source(s) of such income.

4. I say that I have set out in the Third Schedule hereto all my debts and/or liabilities and the persons to whom such debts and liabilities are due.

5. I say that my weekly out goings amount to the sum of £   and I say that the details of such out goings have been set out in the Fourth Schedule hereto.

6. I say that to the best of my knowledge, information and belief, all pension information known to me relevant to the within proceedings is set out in the Fifth Schedule hereto. [Where information has been obtained from the trustees of the pension scheme concerned under the Pensions Act, 1990, such information should be exhibited and where such information has not been obtained, the Deponent should depose to the reason(s) why such information has not been obtained].

First Schedule

[Here set out in numbered paragraphs all assets whether held in the Applicant/Respondent's sole name or jointly with another, whether held legally or beneficially, the manner in which the assets are held, whether they are subject to a mortgage or other charge or lien and such further and other details as are appropriate].

Second Schedule

[Here set out in numbered paragraphs all income from whatever source(s)].

J769

Third Schedule

[Here set out in numbered paragraphs all debts and/or liabilities and the persons/ institutions to which such debts and/or liabilities are due].

Fourth Schedule

[Here set out full details of weekly personal outgoings].

Fifth Schedule

[Here full details of nature of pension scheme, benefits payable thereunder, normal pensionable age and period of reckonable service should be listed to the best of the Deponent's knowledge, information and belief].

SWORN etc.

FORM NO. 6   **J–435**

THE HIGH COURT
FAMILY LAW

[Insert as appropriate]
IN THE MATTER OF THE JUDICIAL SEPARATION AND FAMILY LAW
REFORM ACT, 1989
IN THE MATTER OF THE FAMILY LAW ACT, 1995
IN THE MATTER OF THE FAMILY LAW (DIVORCE) ACT, 1996

BETWEEN/

A.B.
                                                              Applicant
-and-

C.D.
                                                              Respondent

AFFIDAVIT OF WELFARE

I,   , [insert occupation],
of   , aged 18 years and upwards MAKE OATH and say as follows:

1. I say that I am the Applicant/Respondent [DELETE AS APPROPRIATE]
in the above entitled proceedings and I make this Affidavit from facts within
my own knowledge save where otherwise appears and where so appearing I
believe the same to be true.

2. I say and believe that the facts set out in the Schedule hereto are true.

[In circumstances in which the Respondent does not dispute the facts deposed
to by the Applicant in his/her Affidavit of Welfare, the following averment shall
be included, replacing paragraph 2 hereof, and in such circumstances, the
Schedule shall not be completed by the Respondent:

2. I say that I am fully in agreement with the facts as averred to by the
Applicant in his/her Affidavit of Welfare sworn herein on the
day of   19   and I say and believe that the facts set out in
the Schedule hereto are true].

FLP R.1: January 2001

SCHEDULE

Part 1–details of the children

1. Details of children born to the Applicant and the Respondent or adopted by both the Applicant and the Respondent.

Forenames   Surname   Date of Birth

2. Details of other children of the family or to which the parents or either of them are in loco parentis

Forenames   Surname   Date of Birth   Relationship to
                                                           Applicant/Respondent

Part II–Arrangements for the children of the family

3. Home details

    (a) The address or addresses at which the children now live.

    (b) Give details of the number of living rooms, bedrooms, etc., at the addresses in (a) above.

    (c) Is the house rented or owned and, if so, name the tenant(s) or owner(s).

    (d) Is the rent or mortgage being regularly paid and, if so, by whom?

    (e) Give the name of all other persons living with the children either on a full-time or part-time basis and state their relationship to the children, if any.

    (f) Will there be any change in these arrangements and, if so, give details.

Part III–Education and Training Details

    (a) Give the names of the school, college or place of training attended by each child.

    (b) Do the children have any special educational needs. If so, please specify.

    (c) Is the school, college or place of training fee paying. If so, give details of how much the fees are per term/year. Are fees regularly paid and, if so, by whom?

    (d) Will there by any change in these circumstances? If so, give details.

Part IV–Childcare Details

    (a) Which parent looks after the children from day to day? If responsibility is shared, please give details.

    (b) Give details of work commitments of both parents.

    (c) Does someone look after the children when the parent is not there? If yes, give details.

    (d) Who looks after the children during school holidays?

    (e) Will there be any change in these arrangements? If yes, give details.

Part V–Maintenance

    (a) Does the Applicant/Respondent pay towards the upkeep of the children? If yes, give details. Please specify any other source of maintenance.

    (b) Is the maintenance referred to at (a) above paid under court order? If yes, give details.

    (c) Has maintenance for the children been agreed? If yes, give details.

J772

(d) If not, will you be applying for a maintenance order from the Court?

Part VI–Details of Contact with the Children

(a) Do the children see the Applicant/Respondent? Please give details.
(b) Do the children stay overnight and/or have holiday visits with the Applicant/Respondent? Please give details.
(c) Will there be any change to these arrangements? Please give details.

Part VII–Details of Health

(a) Are the children generally in good health? Please give details of any serious disability or chronic illness suffered by any of the children.
(b) Do the children or any of them have any special health needs? Please give details of the care needed and how it is to be provided.
(c) Are the Applicant or Respondent generally in good health? If not, please give details.

Part VIII–Details of Care and Other Court Proceedings

(a) Are the children or any of them in the care of a health board or under the supervision of a social worker or probation officer? If so, please specify.
(b) Are there or have there been any proceeding in any Court involving the children or any of them? If so, please specify. (All relevant court orders relating to the children or any of them should be annexed hereto).

Part IX–Declaration

I, _____, Applicant/Respondent [delete as appropriate], declare that the information I have given herein is correct and complete to the best of my knowledge.

Signed: _____

                Applicant/Respondent

Witnessed: _____

Date: _____

Part X–Agreement of Respondent (where applicable)

I, _____, Respondent, declare that the information given by the Applicant herein is correct and complete to the best of my knowledge and I agree with the arrangements and proposals contained herein.

Signed: _____

                Respondent

Witnessed: _____

Date: _____

FLP R.1: January 2001

J–436

FORM NO. 7

THE HIGH COURT
FAMILY LAW

[Insert as appropriate]
IN THE MATTER OF THE JUDICIAL SEPARATION AND FAMILY LAW
REFORM ACT, 1989
IN THE MATTER OF THE FAMILY LAW ACT, 1995
IN THE MATTER OF THE FAMILY LAW (DIVORCE) ACT, 1996

BETWEEN/

A.B.

Applicant

- and -

C.D.

Respondent

NOTICE TO TRUSTEES

TAKE NOTICE that relief has been claimed by the Applicant/Respondent in the
above entitled proceedings pursuant to section(s) 12 and/or 13 of the Family Law
Act, 1995 or section 17 of the Family Law (Divorce) Act, 1996 or section 8B of the
Family Law (Maintenance of Spouses) Act, 1976 and in particular in relation to
.... [here insert details of pension in respect of which relief is
claimed].

AND FURTHER TAKE NOTICE that any representations to be made to the
Court pursuant to section 12(18) or section 13(2) of the 1995 Act or section 17(18)
of the 1996 Act may be made by way of Affidavit of Representation to be filed and
served on all parties herein within 28 days of the date of service of this Notice upon
you.

Dated the   day of   19   .

Signed: _____
             Solicitors for the Applicant/Respondent

To: The County Registrar
and
To: The Trustees of the pension scheme concerned
and
To: Applicant/Respondent [or solicitors where appropriate].

FLP R.1: January 2001

S.I. No. 84 of 1997

CIRCUIT COURT RULES (No. 1) 1997 (JUDICIAL SEPARATION AND FAMILY LAW REFORM ACT, 1989 AND FAMILY LAW ACT, 1995 AND FAMILY LAW (DIVORCE) ACT, 1996)

*This statutory instrument is due to be amended. The amendments will be examined and included in a future release.

1. These Rules may be cited as the Circuit Court Rules (No. 1), 1997 **J–450** and shall come into operation on the 27th day of February, 1997.

2. The Order referred to in these Rules shall be added to and construed together with those orders contained in the Circuit Court Rules, 1950, as amended.

ORDER 78

JUDICIAL SEPARATION AND FAMILY LAW REFORM ACT, 1989 AND FAMILY LAW ACT, 1995 AND FAMILY LAW (DIVORCE) ACT, 1996

Introduction, Substitution and Revocation

1. In this Order "the 1996 Act" means the Family Law (Divorce) Act, **J–451** 1996 (No. 33 of 1996) and "the 1995 Act" means the Family Law Act, 1995 (No. 26 of 1995) and "the 1989 Act" means the Judicial Separation and Family Law Reform Act, 1989 (No. 6 of 1989). These Rules shall be substituted for the Rules contained in Circuit Court Rules (No. 1) of 1989 (S.I. No. 289 of 1989) and Circuit Court Rules (No. 1) of 1994 (S.I. 225 of 1994) which are hereby revoked, subject only to the provisions contained in Rule 2 hereof.

Transitional

2. All applications made or proceedings taken before these Rules shall **J–452** have come into operation but which are in accordance with the then existing Rules and practice of the Court shall have the same validity as applications made or proceedings taken in accordance with these Rules.

Venue

3. Any proceedings under this Order shall be brought in the County **J–453** where any party to the proceedings ordinarily resides or carries on any profession, business or occupation.

Commencement

4. (*a*) All proceedings for divorce, judicial separation, relief after **J–454** foreign divorce or separation outside the State, nullity, declarations of marital status, the determination of property issues

J775

between spouses pursuant to section 36 of the 1995 Act/ formerly engaged couples pursuant to section 44 of the 1996 Act and relief pursuant to section 25 of the 1995 Act, section 18 of the 1996 Act or section 15A of the 1995 Act under this Order, shall be instituted by the issuing out of the Office of the County Registrar for the appropriate County (hereinafter referred to as "the appropriate Office") of the appropriate Family Law Civil Bill in the format and manner hereinafter provided save that no Family Law Civil Bill for relief after foreign divorce or separation outside the State shall be issued until requirements set down in Rule 4(b) of these Rules have been complied with. Upon issue, the Family Law Civil Bill shall be served in a manner provided for hereunder.

(b) No proceedings for a relief order after foreign divorce or separation outside the State shall issue without the leave of the appropriate Court in accordance with section 23(3) of the 1995 Act. Such application for leave to issue proceedings shall be made *ex parte* by way of *ex parte* docket grounded upon the Affidavit of the Applicant or another appropriate person. The aforementioned Affidavit shall exhibit a draft of the Family Law Civil Bill for relief after divorce or separation outside the State which the Applicant seeks leave to issue as well as the foreign divorce or separation decree, shall set forth fully the reasons why relief is being sought and shall make specific averment to the fact that, to the knowledge, information and belief of the Applicant, the jurisdictional requirements of section 27 of the 1995 Act are complied with in the particular case, specifying the particular basis of jurisdiction being relied upon.

Form of proceedings

J–455   5. Every Family Law Civil Bill shall be in numbered paragraphs setting out the relief sought and the grounds relied upon in support of the application. The Civil Bill shall be in accordance with the form set out in Form 1 herein or such modification thereof as may be appropriate, subject to the requirements hereinafter set out.

(a) A Family Law Civil Bill for a Decree of Divorce shall, in all cases, include the following details:
(i) the date and place of marriage of the parties;
(ii) the length of time the parties have lived apart, including the date upon which the parties commenced living apart, and the addresses of both of the parties during that time, where known;
(iii) details of any previous matrimonial relief sought and/or obtained and details of any previous separation agreement entered into between the parties (where appropriate a certified copy of any relevant court order and/or deed of separation/ separation agreement should be annexed to the Civil Bill);

(iv) the names and ages and dates of birth of any dependent children of the marriage;

(v) details of the family home(s) and/or other residences of the parties including, if relevant, details of any former family home/residence to include details of the manner of occupation/ownership thereof;

(vi) where reference is made in the Civil Bill to any immovable property, whether it is registered or unregistered land and a description of the land/premises so referred to;

(vii) the basis of jurisdiction under the 1996 Act;

(viii) the occupation(s) of each party;

(ix) the grounds relied upon for the relief sought;

(x) each section of the 1996 Act under which relief is sought.

(b) A Family Law Civil Bill for a Decree of Judicial Separation shall, in all cases, include the following details:

(i) the date and place of marriage of the parties;

(ii) the names and ages and dates of birth of any dependent children of the marriage;

(iii) details of the family home(s) and/or other residences of the parties including, if relevant, details of any former family home/residence to include details of the manner of occupation/ownership thereof;

(iv) where reference is made in the Civil Bill to any immovable property, whether it is registered or unregistered land and a description of the land/premises so referred to;

(v) the basis of jurisdiction under the Act;

(vi) the occupation(s) of each party;

(vii) the grounds relied upon for the decree and any other relief sought;

(viii) each section of the Act under which relief is sought including whether or not an Order pursuant to section 54(3) of the 1995 Act is sought.

(c) A Family Law Civil Bill for relief after foreign divorce or separation outside the State pursuant to section 23 of the 1995 Act shall, in all cases, include the following details:

(i) the date and place of marriage and divorce/separation of the parties (a certified copy of the decree absolute or final decree of divorce/separation together with, where appropriate an authenticated translation thereof shall be annexed to the Family Law Civil Bill);

(ii) financial and property and custodial/access arrangements operating ancillary to the said decree, whether such arrangements were made by agreement or by Order of the Court or otherwise and whether such arrangements were made contemporaneous to the decree or at another time and the extent of compliance therewith;

(iii) the names and ages and dates of birth of any dependent children of the marriage;

    (iv) details of the family home(s) and/or other residences of the parties including, if relevant, details of any former family home/residence to include details of the manner of occupation/ownership thereof;

    (v) where reference is made in the Civil Bill to any immovable property within the State, whether it is registered or unregistered land and a description of the land/premises so referred to;

   (vi) the basis of jurisdiction under section 27 of the 1995 Act;

  (vii) the present marital status and occupation(s) of each party;

 (viii) the grounds relied upon for the relief sought;

   (ix) each section of the 1995 Act under which relief is sought;

    (x) details relevant to the matters referred to in section 26 of the 1995 Act.

(d) A Family Law Civil Bill for nullity shall, in all cases, include the following details:

    (i) the date and place of marriage of the parties;

   (ii) the domicile of the spouses on the date of the marriage and on the date of the institution of proceedings and, where either spouse has died prior to the institution of proceedings, the domicile of the said spouse at the date of death;

  (iii) whether or not the spouses or either of them has been ordinarily resident in the State throughout the period of one year prior to the date of institution of proceedings and, where either spouse has died prior to the institution of proceedings, whether or not the said spouse was ordinarily resident in the State throughout the period of one year prior to his/her death;

  (iv) the address and description of each party;

   (v) the number of children of the marriage;

  (vi) the grounds upon which the decree and any other relief is sought;

  (vii) the relief sought (including whether or not a declaration relating to the custody of a dependent member of the family pursuant to section 46 of the 1995 Act is being sought) and the issues to be tried.

(e) A Family Law Civil Bill for Declaration of Marital Status shall, in all cases, include the following details:

    (i) the nature of the Applicant's reason for seeking such a declaration;

   (ii) full details of the marriage/divorce/annulment/ legal separation in respect of which the declaration is sought including the date and place of such marriage/divorce/annulment/legal separation (where possible, a certified copy of the marriage certificate/decree of divorce/annulment/legal separation should be annexed to the Civil Bill);

  (iii) the manner in which the jurisdictional requirements of section 29(2) of the 1995 Act are satisfied;

  (iv) particulars of any previous or pending proceedings in relation to any marriage concerned or to the matrimonial status of a party to any such marriage in accordance with section 30 of the 1995 Act;

(v) the relief being sought;

(vi) any other relevant facts.

(f) A Family Law Civil Bill for the determination of property issues between spouses, pursuant to section 36 of the 1995 Act/formerly engaged couples, pursuant to section 44 of the 1996 Act, shall, in all cases, include the following details:

(i) the description, nature and extent of the disputed property or monies:

(ii) the state of knowledge of the Applicant spouse in relation to possession and control of the disputed property or monies at all relevant times;

(iii) the nature and extent of the interest being claimed by the Applicant in the property or monies and the basis upon which such a claim is made;

(iv) the nature and extent of any claim for relief being made and the basis upon which any such claim for relief is being made;

(v) where reference is made in the Civil Bill to any immovable property, whether it is registered or unregistered land and a description of the land/premises so referred to;

(vi) the manner in which it is claimed that the Respondent spouse has failed, neglected or refused to make to the Applicant spouse such appropriate payment or disposition in all of the circumstances and details of any payment or disposition made;

(vii) that the time limits referred to at section 36(7) of the 1995 Act have been complied with;

(viii) any other relevant matters.

(g) A Family Law Civil Bill for relief pursuant to section 18 of the Family Law (Divorce) Act, 1996 or section 15A or section 25 of the Family Law Act, 1995 shall, in all cases include the following details:

(i) the date and place of marriage and the date of any decree of divorce/judicial separation and the marriage certificate and a certified copy of the decree of divorce/separation shall be annexed to the Civil Bill (with authenticated translations, where appropriate);

(ii) details of previous matrimonial relief obtained by the Applicant and in particular lump sum maintenance orders and property adjustment orders, if any;

(iii) details of any benefits previously received from or on behalf of the deceased spouse whether by way of agreement or otherwise and details of any benefits accruing to the Applicant under the terms of the Will of the deceased spouse or otherwise;

(iv) the date of death of the deceased spouse, the date on which representation was first granted in respect of the estate of the said spouse and, if applicable, the date upon which notice of the death of the deceased spouse was given to the Applicant spouse and the date upon which the Applicant spouse notified the personal representative of his/her intention to apply for relief pursuant to section 18(7) of the 1996 Act and section 15A(7) of the 1995 Act;

(v) the nature and extent of any claim for relief being made and the basis upon which any such claim for relief is being made;

(vi) the marital status of the deceased spouse at the date of death and the marital status of the Applicant at the date of the application and whether the Applicant has remarried since the dissolution of the marriage between the Applicant and the deceased spouse;

(vii) details of all dependents of the deceased spouse at the date of death and of all dependents of the Applicant at the date of the application together with details of any other interested persons;

(viii) that no Order pursuant to section 18(10) of the 1996 Act or section 15A(10) of the 1995 Act has previously been made;

(ix) details of the value of the estate of the deceased spouse, where known;

(x) any other relevant facts.

Applications pursuant to section 15A(6) or section 25(7) of the 1995 Act or section 18(6) of the 1996 Act by the personal representative in relation to the distribution of the estate shall be by motion, grounded on Affidavit, on notice to the Applicant spouse and such other persons as the Court shall direct.

6. All Family Law Civil Bills shall be dated and shall bear the name, address and description of the Applicant and an address for service of proceedings, and shall be signed by the party's solicitor, if any, or, where the Applicant does not have a solicitor, by that party personally. The address to which a Respondent should apply in order to receive information in relation to legal aid shall also be included in such Civil Bills.

Issuing and Entry

J–456   **7.** On the issuing of a Family Law Civil Bill the original thereof shall be filed, together with the appropriate certificate (pursuant to section 5 of the 1989 Act or section 6 of the 1996 Act), an Affidavit of Means in the intended action sworn by the Applicant in compliance with Rules 18 and 19 hereof and, in all circumstances where there are dependent children, an Affidavit of Welfare in the intended action in compliance with Rule 20 hereof, and the County Registrar shall thereupon enter same.

Service

J–457   **8.**   (a) All Family Law Civil Bills shall be served by registered post on the Respondent at his/her last known address or alternatively shall be served personally on the Respondent by any person over the age of eighteen years together with the appropriate certificate in the form set out in Forms 7 and 9 herein (pursuant to section 5 of the 1989 Act or section 6 of the 1996 Act), an Affidavit of Means in compliance with Rules 18 and 19 hereof in the form set out in Form 2 herein or such modification thereof as may be appropriate and in all cases where there are dependent children, an Affidavit of Welfare in compliance with Rule 20 hereof in the form set out in Form 3 herein. Where relief pursuant to section 12 and/or section 13 of the 1995 Act or section 17 of the 1996 Act is sought, notice thereof in accordance with Form 4 herein shall also be served on the trustees of the pension scheme in question by registered post at their registered office or other appropriate address and an Affidavit of such service shall be sworn and filed within fourteen days of service of the Civil Bill. Service shall be endorsed upon all Family Law Civil Bills in accordance with the provisions of Order 10, Rule 22 of the Circuit Court Rules, 1950, as amended. All other pleadings may be served by ordinary pre-paid post.

(*b*) In all cases in which a declaration of marital status under section 29 of the 1995 Act is sought, the Family Law Civil Bill shall, in addition to the provisions of Rule 8(a) hereof, be served upon the parties to the marriage or, where no longer living, their personal representatives (all of whom shall be parties to the proceedings) and to such other persons as the Court may direct, including the Attorney General, in accordance with the provisions as to service of Family Law Civil Bills hereinbefore set out in respect of the Respondent to proceedings which said persons (excepting the Attorney General) may be made parties to the application in accordance with section 29(6) of the 1995 Act. The Attorney General shall, however, be entitled to interplead in such proceedings.

(*c*) Where relief is sought pursuant to sections 15A or 25 of the 1995 Act or section 18 of the 1996 Act, the Family Law Civil Bill shall be served in accordance with these Rules on the personal representative of the deceased and on the spouse (if any) of the deceased and on such other person or persons as the Court shall direct.

Appearance

9. If a Respondent intends to contest the application, or participate in J–458 proceedings, or any part thereof, he/she shall enter an Appearance in the Office within 10 days of the service upon him/her of the Family Law Civil Bill and shall serve a copy of the Appearance on the Applicant's solicitors or, where appropriate, on the Applicant. The Appearance shall bear an address for service of any interlocutory applications and shall be signed by the Respondent's solicitor or, if the Respondent does not have a solicitor, by the Respondent personally.

Defence

J–459   10. (*a*) A Respondent shall at the same time as entering an Appearance, or within 10 clear days from the date of service of the Appearance, or such further time as may be agreed between the parties or allowed by the Court, file and serve a Defence, together with the appropriate certificate in the form set out in Forms 8 and 10 herein (pursuant to section 6 of the 1989 Act and section 7 of the 1996 Act), an Affidavit of Means in compliance with Rules 18 and 19 hereof and, in all cases where there are dependent children, an Affidavit of Welfare in compliance with Rule 20 hereof in the form set out in Form 3 herein, on the Applicant, or the Applicant's solicitor, if any, and on the County Registrar in the form set out in Form 2 herein or such modification thereof as may be appropriate. Where relief pursuant to section 12 and/or section 13 of the 1995 Act or section 17 of the 1996 Act is sought by way of Counterclaim, notice thereof in accordance with Form 4 herein shall also be served on the trustees of the pension scheme in question by registered post at their registered office and an Affidavit of such service shall be sworn and filed within 7 days of service of the Defence and Counterclaim.

(*b*) No Appearance or Defence shall be entered after the time specified in these Rules without the leave of the Court or of the County Registrar or the agreement of the parties, and no Defence shall be entered unless the Respondent has previously entered an Appearance as required by these Rules.

(*c*) Whether or not a Defence is filed and served in any proceedings, the Respondent shall, where appropriate, in any event be obliged to file and serve an Affidavit of Means and a Welfare Statement in accordance with these Rules of Court within 20 days after the service of the Family Law Civil Bill upon him/her subject to Rule 36 hereof.

(*d*) Without prejudice to the entitlement of the Court to permit representations in relation to the making or refusal of an attachment of earnings order at the hearing of the action, such representations for the purposes of section 8(6)(*b*) of the 1995 Act or section 13(6)(*b*) of the 1996 Act may be included in the Defence and for the purposes of section 10(3)(*a*) of the Family Law (Maintenance of Spouses and Children) Act, 1976 may be included in the Answer provided for by Rule 15 of the Circuit Court Rules (No. 6) of 1982 (S.I. No. 158 of 1982) and Form 9 scheduled thereto.

Motions for Judgment

J–460   11. (*a*) In any case in which a Respondent has made default in entering an Appearance or filing a Defence, as the case may be, the Applicant may, subject to the provisions of the following sub-rules of this Rule, at any time after such default, on notice to be served on the Respondent and, where relief pursuant to section 12 and/or 13 of the 1995 Act and section 17 of the 1996 Act is sought, on the trustees of the pension scheme concerned, not less than fourteen clear days before the hearing, apply to the Court for judgment in default of appearance/defence.

(b) No notice of motion for Judgment in default of defence shall be served unless the Applicant has, at least fourteen days prior to the service of such notice, written to the Respondent giving him/her notice of his/her intention to serve a notice of motion for Judgment in default of appearance/defence and at the same time consenting to the late filing of a Defence within fourteen days from the date of the letter.

(c) If no defence is delivered within the said period the Applicant shall be at liberty to serve a notice of motion for Judgment in default of defence which shall be returnable to a date not less than fourteen clear days from the date of the service of the notice, such notice of motion to be filed not later than six days before the return date.

(d) If, not later than seven days after the service of such notice of motion for Judgment in default of appearance/defence, the defendant delivers a Defence to the Applicant and not less than six days before the return date lodges a copy thereof in the appropriate Office with a certified copy of the said notice of motion attached thereto, the said motion for Judgment shall not be put in the Judge's List but shall stand struck out and the Respondent shall pay to the Applicant the appropriate sum for his/her costs of the said motion for Judgment.

(e) If in any case the Applicant can establish special reasons for making it necessary to serve a notice of motion for Judgment in default of appearance/defence in the cases provided for by this Rule with greater urgency than in accordance with the provisions hereinbefore contained, he/she may apply ex parte to the Court or the County Registrar for an Order giving him/her liberty to serve a notice of motion for Judgment in default of appearance/defence giving not less than four clear days' notice to the Respondent, or in the alternative the Judge or the County Registrar may deem good the service of a Notice of Motion giving not less than four clear days' notice to the Respondent.

(f) Upon the hearing of such application the Court may, on proof of such default as aforesaid, and upon hearing such evidence, oral or otherwise, as may be adduced, give judgment upon the Applicant's claim endorsed upon the Family Law Civil Bill, or may give leave to the Respondent to defend the whole or part of the claim upon such terms as he or she may consider just.

(g) Upon the hearing of an application for judgment under this Order the Court may make such order as to costs as the Court considers just.

(*h*) In any case in which the parties are agreed in respect of all of the reliefs being sought and a Defence in accordance with Rule 10 hereof has been filed and served by the Respondent which reflects this agreement, the Applicant or the Respondent may, subject to the provisions of the following sub-rules of this Rule, at any time after such Defence has been filed and served, on notice to be served on the other party and, where relief pursuant to section 12 and/or 13 of the 1995 Act and section 17 of the 1996 Act is sought, on the trustees of the pension scheme concerned, not less than fourteen clear days before the hearing, apply to the Court for judgment, the application to be by way of motion on notice.

(*i*) Upon the hearing of such application the Court may, upon hearing such evidence, oral or otherwise, as may be adduced
  (i) give judgment in the terms agreed between the parties or,
  (ii) give such directions in relation to the service of a Notice of Trial/Notice to fix a date for Trial as to the Court appears just.

(*j*) Upon the hearing of an application for judgment under this Order the Court may make such order as to costs as the Court considers just.

Notice of trial/Notice to fix a date for trial

J–461   12. Subject to Rule 11(*h*), (*i*) and (*j*) herein, when a Defence has been duly entered and served, the Applicant may serve a notice of trial or a notice to fix a date for trial, as appropriate.

Notice of trial (Circuits other than Dublin Circuit)

J–462   13. Not less than ten days' notice of trial shall be served upon the Respondent and all other necessary parties and, where relief is sought under sections 12 and/or 13 of the 1995 Act or section 17 of the 1996 Act, upon the trustees of the pension scheme in question, and shall be for the Sittings next ensuing after the expiration of the time mentioned in the said notice, and same shall be filed at the appropriate Office not later than seven days before the opening of such Sittings. Such notice of trial and filing thereof shall operate to set down the action or matter (including Counterclaim if any) for hearing at the next ensuing Sittings. This Rule shall not apply to the Dublin Circuit.

Notice to fix a date for trial (Dublin Circuit)

J–463   14. This Rule shall apply only to the Dublin Circuit. Ten days' notice to fix a date for trial shall be necessary and sufficient and shall be served upon the Respondent and all other necessary parties and, where relief is sought under sections 12 and/or 13 of the 1995 Act or section 17 of the 1996 Act, upon the trustees of the pension scheme in question, and filed at the appropriate Office. Such notice to fix a date for a trial shall set out the date upon which a date for hearing shall be fixed by the County Registrar and shall operate to set down the action or matter (including a Counterclaim if any) for hearing upon such date as may be fixed by the County Registrar. A notice to fix a date for trial shall be in accordance with Form 5 herein.

Service by Respondent

15. Where the Applicant has failed to serve a notice of trial or notice to fix a date for trial, as appropriate, within ten days after the service and entry of the Defence, the Respondent may do so and may file the same in accordance with these Rules. **J–464**

Joinder

16. The Court, if it considers it desirable, may order that two or more actions be tried together, and on such terms as to costs as the Court shall deem just. **J–465**

Affidavits of Representation

17. (*a*) Save where the Court shall otherwise direct, any notice party, including the trustees of a pension scheme, who wishes to make representations to the Court pursuant to section 12(18) and/or section 13(2) of the 1995 Act or section 17(18) of the 1996 Act shall make such representations by Affidavit of Representation to be filed and served on all parties to the proceedings within 28 days of service upon them of notice of the application for relief under section 12 and/or 13 of the 1995 Act or section 17 of the 1996 Act in accordance with Rules 8 and 10 hereof or within such time or in such manner as the Court may direct. **J–466**

(*b*) Without prejudice to the entitlement of the Court to permit representations by persons having a beneficial interest in property (not being the other spouse) pursuant to section 15(5) of the 1995 Act and section 19(5) of the 1996 Act or by interested persons pursuant to section 15A(5) or section 25(6) of the 1995 Act and section 18(5) of the 1996 Act at the hearing of the action, such representations may be made by way of Affidavit of Representation to be filed and served on all parties to the proceedings as directed by the Court.

Affidavit of Means

18. Without prejudice to the right of each party to make application to the Court for an Order of Discovery pursuant to the Rules of this Honourable Court and without prejudice to the jurisdiction of the Court pursuant to section 12(25) of the 1995 Act and section 17(25) of the 1996 Act, in any case where financial relief under the Acts is sought, the parties shall file Affidavits of Means in accordance with Rules 7 and 10 hereof in respect of which the following Rules shall be applicable— **J–467**

(*a*) either party may request the other party to vouch any or all items referred to therein within 14 days of the request;

(b) in the event of a party failing to properly comply with the provisions in relation to the filing and serving of Affidavits of Means as set down in these Rules or failing to properly vouch the matters set out therein the Court may on application grant an Order for Discovery and/or may make such Orders as the Court deems appropriate and necessary (including an Order that such party shall not be entitled to pursue or defend as appropriate such claim for any ancillary reliefs under the Acts save as permitted by the Court upon such terms as the Court may determine are appropriate and/or adjourning the proceedings for a specified period of time to enable compliance) and furthermore and/or in the alternative relief pursuant to section 38(8) of the 1995 Act or section 38(7) of the 1996 Act may be sought in accordance with Rule 24 hereof.

19. The Affidavit of Means shall set out in schedule form details of the party's income, assets, debts, expenditure and other liabilities wherever situated and from whatever source and, to the best of the deponent's knowledge, information and belief the income, assets, debts, expenditure and other liabilities wherever situated and from whatever source of any dependent member of the family and shall be in accordance with the form set out in Form 2 herein or such modification thereof as may be appropriate. Where relief pursuant to section 12 of the 1995 Act is sought, the Affidavit of Means shall also state to the best of the deponent's knowledge, information and belief, the nature of the scheme, the benefits payable thereunder, the normal pensionable age and the period of reckonable service of the member spouse and where information relating to the pension scheme has been obtained from the trustees of the scheme under the Pensions Acts 1990–1996, such information should be exhibited in the Affidavit of Means and where such information has not been obtained a specific averment shall be included in the Affidavit of Means as to why such information has not been obtained.

Affidavit of Welfare

J–468   **20.** An Affidavit of Welfare shall be in the form set out in Form 3 herein. In circumstances in which the Respondent agrees with the facts as averred to in the Affidavit of Welfare filed and served by the Applicant, the Respondent may file and serve an Affidavit of Welfare in the alternative form provided for in Form 3 herein. In circumstances in which the Respondent disagrees with the Affidavit of Welfare filed and served by the Applicant, a separate Affidavit of Welfare, including the schedule provided for in the form set out in Form 3 herein shall be sworn, filed and served by the Respondent in accordance with Rule 10 hereof.

Counterclaims

J–469   **21.** Save where otherwise directed by the Court, a Counterclaim, if any, brought by a Respondent shall be included in and served with the Defence, in accordance with the provisions of these Rules relating thereto, and shall, in particular, set out in numbered paragraphs

(a) in the case of an application for a decree of divorce
  (i) the facts specified at Rule 5(a) hereof in like manner as in the Family Law Civil Bill;
  (ii) outline the ground(s) for a decree of divorce, if sought;
  (iii) specify any ground upon which the Respondent intends to rely in support of any ancillary relief claimed; and
  (iv) the relief sought pursuant to the 1996 Act;
(b) in the case of an application for a decree of judicial separation
  (i) the facts specified at Rule 5(b) hereof in like manner as in the Family Law Civil Bill;
  (ii) outline the ground(s) for a decree of judicial separation, if sought;
  (iii) specify any additional ground upon which the Respondent intends to rely in support of any ancillary relief claimed; and
  (iv) the relief sought pursuant to the 1995 Act;
(c) in the case of an application for relief after divorce or separation outside the State
  (i) the facts specified at Rule 5(c) hereof in like manner as in the Family Law Civil Bill;
  (ii) specify any additional ground upon which the Respondent intends to rely in support of any ancillary relief claimed; and
  (iii) the relief sought pursuant to the 1995 Act;
(d) in the case of an application for a decree of nullity
  (i) outline the ground(s) for a decree of nullity, if sought;
  (ii) specify any additional ground upon which the Respondent intends to rely in support of any relief claimed; and
  (iii) the relief sought (including whether or not a declaration relating to the custody of a dependent member of the family pursuant to section 46 of the 1995 Act is being sought) and any additional issues to be tried;
(e) in the case of an application for a Declaration of Marital Status
  (i) the facts specified at Rule 5(e) hereof in like manner as in the Family Law Civil Bill;
  (ii) specify any additional ground upon which the Respondent intends to rely in support of any relief claimed; and
  (iii) the relief sought pursuant to the 1995 Act;

(f) in the case of an application for the determination of property issues between spouses, pursuant to section 36 of the 1995 Act/formerly engaged couples pursuant to section 44 of the 1996 Act
  (i) the facts specified at Rule 5(f) hereof in like manner as in the Family Law Civil Bill;
  (ii) specify any additional ground upon which the Respondent intends to rely in support of any relief claimed; and
  (iii) the relief sought pursuant to the 1995 Act;
and shall be in the form set out in Form 6 herein or such modification thereof as may be appropriate.

Evidence

J–470 **22.** Save where the Court otherwise directs and subject to Rules 17, 23 or 26 hereof, every Application under this Order shall be heard on oral evidence, such hearings to be held in camera.

23. Nothwithstanding the provisions of Rule 22 hereof, where relief pursuant to section 12 of the 1995 Act or section 17 of the 1996 Act is sought by the Applicant or the Respondent, evidence of the actuarial value of a benefit under the scheme (as defined in section 12(1) of the 1995 Act and section 17(1) of the 1996 Act) may be by Affidavit filed on behalf of the Applicant/Respondent, such Affidavit to be sworn by an appropriate person and served on all parties to the proceedings and filed at least 14 days in advance of the hearing and subject to the right of the Respondent/ Applicant to serve Notice of cross-examination in relation to same. Where one of the parties has adduced evidence of the actuarial value of a benefit by Affidavit as provided for herein and the other party intends to adduce similar or contra oral evidence, notice of such intention shall be served by the disputing party upon all other parties at least 10 days in advance of the hearing.

Interim and Interlocutory Applications

J–471 **24.** (*a*) An application for Preliminary Orders pursuant to section 6 of the 1995 Act or section 11 of the 1996 Act or for maintenance pending suit/relief pursuant to section 7 or section 24 of the 1995 Act or section 12 of the 1996 Act or for information pursuant to section 12(25) of the 1995 Act of section 17(25) of the 1996 Act or for relief pursuant to section 35 of the 1995 Act or section 37 of the 1996 Act or for relief pursuant to section 38(8) of the 1995 Act or section 38(7) of the 1996 Act or for a report pursuant to section 47 of the 1995 Act or section 42 of the 1995 Act or for any other interlocutory relief shall be by Notice of Motion to be served upon the parties to the proceedings and, in the case of applications pursuant to section 12(25) of the 1995 Act or section 17(25) of the 1996 Act, upon the trustees of the pension scheme concerned.

(*b*) Prior to any interlocutory application for discovery or for information pursuant to section 12(25) of the 1995 Act or section 17(25) of the 1996 Act being made, the information being sought shall be requested in writing voluntarily at least 14 days prior to the issuing of the motion for the relief concerned and upon failure to make such a request, the judge may adjourn the motion or strike out the motion or make such other order, including an order as to costs, as to the Court may appear appropriate.

(*c*) An application for alimony pending suit in nullity proceedings shall be by Notice of Motion grounded upon Affidavit setting out the assets, liabilities, income, debts and expenditure of the

Applicant for alimony and, in so far as same is known to the Applicant, the assets, liabilities, income, debts and expenditure of the Respondent to the said Motion. In every case in which the Respondent wishes to defend such an application for alimony, the Respondent shall file a replying Affidavit setting out details of his assets, liabilities, income, debts and expenditure.

(d) Applications for the appointment of medical and/or psychiatric inspectors in respect of the Applicant and/or the Respondent shall be made by Motion on Notice to the other party and such Motion shall be issued not later than 14 days after the elapsing of the times for the entry of an Appearance and delivery of a Defence save with the leave of the Court or the County Registrar. Where medical and/or psychiatric inspectors are appointed by the Court or the County Registrar, the solicitors for the parties shall attend with the parties on the appointed day at the place in which the inspection is to take place for the purpose of identifying the parties to the County Registrar or his/her nominee. In any circumstances in which a party is unrepresented, appropriate photographic proof of identity must be produced sufficient to satisfy the County Registrar or his/her nominee of the identity of the party concerned. No inspection shall be carried out unless the procedures contained herein are satisfied. Upon completion of the inspection, a report thereof shall be sent by the inspector directly to the County Registrar for the County in which the proceedings have issued.

(e) In any case where the Court is satisfied that the delay caused by proceeding by Motion on Notice under this Order would or might entail serious harm or mischief, the Court may make an Order ex parte as it shall consider just. Urgent applications under this Rule may be made to a Judge at any time or place approved by him, by arrangement with the County Registrar for the County in question.

(f) Interim and interlocutory applications shall where appropriate be made to the County Registrar in accordance with the Second Schedule to the Courts and Court Officers Act, 1995 and Orders 15 and 16 of the Circuit Court Rules, 1950, as amended.

25. If on the date for hearing of any application under this Order the matter is not dealt with by the Court for any reason, and, in particular, on foot of an adjournment sought by either party, the other party, whether consenting to the adjournment or not, may apply for, and the Court may grant, such interim or interlocutory relief as to it shall seem appropriate without the necessity of service of a Notice of Motion.

26. Any interim or interlocutory application shall be heard on Affidavit, unless the Court otherwise directs, save that the Deponent of any Affidavit must be available to the Court to give oral evidence or to be cross-examined as to the Court shall seem appropriate, save that a Motion for Discovery and a Motion in the course of nullity proceedings for the appointment of medical/psychiatric inspectors shall be heard on a Notice of Motion only. Where any oral evidence is heard by the Court in the course of such applications *ex parte*, a note of such evidence shall be prepared by the Applicant or the Applicant's solicitor and approved by the judge and shall be served upon the Respondent forthwith together with a copy of the Order made (if any), unless otherwise directed by the Court.

Further relief and applications on behalf of dependent persons

J–472   27.   (*a*) Where either party or a person on behalf of a dependent member of the family wishes at any time after the hearing of the application to seek further relief as provided for in the 1995 Act or the 1996 Act or to vary or discharge an Order previously made by the Court, that party shall issue a Notice of Motion to re-enter or to vary or discharge as the case may be grounded upon an Affidavit seeking such relief. Such Motions shall be subject to the provisions of Rules 8, 17, 18, 19, 22 and 23 hereof, as appropriate.

           (*b*) Where a person on behalf of a dependent member of the family wishes to make application for ancillary reliefs at the hearing of the action, such application shall be by way of Notice of Motion to be served on all other parties to the proceedings setting out the reliefs sought grounded on Affidavit which said Motion shall be listed for hearing on the same date as the hearing of the action contemporaneously therewith. Such Motions shall be subject to the provisions of Rules 8, 17, 18, 19, 22 and 23 hereof, as appropriate.

28. Where any party to proceedings for a declaration under section 29 of the 1995 Act alleges that the marriage in question was void or voidable and the Court decides to treat the application as one for annulment of the marriage, the provisions of these Rules in relation to the procedures applicable to decrees of nullity may be adapted in such manner as the Court shall direct.

Relief under section 33 of the 1995 Act

J–473   29. Applications under section 33 of the 1995 Act for an order or orders exempting the marriage from the application of section 31(1)(*a*) or section 32(1)(*a*) of the 1995 Act may be made ex parte by the parties where both are over the age of 18 years, by the legal guardians of the parties to the intended marriage where both are under the age of 18 years or, where one of the parties is over the age of 18 years, by that party and the legal guardian or guardians of the other party, and further, where deemed appropriate by the Court, a guardian or guardians *ad litem* may be appointed by the Court to represent either or both of the parties. Such applications may be grounded upon Affidavit or upon oral evidence given by or on behalf of the parties, as the Court may direct, which evidence shall set out the reasons justifying the exemption and the basis upon which it is claimed that the application is in the interests of the parties to the intended marriage.

Applications under section 8 of the Family Law (Maintenance of Spouses and Children) Act, 1976 (as amended) (hereinafter "the 1976 Act")

30. Applications pursuant to section 8 of the Family Law (Maintenance **J–474** of Spouses and Children) Act, 1976 may be by way of originating Notice of Motion, grounded upon Affidavit.

31. For the purposes of Rule 30 hereof, the Notice of Motion shall be entitled in the matter of the 1976 Act (as amended) and shall state the relief sought (including whether or not relief pursuant to section 8B of the 1976 Act, as inserted by section 43 of the 1995 Act is sought); state the name and place of residence or address for service of the Applicant; the date upon which it is proposed to apply to the Court for relief and shall be filed in the appropriate Office.

32. For the purposes of Rule 30 hereof, without prejudice to the jurisdiction of the Court to make an Order for substituted service, the Motion shall be served by registered post on the Respondent at his last-known address or alternatively shall be served personally on the Respondent by any person over the age of eighteen years. Where relief pursuant to section 8B of the 1976 Act is sought, the Motion shall be served upon the trustees of the pension scheme also. There must be at least ten clear days between the service of the Notice and the day named therein for the hearing of the Motion.

33.   (a) Subject to the right of the Court to give such directions as it considers appropriate or convenient, evidence at the hearing of the Motion under Rule 30 shall be by Affidavit.

   (b) Any Affidavit to be used in support of the Motion shall be filed in the appropriate Office and a copy of any such Affidavit shall be served with the Notice. Any Affidavit to be used in opposition to the application shall be filed in the appropriate Office and served upon the Applicant and, where relief pursuant to section 8B of the 1976 Act is sought, upon the trustees of the pension scheme by the Respondent following the service on him of the Applicant's Affidavit and any Affidavit of Representation to be used by the trustees of the pension scheme shall be filed in the appropriate Office and served upon the Applicant and the Respondent.

34. The plaintiff in proceedings wherein it is sought to have a conveyance declared void pursuant to the provisions of section 3 of the Family Home Protection Act, 1976 (as amended by section 54 of the Family Law

Act, 1995) (which said proceedings shall be instituted by way of Equity Civil Bill seeking declaratory relief) shall forthwith and without delay following the institution of such proceedings cause relevant particulars of the proceedings to be entered as a *lis pendens* upon the property and/or premises in question under and in accordance with the Judgments (Ireland) Act, 1844.

Costs

35. (*a*) The costs as between party and party may be measured by the Judge, and if not so measured shall be taxed, in default of agreement by the parties, by the County Registrar according to such scale of costs as may be prescribed. Any party aggrieved by such taxation may appeal to the Court and have the costs reviewed by it.

(*b*) Where necessary, the Court may make an order determining who shall bear any costs incurred by trustees of a pension scheme pursuant to section 12(22) of the 1995 Act or section 17(22) of the 1996 Act and in making such determination the Court shall have regard, *inter alia*, to the representations made by the trustees pursuant to Rule 17 hereof, if any.

General

J–475   **36.** The Court may, upon such terms (if any) as it may think reasonable, enlarge or abridge any of the times fixed by these Rules for taking any step or doing any act in any proceeding, and may also, upon such terms as to costs or otherwise as it shall think fit, declare any step taken or act done to be sufficient, even though not taken or done within the time or in the manner prescribed by these Rules.

Certificates

J–476   **37.** (*a*) The Certificate required by section 5 of the 1989 Act shall be in accordance with Form No. 7 in the Schedule attached hereto.

(*b*) The Certificate required by section 6 of the 1989 Act shall be in accordance with Form No. 8 in the Schedule attached hereto.

(*c*) The Certificate required by section 6 of the 1996 Act shall be in accordance with Form No. 9 in the Schedule attached hereto.

(*d*) The Certificate required by section 7 of the 1996 Act shall be in accordance with Form No. 10 in the Schedule attached hereto.

Service of orders by the Registrar of the Court

J–477   **38.** In all circumstances in which the Registrar of the Court and/or the County Registrar is required to serve or lodge a copy of an order upon any person(s) or body such service of lodgment shall be satisfied by the service of a certified copy of the said order by registered post to the said person(s) or body.

SCHEDULE

FORM NO. 1   **J–478**

AN CHUIRT TEAGHLAIGH CHUARDA
(THE CIRCUIT FAMILY COURT)

CIRCUIT   COUNTY OF
[Insert as appropriate]

IN THE MATTER OF THE JUDICIAL SEPARATION AND
FAMILY LAW REFORM ACT, 1989

IN THE MATTER OF THE FAMILY LAW ACT, 1995

IN THE MATTER OF THE FAMILY LAW (DIVORCE) ACT, 1996

BETWEEN

A.B.
                                              Applicant
And

C.D.
                                              Respondent

FAMILY LAW CIVIL BILL
INDORSEMENT OF CLAIM

YOU ARE HEREBY REQUIRED within ten days after the service of this Civil
Bill upon you, to enter, or cause to be entered with the County Registrar, at his or
her Office at ....

an Appearance to answer the Claim of ....

of .... in the County of ....
the Applicant herein as indorsed hereon.

AND TAKE NOTICE THAT unless you do enter an Appearance, you will be held
to have admitted the said claim and the Applicant may proceed therein and
judgment may be given against you in your absence without further notice.

AND FURTHER TAKE NOTICE THAT if you intend to defend the proceedings
on any grounds, you must not only enter an Appearance as aforesaid, but also
within ten days after the Appearance deliver a statement in writing showing the
nature and grounds of your Defence.

J793

The Appearance and Defence may be entered by posting same to the said Office and by giving copies to the Applicant and his/her Solicitor by post.

Dated the   day of   , 19 .

To: The Respondent

Signed: ....
Applicant/Solicitor for the Applicant

[Here set out in numbered paragraphs details of the relief(s) being claimed by the Applicant specifying the matters required by Rule 5 of these Rules.]

AND THE APPLICANT CLAIMS:
[Here set out in numbered paragraphs the reliefs (including decrees and declarations) being claimed pursuant to the 1989 Act, the 1995 Act or the 1996 Act specifying, where appropriate, the statutory basis upon which each such relief is sought].

AND FURTHER TAKE NOTICE that, in any cases where financial relief is sought by either party you must file with the Defence herein or in any event within 20 days after the service of this Civil Bill upon you at the aforementioned Circuit Court Office an Affidavit of Means and, where appropriate, an Affidavit of Welfare in the Manner prescribed by the Rules of this Court and serve a copy of same as provided by the Rules of this Court on the Applicant or his/her Solicitor at the address provided below.

Dated the   day of   , 19 .

The address for service of proceedings upon the Applicant is as follows:

(here insert address of Applicant or his/her Solicitor)

Signed: ....
Applicant or Solicitor for the Applicant

To: The Registrar Circuit Family Court
    Address

and

To: Respondent or Solicitor for Respondent
    Address

TAKE NOTICE that it is in your interest to have legal advice in regard to these proceedings. If you cannot afford a private solicitor, you may be entitled to legal aid provided by the State at a minimum cost to you. Details of this legal aid service are available at the following address:

Legal Aid Board,
St. Stephen's Green House,
Dublin 2.
Telephone No. (01) 6615811

where you can obtain the addresses and telephone numbers of the Legal Aid Centres in your area.

J794

FLP R.1: January 2001

FORM NO. 2   **J–479**

AN CHUIRT TEAGHLAIGH CHUARDA
(THE CIRCUIT FAMILY COURT)

CIRCUIT   COUNTY OF
[Insert as appropriate]

IN THE MATTER OF THE JUDICIAL SEPARATION AND
FAMILY LAW REFORM ACT, 1989

IN THE MATTER OF THE FAMILY LAW ACT, 1995

IN THE MATTER OF THE FAMILY LAW (DIVORCE) ACT, 1996

BETWEEN

A.B.
                                                       Applicant
And

C.D.
                                                       Respondent

AFFIDAVIT OF MEANS

I,   , [insert occupation]
                   , of
aged 18 years and upwards MAKE OATH and say as follows:

1. I say that I am the Applicant/Respondent [delete as appropriate] in the above entitled proceedings and I make this Affidavit from facts within my own knowledge save where otherwise appears and where so appearing I believe the same to be true.

2. I say that I have set out in the First Schedule hereto all the assets to which I am legally or beneficially entitled and the manner in which such property is held.

3. I say that I have set out in the Second Schedule hereto all income which I receive and the source(s) of such income.

4. I say that I have set out in the Third Schedule hereto all my debts and/or liabilities and the persons to whom such debts and liabilities are due.

5. I say that my weekly outgoings amount to the sum of £   and I say that the details of such outgoings have been set out in the Fourth Schedule hereto.

6. I say that to the best of my knowledge, information and belief, all pension information known to me relevant to the within proceedings is set out in the Fifth Schedule hereto. [Where information has been obtained from the trustees of the pension scheme concerned under the Pensions Act, 1990, such information should be exhibited and where such information has not been obtained, the Deponent should depose to the reason(s) why such information has not been obtained].

J795

First Schedule

[Here set out in numbered paragraphs all assets whether held in the Applicant/ Respondent's sole name or jointly with another, whether held legally or beneficially, the manner in which the assets are held, whether they are subject to a mortgage or other charge or lien and such further and other details as are appropriate.]

Second Schedule

[Here set out in numbered paragraphs all income from whatever source(s).]

Third Schedule

[Here set out in numbered paragraphs all debts and/or liabilities and the persons/ institutions to which such debts and/or liabilities are due.]

Fourth Schedule

[Here set out full details of weekly personal outgoings.]

Fifth Schedule

[Here full details of nature of pension scheme, benefits payable thereunder, normal pensionable age and period of reckonable service should be listed to the best of the Deponent's knowledge, information and belief.]

SWORN etc.

FORM NO. 3   **J–480**

AN CHUIRT TEAGHLAIGH CHUARDA
(THE CIRCUIT FAMILY COURT)

CIRCUIT   COUNTY OF
[Insert as appropriate]

IN THE MATTER OF THE JUDICIAL SEPARATION AND
FAMILY LAW REFORM ACT, 1989

IN THE MATTER OF THE FAMILY LAW ACT, 1995

IN THE MATTER OF THE FAMILY LAW (DIVORCE) ACT, 1996

BETWEEN

A.B.
                                               Applicant
And

C.D.
                                               Respondent

AFFIDAVIT OF WELFARE

I,   , [insert occupation]

                    , of

aged 18 years and upwards MAKE OATH and say as follows:

1. I say that I am the Applicant/Respondent [delete as appropriate] in the above entitled proceedings and I make this Affidavit from facts within my own knowledge save where otherwise appears and where so appearing I believe the same to be true.

2. I say and believe that the facts set out in the Schedule hereto are true.

[In circumstances in which the Respondent does not dispute the facts as deposed to by the Applicant in his/her Affidavit of Welfare, the following averment shall be included, replacing Paragraph 2 hereof, and in such circumstances, the Schedule shall not be completed by the Respondent:

3. I say that I am fully in agreement with the facts as averred to by the Applicant in his/her Affidavit of Welfare sworn herein on the   day of   19   and I say and believe that the facts set out in the Schedule thereto are true.]

J797

SCHEDULE

PART I—DETAILS OF THE CHILDREN

1. Details of children born to the Applicant and the Respondent or adopted by both the Applicant and the Respondent

  Forenames   Surname   Date of Birth

2. Details of other children of the family or to which the parties or either of them are in loco parentis

  Forenames   Surname   Date of Birth   Relationship to
                          Applicant/
                          Respondent

PART II—ARRANGEMENTS FOR THE CHILDREN OF THE FAMILY

3. Home Details

(a) The address or addresses at which the children now live.

(b) Give details of the number of living rooms, bedrooms, etc. at the addresses in (a) above.

(c) Is the house rented or owned and, if so, name the tenant(s) or owners(s)?

(d) Is the rent or mortgage being regularly paid and, if so, by whom?

(e) Give the names of all other persons living with the children either on a full-time or part-time basis and state their relationship to the children, if any.

(f) Will there be any change in these arrangements and, if so, give details.

PART III—EDUCATION AND TRAINING DETAILS

(a) Give the names of the school, college or place of training attended by each child.

(b) Do the children have any special educational needs? If so, please specify.

(c) Is the school, college or place of training fee-paying? If so, give details of how much the fees are per term/year. Are fees being regularly paid and, if so, by whom?

(d) Will there be any change in these circumstances? If so, give details,

FLP R.1: January 2001

Part IV—Childcare Details

(*a*) Which parent looks after the children from day to day? If responsibility is shared, please give details.

(*b*) Give details of work commitments of both parents.

(*c*) Does someone look after the children when the parent is not there? If yes, give details.

(*d*) Who looks after the children during school holidays?

(*e*) Will there be any changes in these arrangements? If yes, give details.

Part V—Maintenance

(*a*) Does the Applicant/Respondent pay towards the upkeep of the children? If yes, give details. Please specify any other source of maintenance.

(*b*) Is the maintenance referred to at (*a*) above paid under court order? If yes. give details.

(*c*) Has maintenance for the children been agreed? If yes, give details.

(*d*) If not, will you be applying for a maintenance order from the Court?

Part VI—Details of contact with the children

(*a*) Do the children see the Applicant/Respondent? Please give details.

(*b*) Do the children stay overnight and/or have holiday visits with the Applicant/ Respondent? Please give details.

(*c*) Will there be any change to these arrangements? Please give details.

Part VII—Details of health

(*a*) Are the children generally in good health? Please give details of any serious disability or chronic illness suffered by any of the children.

(*b*) Do the children or any of them have any special health needs? Please give details of the care needed and how it is to be provided.

(*c*) Are the Applicant or Respondent generally in good health? If not, please give details.

FLP R.1: January 2001

PART VIII—DETAILS OF CARE AND OTHER COURT PROCEEDINGS

(*a*) Are the children or any of them in the care of a health board or under the supervision of a social worker or probation officer? If so, please specify.

(*b*) Are there or have there been any proceedings in any Court involving the children or any of them? If so, please specify. (All relevant Court Orders relating to the children or any of them should be annexed hereto.)

SWORN etc.

FORM NO. 4   **J–481**

AN CHUIRT TEAGHLAIGH CHUARDA
(THE CIRCUIT FAMILY COURT)

CIRCUIT   COUNTY OF
[Insert as appropriate]

IN THE MATTER OF THE JUDICIAL SEPARATION AND
FAMILY LAW REFORM ACT, 1989

IN THE MATTER OF THE FAMILY LAW ACT, 1995

IN THE MATTER OF THE FAMILY LAW (DIVORCE) ACT, 1996

BETWEEN

A.B.
                                                          Applicant
And

C.D.
                                                          Respondent

NOTICE TO TRUSTEES

TAKE NOTICE that relief has been claimed by the Applicant/Respondent in the above entitled proceedings pursuant to section(s) 12 and/or 13 of the Family Law Act, 1995 or section 17 of the Family Law (Divorce) Act, 1996 or section 8B of the Family Law (Maintenance of Spouses and Children) Act, 1976 and in particular in relation to ....
[here insert details of pension in respect of which relief is claimed].

AND FURTHER TAKE NOTICE that a Notice of Trial or a Notice to fix a date for Trial will be served upon you in due course in accordance with the Rules of the Circuit Court.

    Dated the   day of   , 19 .

Signed: ....
              Solicitors for the Applicant/Respondent

To: The County Registrar

and

To: The trustees of the pension scheme concerned

and

To: Applicant/Respondent [or Solicitors where appropriate]

J801

FLP R.1: January 2001

J–482

FORM NO. 5

AN CHUIRT TEAGHLAIGH CHUARDA
(THE CIRCUIT FAMILY COURT)

CIRCUIT   COUNTY OF
[Insert as appropriate]

IN THE MATTER OF THE JUDICIAL SEPARATION AND
FAMILY LAW REFORM ACT, 1989

IN THE MATTER OF THE FAMILY LAW ACT, 1995

IN THE MATTER OF THE FAMILY LAW (DIVORCE) ACT, 1996

BETWEEN

A.B.
                                                                    Applicant
And

C.D.
                                                                    Respondent

NOTICE TO FIX A DATE FOR TRIAL

TAKE NOTICE that the above matter will be listed before this Honourable Court/ the County Registrar sitting at   on the   day of 19   at   o'clock in the forenoon for the purpose of fixing a date for the trial hereof.

    Dated the   day of   , 19   .

Signed: . . . .
              Solicitor for Applicant/Respondent (delete as appropriate)

To: The County Registrar

and

To: The Respondent/Applicant (delete as appropriate) or the solicitors for the Respondent/Applicant, if appropriate.

To: The trustees of the pension scheme concerned if relief is sought under sections 12 and/or 13 of the 1995 Act of section 17 of the 1996 Act.

FLP R.1: January 2001

FORM NO. 6   **J–483**

AN CHUIRT TEAGHLAIGH CHUARDA
(THE CIRCUIT FAMILY COURT)

CIRCUIT   COUNTY OF
[Insert as appropriate]

IN THE MATTER OF THE JUDICIAL SEPARATION AND
FAMILY LAW REFORM ACT, 1989

IN THE MATTER OF THE FAMILY LAW ACT, 1995

IN THE MATTER OF THE FAMILY LAW (DIVORCE) ACT, 1996

BETWEEN

                         A.B.
                                                          Applicant
                         And

                         C.D.
                                                          Respondent

DEFENCE AND COUNTERCLAIM

TAKE NOTICE that the Respondent   of
                    in the County of
disputes the claims made in the Applicant's Family Law Civil Bill pursuant to
sections   of the above entitled Acts, which Civil Bill was served on the
Respondent on the   day of   19 .

AND TAKE NOTICE that the Respondent will rely upon the following matters in
disputing the Applicant's claim:

[Here set out in numbered paragraphs the matters disputed or denied by the
Respondent. Indicate clearly the extent (if any) to which the Applicant's claim or
claims are admitted]

COUNTERCLAIM

AND TAKE NOTICE that the Respondent will rely on the following matters in
support of his/her Counterclaim:

[Here set out in numbered paragraphs details of the relief(s) being claimed by the
Respondent specifying the matters required by Rule 21 of these Rules.]

J803

AND THE RESPONDENT CLAIMS;

[Here set out in numbered paragraphs the reliefs (including decrees and declarations) being claimed pursuant to the 1989 Act, the 1995 Act or the 1996 Act specifying, where appropriate, the statutory basis upon which each such relief is sought.]

Dated the   day of   , 19 .

The address for the service of proceedings on the Respondent is as follows:
[Here insert address of Respondent/Solicitor for the Respondent]

Signed: . . . .
Respondent/Solicitor for Respondent

To: The County Registrar

Address

and

To: The Applicant/Solicitors for the Applicant

Address

FORM NO. 7   **J–484**

AN CHUIRT TEAGHLAIGH CHUARDA
(THE CIRCUIT FAMILY COURT)

CIRCUIT   COUNTY OF

IN THE MATTER OF THE JUDICIAL SEPARATION AND
FAMILY LAW REFORM ACT, 1989 AND IN THE MATTER OF
THE FAMILY LAW ACT, 1995

BETWEEN

A.B.

                                            Applicant
And

C.D.

                                            Respondent

CERTIFICATE PURSUANT TO SECTION 5 of THE JUDICIAL
SEPARATION AND FAMILY LAW REFORM ACT, 1989

I,   , the
Solicitor acting for the above Applicant do hereby certify as follows:

1. I have discussed with the Applicant the possibility of reconciliation with the Respondent and I have given the Applicant the names and addresses of persons qualified to help effect a reconciliation between spouses who have become estranged.

2. I have discussed with the Applicant the possibility of engaging in mediation to help effect a separation on an agreed basis with the Respondent and I have given the Applicant the names and addresses of persons and organisations qualified to provide a mediation service.

3. I have discussed with the Applicant the possibility of effecting a separation by the negotiation and conclusion of a Separation Deed or written Separation Agreement with the Respondent.

Dated the   day of   , 19 .

Signed: . . . .
                        Solicitor

Address:

J805

J–485

FORM NO. 8

AN CHUIRT TEAGHLAIGH CHUARDA
(THE CIRCUIT FAMILY COURT)

CIRCUIT   COUNTY OF

IN THE MATTER OF THE JUDICIAL SEPARATION AND
FAMILY LAW REFORM ACT, 1989 AND IN THE MATTER OF
THE FAMILY LAW ACT, 1995

BETWEEN

A.B.

                                                                Applicant
And

C.D.

                                                                Respondent

CERTIFICATE PURSUANT TO SECTION 6 of THE JUDICIAL
SEPARATION AND FAMILY LAW REFORM ACT, 1989

I,   , the
Solicitor acting for the above Respondent do hereby certify as follows:

1. I have discussed with the Respondent the possibility of reconciliation with the Applicant and I have given the Respondent the names and addresses of persons qualified to help effect a reconciliation between spouses who have become estranged.

2. I have discussed with the Respondent the possibility of engaging in mediation to help effect a separation on an agreed basis with the Applicant and I have given the Respondent the names and addresses of persons and organisations qualified to provide a mediation service.

3. I have discussed with the Respondent the possibility of effecting a separation by the negotiation and conclusion of a Separation Deed or written Separation Agreement with the Applicant.

Dated the   day of   , 19 .

Signed: ....

Solicitor

Address:

J806

FORM NO. 9   **J–486**

AN CHUIRT TEAGHLAIGH CHUARDA
(THE CIRCUIT FAMILY COURT)

CIRCUIT   COUNTY OF

IN THE MATTER OF THE FAMILY LAW (DIVORCE) ACT, 1996

BETWEEN

A.B.

                                          Applicant

And

C.D.

                                          Respondent

CERTIFICATE PURSUANT TO SECTION 6 OF THE FAMILY LAW (DIVORCE) ACT, 1996

I,   ,the
Solicitor acting for the above Applicant do hereby certify as follows:

1. I have discussed with the Applicant the possibility of reconciliation with the Respondent and I have given the Applicant the names and addresses of persons qualified to help effect a reconciliation between spouses who have become estranged.

[The following paragraphs to be inserted where appropriate.]

2. I have discussed with the Applicant the possibility of engaging in mediation to help effect a separation on an agreed basis (the spouses the parties hereto not being separated) or a divorce on a basis agreed between the Applicant with the Respondent and I have given the Applicant the names and addresses of persons and organisations qualified to provide a mediation service for spouses who have become estranged.

3. I have discussed with the Applicant the possibility of effecting a separation by the negotiation and conclusion of a Separation Deed or written Separation Agreement with the Respondent.

4. I have ensured that the Applicant is aware of judicial separation as an alternative to divorce, no decree of judicial separation in relation to the Applicant and the Respondent being in force.

       Dated the   day of   , 19   .

Signed: ....
                                 Solicitor

Address:

FLP R.1: January 2001

J–487

FORM NO. 10

AN CHUIRT TEAGHLAIGH CHUARDA
(THE CIRCUIT FAMILY COURT)

CIRCUIT   COUNTY OF

IN THE MATTER OF THE FAMILY LAW (DIVORCE) ACT, 1996

BETWEEN

A.B.

Applicant

And

C.D.

Respondent

CERTIFICATE PURSUANT TO SECTION 7 OF THE FAMILY LAW
(DIVORCE) ACT, 1996

I,   , the
Solicitor acting for the above Respondent do hereby certify as follows:

1. I have discussed with the Respondent the possibility of reconciliation with the Applicant and I have given the Respondent the names and addresses of persons qualified to help effect a reconciliation between spouses who have become estranged.

[The following paragraphs to be inserted where appropriate.]

2. I have discussed with the Respondent the possibility of engaging in mediation to help effect a separation on an agreed basis (the spouses the parties hereto not being separated) or a divorce on a basis agreed between the Respondent with the Applicant and I have given the Respondent the names and addresses of persons and organisations qualified to provide a mediation service for spouses who have become estranged.

3. I have discussed with the Respondent the possibility of effecting a separation by the negotiation and conclusion of a Separation Deed or written Separation Agreement with the Applicant.

4. I have ensured that the Respondent is aware of judicial separation as an alternative to divorce, no decree of judicial separation in relation to the Respondent and the Applicant being in force.

Dated the   day of   , 19 .

Signed: ....
Solicitor

Address:

FLP R.1: January 2001